THIS
OLD
HOUSE

To Gram Gerry —
Merry Christmas '76

Love — Dirk & Candy

THIS OLD HOUSE
the story of
Clara Rust

Jo Anne Wold

ALASKA NORTHWEST PUBLISHING COMPANY
Anchorage, Alaska

Published September 1976
Second printing October 1976

Library of Congress cataloging in publication data:

Rust, Clara, 1890-
    This old house : the story of Clara Rust.

    1. Fairbanks, Alaska—History.   2. Frontier and
pioneer life—Alaska—Fairbanks.   3. Rust, Clara,
1890-   I. Wold, Jo Anne, joint author.   II. Title.
F914.F16R87   979.8'6   76-22728
ISBN 0-88240-069-X

Design by David A. Shott
Alaska Northwest Publishing Company
Box 4-EEE, Anchorage, Alaska 99509
Printed in U.S.A.

Dedicated in memory of Jesse W. Rust Sr.
And to Lila, Cora, June, Jess Jr., George
and Beth.

FOREWORD

This story about Clara Hickman Rust is true. It is based on her journals—which number 12—and my conversations with her during the past 3 years. Most of the pictures in this book, dating back to 1908 when Clara first came to Fairbanks, were taken by Jess Rust. (Jess died in March 1956.)

Now Clara is in her 86th year. She lives at the Pioneer Home in Fairbanks in a sunny room surrounded by her books, pictures and memorabilia. Her life is active—how she loves parties and plays, concerts and meetings. This spring she started swimming lessons.

To write this story I have relied on her writings and her memory of people and events so long ago. Her memory has never failed me. "What year was the old house flooded? When did you start work at the laundry? Who owned the grocery store on Cushman Street?" I ask. The answers, inscribed with an indelible pen on her memory, come intact. So, story by story, and line by line, we have recreated the time and the place and the people with details that make the past live again.

"When you're young, there is an innate curiosity that drives you on," Clara said. "That happened to me when I first came to Fairbanks. I felt that here I could be somebody. People cared about me as a person. That is a feeling I shall never forget."

In the early years, nothing came easy for Clara and her family. Life then was a demonstration of the old fashioned philosophy: The harder you work, the more you get. Clara said, "Many times it was difficult, but we met each challenge with the thought that things will be better tomorrow."

And things did get better tomorrow. Not by any giant step, or by any stroke of luck, but by small drops of labor that dissolve the hard times.

There is always something to be done. At the age of 76 Clara started writing a newspaper column. She writes it weekly for the Fairbanks *Daily News-Miner*. During the past 8 years she has served as hostess at the Alaskaland Pioneer Museum. Then there has been work on this book.

And to think, when Clara sailed for Alaska she was going to stay 1 year. It has been 68 years. So much has happened. I would like to tell you about it.

Jo Anne Wold

chapter 1

The 10th day. Gray rain swept out of a swollen sky. The sun was lost forever, a yellow disk now dulled to an occasional white spot in the mass of misty, steaming clouds almost low enough for me to touch from where I stood on the deck of the steamship *Northwestern.*

As I peered into the leaping black waves of the Pacific Ocean, I felt the wind rushing across my face and tugging at my proper pompadour. Water rolled toward me in rivulets, dampening the hem of my long wool skirt. The cloth coat I had bought in Seattle was totally inadequate for such a voyage, as was my scarf I fancied so fashionable before the rain started.

It was the year 1908 and the *Northwestern,* with railings rusting and sides bubbly with flaking paint, lumbered through the high seas, doggedly pursuing its course for Nome, Alaska. Early in the voyage the jogging and rolling of the ship had sent most of the passengers to their staterooms. Except me.

I turned and left the deck for the protection of the main salon before the captain could scold me again for being out in such weather. I didn't tell him, but his concern for me was comforting. At least there was someone I could turn to on this long journey. Captain John Trubridge was an old friend of the family and a former neighbor of ours in Seattle.

Several weeks earlier when I received Dad's letter telling me of the death of my older brother, Thayne, he instructed me to join the family in Fairbanks. I was not looking forward to the reunion; our happy times as a family had been so few. The thought of seeing my 9-year-old sister, Beth, was the only thing that made it easier for me to get on the boat and sail away from my friends in Seattle.

Many times during the journey I was filled with doubt and apprehension. How often during my 18 years had we moved? I had lost count years ago. I was tired of pulling up stakes while Mother

The steamship Northwestern *carried Clara and her new friend, Marie, from Seattle to Nome and then on to Saint Michael across Norton Sound. A succession of river boats took them from there up the Yukon and Tanana rivers to Fairbanks.*

became more unhappy with each move. We were always starting over. When would it end?

Ever since Dad had been 13 years old he had been on the run. At that age he left his home in Ohio and the strict control of his Baptist minister father, without a backward glance. After a number of years of apprenticeship in the printing business, Dad became editor and then manager of a small newspaper in Leesburg, Ohio. It was while he was covering a story in the small town of Washington Courthouse, Ohio, that he met and married Martha de Lila Thurston.

"I remember the day I met your mother," Dad used to say to me. "I thought she was the most beautiful woman I had ever seen."

And she was beautiful. Everyone said so. That glorious auburn hair of hers was thick and heavy, coiled in a neat bun on the nape of her neck. She had translucent skin, and just enough color in her cheeks for a healthy glow. Her eyes were widely spaced and framed with dark lashes. And I, her eldest daughter, was an awkward lump beside her, much too fat. When I was a little girl Mother became discouraged trying to make me look pretty. "Oh, Clara," she would say, "you are like a meal sack with a string tied in the middle."

All the years they were married Dad idolized Mother, though he could not settle down, no matter how much she complained and no matter how unhappy she became. Their life together was not easy; even as a child I knew that. Dad was gone months at a time. Mother never knew when he would send money, nor when he would return. And when he did, it was only to launch some new scheme halfway across the state, or the country, and the moving would begin again.

Soon after they were married in Ohio, Dad had a yen to travel west. They worked their way to the coast on the Great Northern Railway, Dad on a tie crew and Mother as a camp cook. When they finally reached Ellensburg, Washington, Mother gave birth to their first child on May 12, 1888, whom they named Thayne Thurston Hickman.

While Mother recovered, Dad was off again, this time to Seattle, where he became a partner in the Sunset Printing Company. When Mother and Thayne joined him they lived in a small room over a Chinese laundry. It was from the window of that apartment that Mother watched the great Seattle fire in 1889, and Dad's printing shop go up in flames.

When the fire alarm sounded, Dad and his partners carried the presses, the stock and office equipment to a barge on Puget Sound to be towed out of the flames' reach. In their haste, they loaded the barge improperly and when a wave rocked the barge it deposited all the cargo on the bottom of the Sound. Everything was lost.

Following the fire came an epidemic of scarlet fever. In the spring of 1890, Mother and Thayne were stricken. While Mother was still ill, I was born on the second of May. They named me Clara Louise.

Fortunately Mother's brother Harry came to live with us about this time. He was studying to become a doctor and he was the one who took care of us and cooked our meals.

Mother's recovery was slow; perhaps her unhappiness had something to do with it. When she was well enough to travel, Uncle Harry took us back to our relatives in Ohio. A year later we were reunited with Dad in a couple of rooms on the fourth floor of the Arlington Hotel. Mother had to go down the hall to the common kitchen to cook our meals, then carry the food to the room. We had to go even farther to the bathroom.

Either Dad's schemes, or Mother's restlessness kept us on the move or up in the air all the time. Mother took Thayne and me to Ohio for another year. Then we returned to Seattle, where my sister, Beth, was born in November 1896.

During this time Dad went into partnership with Pliny Allen, George Allen and C. W. Frankland to form the Metropolitan Printing and Binding Company. They built it into one of the largest printing companies in the state of Washington. It was housed in a four-story brick building on the corner of Third Avenue and Main Street and I remember how proud I was whenever we went to visit Dad there.

When news of the Klondike gold strike hit Seattle in 1897, my father talked his partners into setting up a newspaper in Dawson, Yukon Territory. Dad helped carry the printing press over the White Pass, and they established the Klondike *Nugget,* the town's first newspaper, in 1898. But just Dad's luck, a rival newspaper, the Dawson *News,* hit the streets an hour later the same day.

That winter while Dad was in Dawson was a difficult one for us at home. We had known for some time that my brother, Thayne, was not well, but the doctors did not know why he was stricken with violent seizures. He was a constant worry to Mother, who was not too well herself.

The Zacharius Hickman family, with Clara at left, in 1897 before Zack went over the Chilkoot Pass to Dawson.

In 1900 when Dad returned from Dawson, he could not settle down, and before we knew it, he was off to Guatemala. When he returned, Mother packed us kids off to the relatives in Ohio, where we stayed for a year.

This time when we went back to Seattle Dad took us to a little house on Queen Anne Hill which he had purchased while we were gone. Although it was freshly papered and painted, it was not modern in any way. There was an old well on the property and we hauled our water up with a rope and pulley.

About this time Dad dropped his interest in the Metropolitan Company, and he and one of the partners formed the Frankland-Hickman Company, but that did not last very long. Pretty soon, much to our regret, we had to give up the house on Queen Anne Hill with its beautiful view of Lake Union and move to Tacoma, where Dad had entered into another printing business.

We were there about a year when Dad decided to go into another new business. This time it was the Graham-Hickman Printing and Paper Box Factory in Seattle.

"I can't take much more of this moving," Mother threatened. "I know, I know," Dad would say. "This is the last time." But it never was. Dad was a brilliant promoter, but after he got a company organized, he could not manage it properly. He either had to sell or go broke, and he did both more often than any of us cared to remember.

One time when Dad was doing quite well financially, he built two modern houses on the Queen Anne Hill property he had retained. We hadn't been settled in our new house very long when, one day in 1905, Dad dropped another bombshell.

"I just bought a partnership in the *Daily News,* a paper in Fairbanks, Alaska," he said.

"Oh, Zack, how could you?" Mother cried.

"Martha, Martha, listen to me," Dad said. "Fairbanks is a booming gold rush town. There is lots of money to be made. You will see."

"When are you leaving?" was all Mother wanted to know.

"Next week," Dad answered. "I will send for you when I get settled and find a place to live."

Dad's intentions were good, but his luck wasn't. In May of 1906, a fire in Fairbanks wiped out half the business district, Dad's newspaper included. Since we never did have enough money when Dad was away, I quit school in the eighth grade and went to work at the Seattle Cracker and Candy Company, where I put in 10 hours a day dipping chocolates. For that I earned $3.50 a week.

Then one night in the summer of 1907 Mother was rushed to the hospital with a ruptured appendix and I had to quit my job to take care of Beth. Thayne had signed up with a crew leaving for Alaska to work on the railroad near Valdez.

As soon as Mother returned from the hospital, Dad began making plans for the family to go north. It wasn't until I overheard a conversation that I realized I was not going with them.

"My daughter, Clara, will be staying in the apartment," I heard Mother say to someone on the telephone. "If you agree, she will keep her bedroom, and in exchange, you can use my furniture."

I was hurt and bewildered, but I kept my feelings to myself so I wouldn't worry Mother, who was still recuperating from her surgery. But I was afraid to be left alone with those strangers who were coming to take over our apartment and belongings.

At the dock the day the boat left, Dad pulled a $10 bill out of his pocket saying, "I'm sorry this is all I can give you. I know you will get a job soon, and this should tide you over."

He kissed me good-by and walked away, and I was glad he did because I did not want him to see me crying. Although it was dark, I stood on the dock until the boat was out of sight. Then I walked home, blinded by my tears.

In less than a week after the couple moved into our apartment, they rented my bedroom to their nephew and put me in the sitting room, where I had no privacy at all. After 2 weeks of job hunting, I went to work at another candy factory. With my first paycheck I put a dollar down on a nice brown coat and a dollar a week for 8 weeks until it was paid for. Then I bought a skirt, paying 50 cents a week, until, little by little, I got myself a small wardrobe. I started going to dances at the dance school where my mother had taught, and thus began a life of my own.

Then I got Dad's letter telling me of Thayne's drowning in the Chatanika River and how mother was grieving. She wanted to leave Fairbanks, but Dad had talked her into staying if I would join them.

That was why I was sailing on the steamship. I was alone, but I was not lonely. When the ship's officers had time, they would walk with me around the deck, and in the evenings we would play card games in the main salon while the lamps overhead swayed with the rocking motion of the ship.

It was good to be young and have skin that was fresh and fair, and dark hair that curled softly on my neck. I was too big, I knew that, with well supplied hips and bosom. But my waist was small, and oh, so tightly cinched by a many-boned corset, and it was my redeeming feature in a figure too big for my height. I was light on my feet and never lacked for a dancing partner. If no one teased me about my weight, I forgot about it, and thought I was just like everybody else.

Marie Thompson, with whom I had made an acquaintance early in the voyage, was bound for Fairbanks to join her widowed mother, so I also had female companionship.

When we reached Nome, a storm had come up. The *Northwestern* lay out in Norton Sound until the next morning when the water had calmed enough for a tugboat to take the mail and passengers to shore.

The storm continued as we made our way across Norton Sound to

Saint Michael. Again we anchored offshore. This time Marie and I and the other passengers bound for Fairbanks were lowered by a swaying platform to the deck of a waiting tugboat. Rain streaked down from a wet and woolly sky, plastering my hair against my cheeks and thoroughly soaking my flimsy coat.

Don't look down, I told myself as the sea water boiled and frothed below me. Instead I looked in vain for the shoreline or any light or building that would be the place they called Saint Michael. A thick fog enveloped the ship, blotting the landmarks until there was nothing but a melding of sky and sea, colorless and dense.

In the cabin of the tugboat I clung to the overhead straps while pressed tightly against my fellow passengers like a sardine in a can. The tugboat rolled and jerked over the rough waves, lurching and dipping until I thought my stomach would turn inside out. What was I doing in such a godforsaken place? What would I do in Fairbanks? Would my family ever find a place to call their own and happiness to go with it? Would I?

With an abrupt *thud* we hit the dock and we were put ashore to make our way against the wetness and the wind to the Northern Navigation Company office. It was good to walk on land again—the first time in 14 days.

Then we were hit with bad news. Our ship, the *Sarah,* which was to take us up the Yukon, the Tanana and the Chena rivers to Fairbanks, had left without us.

"It will be a week before the next boat gets here," the steamship company agent said.

"A week!" I said. Marie and I exchanged stricken looks. "What will we do for a whole week?"

Wait. That was all we could do.

After we were directed to the steamship company dormitory, Marie and I tried to make ourselves presentable. We shared a bare room with no modern conveniences except a washbowl and pitcher of water. Our clothes were rumpled and musty smelling after our long ocean voyage, and we rinsed things out as best we could.

For our meals we walked to the steamship company mess hall up the street. There we ate at long tables, family style. The food was tasty and hot—and plenty of it—even though it was served on tin plates.

Although Marie and I were anxious to reach Fairbanks, we tried to make the best of our enforced stay in Saint Michael. True, the

"The good ship Susie," *as Clara fondly calls it, the sternwheeler on which Clara and her shipmate, Marie, traveled up the Yukon River into the Interior of Alaska. The kindness of its captain and the friendship of two of the ship's officers, Ralph Newcombe Jr. and Handsome Harry Webber, made this leg of the journey memorable. At Fort Gibbon, 3 days' journey from Fairbanks at the confluence of the Yukon and Tanana rivers, they transferred reluctantly to the smaller, woodburning vessel* Tanana.

August days were dwindling fast, and in this northern climate there was heavy frost in the mornings. Still there was much we enjoyed about that coast town with its docks and warehouses, trading posts and saloons, its onion-domed Russian church and log cabins—many built on stilts above the mud. Elevated boardwalks tied the town together and we clattered over them wherever they might lead.

One day while Marie and I were having lunch at the mess hall, a man came to our table and said, "Which one of you girls is Clara Hickman?"

I was so astonished that anyone would know me out in the middle of the Alaskan wilderness, I could hardly speak. He introduced himself as Mr. Huey, a free-lance photographer, who had come down from Fairbanks.

"Your father told me to be on the lookout for you," he said. "I will be in Saint Michael a few days, and I would be happy to be your escort."

Marie and I spent several pleasant afternoons with Mr. Huey, visiting the home of a white trader and his Eskimo wife and children, and having our pictures taken. Many early day photographs bear the Huey-Hyland credit line.

Several days later, Marie and I heard whistles blowing and a great commotion coming from the direction of the docks.

"Let's go!" I cried, and we flew out the door.

At last the good ship *Susie* had arrived, and how magnificent she was with her gleaming white paint and gold trim on the wide double decks and ornamental posts. Here was one of the finest sternwheelers on the Yukon.

From the talk we heard around us, Marie and I gathered that the *Susie* had suffered some damage to her hold due to the low level of the water.

"I doubt she will make it back upriver," one man speculated. "She has to make it," another man replied. "There is a ton of freight in the warehouse that has to be delivered before freezeup."

While we were standing on the dock, Mr. Huey joined us and introduced us to two officers from the *Susie*. They were Ralph Newcombe Jr., the ship's pilot, and Harry Webber ("Handsome Harry" they called him), the deck clerk. They were both young, they were friendly, and how good-looking they were in their uniforms. Ralph's father was the captain and before the journey of 1,000 miles was over, we would be friends.

It was two days before we were allowed to board the ship. Since there were so few of us (nine male passengers and two female), Marie and I had private staterooms across the hall from each other. Our rooms, with windows on the deck and doors that opened on an inside corridor, had comfortable bunks with spanking white sheets and clean blankets, and, best of all, hot running water.

The *Susie* was one of the queens of the Yukon. She could accommodate 225 passengers, so we were not wanting for space on our trip. On the main deck, where the deck hands had their quarters, were the engines and boilers. The *Susie* was one of the first sternwheelers on the Yukon to convert to oil. On this last trip of the season, the deck would be piled high with cargo, covered with heavy tarpaulins to protect it from the rain.

That evening in the dining salon, which was on the same deck as our staterooms, we sat on chairs covered with red plush and we were attended by waiters in white jackets, who were also our cabin boys. Red velvet draped the windows and matched the red carpet on the floor. The white woodwork, trimmed with gold, contrasted with the walls of rich mahogany. In summer, hanging baskets of flowers decorated the passageways, I was told.

By the time Marie and I got settled in our bunks it was after midnight. I was so exhausted from our excitement of the day that I went to sleep instantly, only to be awakened abruptly a few hours later. Bells were ringing madly, whistles pierced the air and loud shouting came from the deck.

"We are on our way!" Marie shouted, pounding on my door.

But it was another disappointment. The *Susie* was being tugged out in the sound for the night due to the high winds that had come up suddenly and begun pounding the boat against the dock.

Marie and I went back to bed, sad and sleepy-eyed. Would we ever be on our way? It was times like those that we realized how far we were from home and cut off from civilization.

In the morning we were tied up to the dock again so the freight could be loaded. Marie and I ate a leisurely breakfast in the dining salon where the sun poured through the windows and set the silverware to sparkling. Our table was covered with a snowy white cloth and was well attended by the courteous waiters. Everyone was so kind to us that we felt like royalty.

When at long last the freight was loaded, including the first two automobiles shipped to Fairbanks, we were towed to deeper water. Then four barges were towed out and two of them were lashed side by side, and placed one in front of the other to be pushed ahead by the sternwheeler.

When we were finally under way, a lookout was posted on the roof of each barge. The water was rough as we headed across Norton Sound with our flotilla of freight. There was much ringing of bells and shouting of the captain and crew. Since the Yukon was so low at that time, we had to enter the river at the Alakanuk entrance. It was quite a feat to get that huge riverboat and the barges into the mouth of the Yukon. Markers and buoys guided us into the deepest water so we would not get hung up on a sand bar.

Despite the skill of our crew, our progress was slow. Marie and I, outfitted in our long coats with scarves tied tightly under our chins, hung over the railing to watch the gray, silty water slip beneath us and to listen to the commotion on deck.

We were just getting into the excitement of it when suddenly everything stopped. The engines died and the huge sternwheeler and the barges ground to a halt.

Just then Officer Webber made his way along the deck and I called, "Why have we stopped?"

"The tide has receded," he said. "There isn't enough water to float the boat and barges."

"How long will we be here?" Marie wanted to know.

"It will be about 48 hours before the tide runs again," he replied and quickly made his exit.

The *Susie* was not alone in this predicament. Up ahead I could see four other boats, their black smokestacks etched neatly against the rosy glow of the morning sky. Their red paddle wheels were as idle as ours. With everything at a standstill, there was no work for the ship's crew.

"Come duck hunting with Harry and me," Ralph invited. "We will take the lifeboat."

"Duck hunting?" I said. What did we know about duck hunting? Absolutely nothing.

"That sounds like a fine idea," Marie said.

"It sure does," I joined in.

So we set off in the splendid sunshine with Ralph rowing and Harry passing around the thermos of hot coffee. It mattered not that we didn't see a single duck that day. Just being out in that small boat bobbing along the muddy Yukon with two handsome sailors was good enough for us.

When the men tired of "duck hunting" they took us boat hopping to the other stranded vessels in the middle of the river. We visited the *W. H. Isom,* the largest and most beautiful boat on Alaskan waters—Marie and I were informed. The *Isom* certainly possessed more gold trim, more red velvet, more mahogany paneling than the *Susie,* and a filigreed smokestack to boot.

Nearly two days passed before the tide returned and the boats were lifted off the sand bars and on their way. As we traveled inland the river narrowed, and the *Susie* grew wider, or so it seemed to me as I eyed the riverbanks closing in on us.

At night the *Susie* was tied to the bank because it was dangerous to navigate the narrow bends in the dark with the barges out front. It wasn't long before we lost sight of the other vessels. Now we had the entire river to ourselves except for an occasional Indian canoe cutting through the dark water from a nearby fish camp.

We stopped at the small villages en route, unloading mail and winter supplies. Even before we could see the village, we heard the howling of the Natives' dogs announcing our arrival. As we pulled to shore the children were the first to greet us, followed by the adults, all so eager to get their mail, help unload the cargo and talk with the crew. Everywhere we stopped Ralph and Harry were treated like royalty.

When there was time Marie and I would go ashore. Each village had a trading post and they all looked the same—a log building set against a wooded bluff, the shelves stacked high with case goods and smelling of fish, tobacco and furs. In the yards would be the boxy, flat-roofed doghouses with the anxious huskies tugging at their chains, yapping and howling.

At these stops we took on bales of dried salmon to be sold as dog food in Fairbanks, and sometimes more oil to fuel the sternwheeler.

There was a kind of leisurely enchantment about the passage of the days, wrapped in the glorious colors of fall that lit up the riverbank as we moved steadily onward. To me the paddle wheel churning, churning, churning was the rhythmic heartbeat of the journey.

One evening Harry and I had a yen to dance, so we rolled up the heavy red carpet in the observation lounge and danced to the music on the Victrola. One of the passengers, Lipman Simpson, had a zither and he came and played for us. On other evenings the passengers and crew members gathered around to sing and listen to Lipman.

Since the *Susie* was behind schedule and the river was wider, the captain gave the order to travel at night.

"There is no danger now," Harry said, "as long as the nights are clear. The moon gives plenty of light."

One night, very late, there was a knock on my stateroom door.

"Who is it?" I called, instantly alert. Even though Marie and I were the only women passengers, we did not fear for our safety. The knock did not signify danger, only excitement.

"It's Ralph," came the muffled reply.

"What do you want?" I asked.

"There is a beautiful moon tonight," he said. "Why don't you join Harry and me in the pilothouse. Marie is coming," he said as an added incentive.

"I'll be ready in a minute," I replied eagerly.

Ralph was waiting outside our doors to lead us along the quiet passageways and up the narrow stairs to the pilothouse. Harry was at the wheel and flashed us a welcome smile, gesturing out the window.

"There it is, girls, all yours," he said.

Marie and I gasped appreciatively. We stepped forward for a better view. The September moon was a golden goblet hanging motionless above low, rolling hills. The midnight sky was swept clean of every cloud to let a million stars shine through. Reflected back in the glassy sheen of the black river was a second moon and a million more stars. In the dazzling moonlight each rock, each bush was etched with a diamondlike sharpness against the riverbank.

Before long the steward brought hot coffee and sandwiches for the officers' midnight snack. The men shared their food with Marie and me, and it tasted so good, partly because we were hungry and partly because there wasn't enough food for the four of us. Everything we said that night was funny, and our voices kept getting louder and louder.

Suddenly, the captain was standing in the doorway. "What is going on here?" he demanded.

The pilothouse was quiet as a tomb, no one spoke. Even the articulate Ralph was silent in the presence of his father's anger.

"Mr. Newcombe," the captain said, his voice sharp with his displeasure, "this is a pilothouse, not a salon for entertaining. You are responsible for the safety of this ship, the passengers and the cargo."

He came forward and took the wheel. Ralph stepped aside obediently. "I will have to ask the ladies to leave," the captain said with a curt nod in our direction.

Marie and I fled down the narrow stairway, tripping on our long skirts in our haste. We went directly to our staterooms, not wishing to encounter the captain again that night. Marie and I slipped into our bunks and each felt guilty for having displeased the captain who had treated us so kindly on this voyage. ◀▬▬

 **chapter 2**

And so our days on board the *Susie* passed while the frost of fall nipped at our heels. The red paddle wheel turned and turned, pushing the sternwheeler and her barges around corkscrew bends, through narrow passages, past grassy plains, rocky outcroppings and the rolling hills vibrant with leaves of ruby red and tawny gold.

Above Holy Cross, the Yukon spreads for miles and miles of flat mud banks with a maze of channels. I marveled at how Captain Newcombe knew which one to travel. Soundings were constantly taken by the men on the barges. They used long poles, plunging them into the river until they touched bottom, and then calling out the depth of water at that point.

In spite of the soundings, there were still times when we got hung up on a sand bar. When that happened the barges had to be unfastened before the boat could be maneuvered free. Sometimes it took an entire day before we were on our way again.

Much to the captain's concern, the water level in the river dipped lower and lower. His destination was Dawson, Yukon Territory, before freezeup. There wasn't time to lose. On and on we went, with stops at Anvik, Kaltag, Koyukuk, Ruby, Birch, Andreafsky.

In one way I was happy when we were delayed; I didn't want my trip on the *Susie* to end. Marie and I were spoiled by all the male attention we got. It made me feel like a princess. But in another way I was anxious to reach my destination before the full grip of winter was on the land. I had been traveling long enough, and all fairy tales must end.

It was a cold, foggy morning with fog rising from the river's warmth when Fort Gibbon came into view. We were three days from Fairbanks. There the Tanana joins the Yukon and it was there we transferred to a smaller boat for the trip deeper into the Territory of Alaska. It was a sad time for Marie and me; how we hated to part with our good friends Ralph and Harry. We stayed on the *Susie* until we practically had to be dragged off.

As we boarded the *SS Tanana,* a wood-burning replica of the *Susie,* snow flurries twirled overhead. The leafless trees were down to the bare bones of winter.

The Tanana River was narrower and swifter than the Yukon. We had as our cargo two of the barges brought upriver by the *Susie.* There were still many stops to make along the way, depositing supplies and taking on cords of wood cut by the Indians.

When I heard the slap, slap, slap of the paddle wheel in the muddy Tanana, I could hardly wait to reach Fairbanks. Now I became impatient with the stops and the piercing howls of the dogs. I was tired of the constant motion of the boat. I was even annoyed at the beat, beat, beat of the paddle wheel.

The sky stayed a sullen gray and threatened snow, and I was afraid we might get wintered in at one of the fish camps, for it was getting late in the season and the water was dangerously low.

My fears were unfounded. After 3 days of uninterrupted travel, we reached the town of Chena. Now we were just a few hours from Fairbanks.

"Just think, Marie," I said. "I shall have dinner with my family tonight."

"And I shall see my mother," she answered happily.

In those days Chena was a thriving community of white settlers, situated at the confluence of the Tanana and Chena rivers 12 miles from Fairbanks. This last waterway, even narrower and more winding than the last, would take me to my destination. In addition to the boating activity, Chena was the terminus of the narrow-gauge Tanana Valley Railroad which carried freight to Fairbanks and north to the mining towns of Fox, Olnes, Gilmore, Fairbanks Creek Camp, and even as far as Chatanika.

While I continued my packing, Marie (with whom I had to share a cabin on this part of the trip) went to find out how long we would stop in Chena. It wasn't long before she came storming into the stateroom.

"We have to leave the boat," she announced in an angry voice.

"What!" I cried. "They can't make us do that. We are almost to Fairbanks."

"Well, they *are* doing it!" Marie said as she jammed clothing into her suitcase. "The captain doesn't think the *Tanana* can get up the river. He says the water is too low."

"Well, what are we going to do?"

"No one knows for sure," Marie said. "There is talk that we will have to wait until tomorrow morning and take the train."

"Tomorrow morning!" I wailed. "I can't wait that long, now that we are this close to Fairbanks."

"They might put us on a smaller boat, the *Reliance,*" Marie said. "It is supposed to leave tonight."

"Oh, I don't think we will ever get to Fairbanks," I said, slumping in my chair. "It has been one delay after another. How much more do we have to take?"

After several hours' discussion, the steamship company officials decided to put us on the *Reliance.* By this time it was past midnight, darker than the ace of spades, with a damp, icy wind blowing. The boat was much smaller than the last one, and I had a feeling it just might not get us where we wanted to go.

While the lights of Chena could still be seen from the deck of the *Reliance,* we felt that well-known, sinking *thud.* We were hung up on a sand bar. The *Reliance* chugged and chugged, but nothing happened. Marie and I and the other passengers stood on the deck to watch the crew tie heavy cables to the tree stumps on the bank in order to maneuver us out of the mud.

While we stood there, the *SS Tanana,* the boat we had been evicted from earlier, steamed past us.

We thronged to the railing and waved our arms and shouted, "Stop! Stop! Come get us!"

With a toot of its whistle the *Tanana* was out of sight. Then we were more upset and impatient than before. We waited an eternity, it seemed, before the *Reliance* was on her way again.

But that wasn't the last sand bar we hit. Our captain, unfamiliar with the river, managed to lead us into a sand bar at almost every turn. Stop and go, stop and go. The 1-hour trip had already taken us 4 hours.

Too excited to sleep, we all gathered in the cabin where the crew served us hot coffee and sandwiches. There was nothing to do but wait.

Daylight was just breaking over the tops of the leafless trees when the first lights of Fairbanks were seen.

"Hooray!!" we cheered.

Then *thud*! The captain had done it again. Another sand bar. I grabbed my coat and hurried out on deck before anyone could see the tears rolling down my cheeks. As I strode up and down the deck, trying to keep warm, I heard someone call my name from the riverbank. Then I saw a young girl dressed in a long coat with a knitted hat on her head. She waved a mittened hand and called again, "Clara, Clara!"

"Beth! Beth!" I cried, and the tears started anew at the sight of my little sister.

Just then the captain came up beside me. "We are launching a lifeboat for some of the men who are anxious to get ashore," he said. "You can go with them if you wish."

Did I ever wish! So there I was making my grand entrance into Fairbanks in a rowboat at 6 o'clock in the morning with a cold wind plucking my hair and sending a chill down my spine. As I scrambled up the slippery riverbank, my long skirts trailing in the mud, I felt most unglamorous. It was not the kind of arrival I had envisioned all those weeks.

Beth and I hugged each other, laughing and crying at the same time.

"We waited up all night for you," Beth said. "Mother and Dad and I met the *Tanana,* and when you were not on it I cried for hours."

"Oh Beth," I said. "I didn't think I would ever get here."

"Let's hurry," Beth said. "We are only a few blocks from home."

A fine powdery snow covered the ground. My clothes were not suitable for this northern climate; I found that out soon enough. I shivered every step of the way.

Most of the log cabins we passed were still dark at that early morning hour with just a thin veil of smoke drifting out of the chimneys. Color was coming into the sky, deep pink and gold as the rays of light spread before us in the snow. Under the tall spruce trees were dark pools of blue, like ink smudges.

"How much farther?" I asked Beth, through chattering teeth.

"We're almost there," she said, hurrying her step.

Up ahead, in a small log cabin with a peaked tarpaper roof, shone a yellow light in the window. Mother stood in the open doorway.

Home at last! My journey of 32 days had ended.

chapter 3

After breakfast my family and I sat leisurely around the small dining room table in our log cabin on Eighth Avenue with a whole year of talking to catch up on. Our circle was incomplete without my brother, Thayne.

Mother told me that while he was working on the railroad out of Valdez he was shot in the hip and hospitalized for several weeks. At that same time one man was killed and several others wounded during the dispute between the Alaska Home Railroad company and the Guggenheim company over a right-of-way in Keystone Canyon.

"After Thayne came home, he was not strong enough to take a job," Mother said, "so Dad let him set up a skate sharpener shop in the newspaper plant.

"This spring he was well enough to work with the Tanana Light and Power Company near the little town of Chatanika as a lineman. He seemed so happy to be on his own again."

Then in early May, about breakup time, the line crew was returning to the bunkhouse after a day's work. Since it had been unusually warm, the men decided not to take the shortcut across the ice, which looked soft. Thayne would not listen to the others; he insisted on crossing the ice as they had always done. Later, when he did not return to camp, the men began searching for him. It was several days before his body was found in the ice. Thayne's drowning, on his 19th birthday, was a sad ending to a difficult life. Now that I was with Mother, I hoped that I could help her get over her grief and that all of us could find happiness together.

When I first saw the cabin, just three rooms and a lean-to that served as the kitchen, I was surprised at its small size and many inconveniences. For this, Mother had left a new and modern house in Seattle. But with her good taste and ingenuity, she had managed to make a cozy nest for the family. I marveled at the log walls covered with burgundy burlap which gave warmth and color to the living room and dining room. On the ceiling was a taut covering of cheesecloth with a cream-colored paper on top of that.

"It is called a balloon ceiling," Beth informed me importantly.

The floors, 12-inch planks covered with newspaper for insulation, were covered with heavy canvas that was tacked down around the edges and painted green. In the living room a light blue rug with bright red roses and green leaves gave a cheery effect.

My Mother's touch could be seen throughout the house—the colorful curtains, the crocheted doilies, the shelves which held her cut-glass vases and fancy china. On the window sills bloomed pansies and geraniums, their petals as soft as velvet in the warm sunshine. Beth's small cot, pushed against the wall in the living room, was covered with a gay cretonne throw. Mother had fixed up and made do—with so many houses, it was a wonder to me that she still had any enthusiasm for it.

"I hate to leave this fine company," Dad said after breakfast that first morning, pushing his chair away from the table, "but I have a newspaper to put out today."

The Fairbanks *Daily News* was housed on the ground floor of the Masonic Temple on First Street, along the river front. The town, with a population of 8,000, had another daily paper, the Fairbanks *Times,* as well as the weekly, the *Alaska Citizen.* Dad had plenty of competition, and his chances of getting rich weren't as good as he had led us to believe, but that was nothing new.

"Oh, by the way, Clara," Dad said, pulling on his coat, "I made some inquiries about jobs for you. I put your application in at the telephone company. You shouldn't have any trouble going to work."

My cheeks burned rosy-red as they always did when I was excited or mad, and then I was mad. Here I had only been in town a few hours and Dad was afraid I wouldn't go to work. Hadn't I taken care of myself in Seattle without any help from him? Well, I would take care of myself in Fairbanks, too.

Instead of snapping out some remark I might regret, I mumbled, "I'll get a job, Dad, don't worry."

There was no need starting a family quarrel the first day. Besides, it was just like him to make a remark like that. I shouldn't have been hurt by it, but I was.

As Dad went out the door, Mother, Beth and I sat in silence at the table. The smell of bacon and eggs that mother had fixed for breakfast hung heavy on the air. In the kitchen the black wood-burning stove ticked contentedly as it cooled.

Bright sprigs of colored flowers brightened the wallpaper in the kitchen, which had originally been a shed at the back of the cabin. Dad had remodeled it by lining the walls with building paper and then with oil paper in a flowery design. Mother had a small work table in there along with wooden boxes nailed to the wall for cupboards. Beneath the only window sat two 5-gallon cans with wooden lids. All the water for our house was contained in those cans, carried in by our neighbor, Joe Brinkman, who had a well of sweet water on his property.

That very morning I had seen Joe with his wooden yoke over his shoulder balancing two cans of water while he trudged down the street to make his deliveries.

"Be careful of the water," was a phrase I would hear over and over again in the weeks to come. All the water for the house had to be carried in—and out. The hot bath I had been waiting for would have to wait until we walked to the bathhouse on Front Street.

Outside the kitchen door there was a porch where Dad kept a neat pile of chopped wood handy for Mother's use. Directly across from that was a tent with board sides and a dirt floor where the cords of wood for winter use were stacked. A narrow path led to the little house with the half-moon cut in the door. Tacked to the toilet seat was a piece of caribou fur—a most welcome innovation on a cold winter's night, I was told.

Everything in this new country was different from the city life I had always known. Then Dad had to make that remark about the job, and for an instant, I wished I hadn't come.

"Don't feel too badly, Clara," Mother said, noting my downcast expression. "You know your father." She squeezed my hand and said, "Why don't you take a nap in my room? Beth and I will clean the kitchen, and then we can walk to town and find out what has happened to your trunk."

"All right," I agreed, too tired to protest.

In Mother's small bedroom there was a chair and a dressing table against one wall. I turned around in dismay. Something was missing.

"Where's the bed?" I hollered.

Mother and Beth came to my rescue; they were both laughing. "It's right here," Mother said.

She pulled back the curtains to reveal a bed on hinges folded against the wall. In a moment the ready-made bed filled the room. It didn't take me long to crawl under those blankets and fall asleep.

By the time the three of us walked to town, the snow, which had been powdery and glistening when I arrived, had turned gray and mushy. In some places there were plate-size black puddles we had to tiptoe around, holding our skirts out of the mud. There were no wooden sidewalks in our neighborhood, which was considered on the fringe of town, so we took to the dirt paths, wherever possible, or out in the middle of the street. Beyond our place on Eighth was an undeveloped wooded area of unsurveyed streets.

As we walked down Cushman Street, the main artery of the town which ran from the Chena River south to join the trail to Valdez, I felt the vitality and daring of this mining town, barely 6 years old, trying to look as grownup and respectable as the places "back home."

In many ways it succeeded, because Fairbanks was not like other stampede towns, built for quick plundering; its roots went deeper. Here the placer gold was buried beneath layers and layers of muck, called overburden, sometimes as much as 150 feet under the ground. It took time to get the gold out. The get-rich-quick crowd had left 4 years earlier, but the pioneers who stayed had to build a town while they were digging for gold. On the heels of the miners came the businessmen, and the doctors, and the lawyers, and even surveyors who laid out the town and named the streets in honor of the first settlers. As a result, Fairbanks was built on a more lasting foundation than the shifting sands of Nome, or the glittering shores of Dawson.

When the first settlers came, after gold was discovered in 1902 by an Italian miner named Felix Pedro, the business district of the

Fairbanks, with cordwood stacked for the winter's use. The Northern Commercial Company power plant is at left.

town naturally took shape along the waterfront. It was there that Eldridge T. Barnette, a merchant man with a reputation for fast wheeling and dealing, set up the first trading post in crude cabins cut from the stand of native spruce.

A few years later Barnette's post was bought out by the Northern Commercial Company, which expanded the enterprise until it occupied almost a square block on First Avenue between Turner and Barnette streets. Their docks and warehouses, conveniently located along the riverbank, handled the freight that came in by the big sternwheelers and barges plying the muddy waters of the Chena River in the summer months.

The Northern Commercial Company owned the power plant, located on Second Avenue, which provided steam heat for the businesses, and electricity for those who could afford it. Here was a town, on the fringes of the Arctic Circle, that had a downtown water system, telephone service (hand crank with 18 pages in the directory), a library, two hospitals, two dairies, a number of churches, several public halls, an indoor swimming pool and the social activities of the Mason, Eastern Star and Eagles lodges.

Fairbanks was a city of contrasts. I soon lost count of the saloons we passed packed side by side along the waterfront in slapdash log buildings, with false fronts, opening onto wooden sidewalks. There were other businesses, too, for the town had to be self-sufficient during the winter's isolation. Some of them were housed in wooden frame buildings, two and three stories high, with signs out front: Owl Drug Store, Sargeant and Pinska's Men's Store, E. R. Peoples Furniture, Horseshoe Saloon, Third Avenue Hotel, Gordon's, Northern Hotel, J. L. Sale, Jewelers, Cribb's Glass Block, and others.

On a grander scale were the banks, three of them, with striped awnings over their plate glass windows. Upstairs were the offices of doctors, lawyers, dentists, assayers and government officials, for Fairbanks was the seat of the Fourth Judicial District.

Men wearing dark suits and hats lounged against the corrugated tin siding of the post office, and as we passed they tipped their hats, but they did not stare.

"Who are those men?" I asked as we crossed the muddy street.

"Most of them are miners," Mother answered. "They are out of work waiting to go Outside."

"Where is Outside?" I asked.

"It means Seattle," Beth said, eager to show off her knowledge.

"Or any place outside Alaska," Mother added. "The last boat of the season leaves next week. Most of those men will be on it."

Somehow I found that piece of news a little disappointing. I hoped that didn't mean *all* the men would be gone. But there I was, getting ahead of myself as usual.

In some places the wooden sidewalks were elevated as much as a foot above the ground to avoid the mud and small sloughs that ran through town. At the corners the sidewalks sloped to the street where horse-drawn wagons and men on horseback passed.

As we walked up Cushman, which was a mercantile district with shops on both sides of the street, we came to Fourth Avenue. At Fourth, there was a 10-foot-high board fence creating, oddly, a walled compound. A gate in the fence was just wide enough to admit wagon deliveries inside the compound.

"What in the world is that?" I asked.

"It's the red-light district," Mother replied above the clatter of our boots on the sidewalk.

"Right in the middle of town?" I asked.

"Yes," Mother said.

Then I noticed a pedestrian entrance to the Line, which was constructed with a blind wall so people could not see inside. Also in

25

this part of town were several dance halls, the Fast Track and the Flora Dora; and up ahead was Tammany Hall.

"Why did they build the Line right in the middle of town?" I wanted to know.

"That's just the way they do things in this town," Mother replied, not wanting to continue the conversation.

Well, it was no matter to me. I still liked this town in the heart of the Tanana Valley, flanked by the Alaska Range to the south and the rolling gold-bearing hills to the north.

There was something in me that wanted to know more about this place and the people in it. But did I dare? Would it only make the parting more painful as it had in the past whenever I got attached to a place and the people in it, and then we had to leave? After so many good-bys, I kept myself apart from things. I didn't want to get hurt again.

"Let's go in here," Mother said, turning in at Mary Anderson's Dry Goods and Dress Shop at Fifth and Cushman. "I want you to meet Mary."

As we entered the store, a boxy, one-story building, a bell sounded over the door. Mary spotted Mother immediately and came bustling toward us. She was in her forties, but with her enthusiasm and energy (along with a petite figure and blond-tinted hair), she gave the impression of a younger woman.

"I'll bet this is Clara," Mary said brightly, giving me a quick pat on the shoulder. "You look just like your mother."

"Thank you," I said. I liked her right away. Her small, heart-shaped face was open and friendly. There was understanding in her bright blue eyes, and a welcome in her warm smile.

While Mother and Mary talked, Beth and I explored the store, which was one large room, with a floor that dipped and heaved from the permafrost, crammed full of merchandise. On the shelves, which went up to the ceiling, were bolts of bright fabrics. Displayed on the counters and in the glass cases were boxes of sewing notions—shiny buttons, belt buckles, lace, velvet ribbons and such.

Ladies' dresses and coats were hung on racks while nearby tables were stacked with skirts, blouses and petticoats. On one table was a display of elegant Gage hats, some with broad brims, others with veils and ostrich feathers, flowers and bows.

"Who buys these kinds of hats way up here?" I asked Beth as I tried one on.

26

"Mostly the girls off the Line," Beth said.

"Oh, and how do you know that, Miss Smarty?" I asked.

"I heard Mother talking," she answered.

Just as we were leaving the store, Mother said, "Oh, Mary, can you use a husky girl? Clara is looking for work."

Mary sized me up with those knowing blue eyes. "Have you ever worked in a dress shop?" she asked.

"No," I replied, "but I worked in a bakery and a candy store. I know how to run a cash register and make change."

It didn't take long for her to make up her mind. "All right," she said, "I will put you to work. Come in Monday morning at 8 o'clock."

There it was, as simple as that. I got my first job in Fairbanks without really trying, and without Dad's help too. I could hardly wait to tell him.

"You don't have to gloat about it, Clara," Dad said that night at dinner. "Your job at Mary's isn't going to be a bed of roses, you know."

"Oh, I know," I answered, "but $50 a month is better than the $4 a week I was making in Seattle."

Mary would make me earn my money, but I knew I could handle the job. Ever since I was in the eighth grade I had worked; it was nothing new to me.

"And don't believe everything Mary Anderson tells you," Dad said as a parting shot before he went back to work that night.

"What does he mean by that?" I asked Mother.

"He means he doesn't approve of everything Mary says and does."

That didn't surprise me. With Dad's pessimism—a professional quirk among newspapermen—I doubted there was a person alive that he approved of wholeheartedly.

After I helped Mother put the kitchen in order (the dishwater was heated on top of the stove), she said, "Clara, I am sorry to leave like this on your first night in town, but I am in a play and I have to go to rehearsal."

I was disappointed. In the past Mother had always put her own interests before any of us. What made me think it would be any different now? I remember one winter when Dad was gone, Mother joined a theater group that went on tour. That left Beth and me home alone in the apartment. We were almost happy when we learned she had broken her shoulder because then we knew she would be home again.

It seemed to me that I was never a real person to my mother, but merely someone she lived with. My self-pity boiled up inside me. Why did she have to run off on my first night home?

Before my tears betrayed my emotions, I left the kitchen abruptly. All right, I thought, I will spend the evening unpacking and washing my clothes. It seemed a big letdown after the excitement of the day.

A few minutes later Mother put her hands on my shoulders. "Clara," she said, "why don't you come with me? I think you would enjoy rehearsal."

It was on the tip of my tongue to refuse, to stay stubbornly at home, nursing my wounded feelings. But I didn't want to stay home. This town seemed to be reaching out to me, offering me more than I had ever had before.

"Yes," I answered. "I would like to go with you."

At Eagles Hall, a spacious auditorium, Mother introduced me to the cast members. They all displayed that same friendliness I had encountered from other people I had met earlier in the day. How would I remember their names? I hoped that would come in time.

Dick Thorne, the director of the play, gave me a quick once-over. He was slight of frame and swift on his feet, dashing madly about the stage giving orders. His snow-white hair was thick and full, like a furry cap.

"Lose some weight and you will be a real looker," he said to me when we were introduced.

I smiled at his well-meant advice. It wasn't the first time I'd been told that.

After rehearsal was under way, Mr. Thorne handed me a script. "Here," he said, "you can be the Irish maid. One of our girls didn't show up."

"I've never been in a play before," I said incredulously.

"You are in one now," he said. "Read the lines with an Irish brogue. No trouble at all."

That night as I lay curled up on the day bed in the living room, with the wood stove flickering firelight on the balloon ceiling, I thought of the events of the day and wondered what could possibly happen tomorrow.

And the next day, and the next.

 **chapter 4**

As the weeks flipped by, like the ruffling of a deck of cards, a pattern emerged from the routine. Early in the morning, 6 days a week, I went to work and returned home in time for dinner. There were many evenings that I went back to work if Mary had merchandise to unpack. In my eagerness to prove equal to the job, I worked during my lunch hour, snatching bites of my sandwich between customers.

"Don't let Mary work you so hard," Dad advised. "You should come home on your lunch hour."

Although I resented Dad telling me what to do, I knew he was right. After that I walked home for lunch, no matter how cold it got.

As soon as I reached the store at 8 o'clock in the morning, I started the fire in Mary's bedroom, which was a cozy area off the main part of the store with a larger sitting room where she entertained her visitors. At that time of the morning Mary would still be asleep under a heap of wool blankets and a wolf robe. She had an intense fear of fire, and she let all the fires go out at night. When I arrived the rooms were like an icebox.

I learned to keep a supply of paper and kindling handy so I could get a quick fire started in Mary's room and in the store. Usually it was midafternoon before that big barn of a room was warmed up. I can still remember how cold those bolts of material were when I rolled them out to cut them for a customer. My hands never did get warm that first winter.

As the temperature in her room went up, Mary would discard one blanket after another until it was warm enough for her to get dressed and make her appearance.

Mrs. Housman, a mild-mannered, old-fashioned woman with wispy gray hair, worked with me. We shared the task of starting the fires, wearing our heavy coats all the while. It was her job to trim the hats and do alterations. Mine was to wait on the customers, most of them married women, the wives of lawyers, dentists, businessmen and government officials. Mary carried very expensive lines of clothing that the average person could not afford.

Just before I left in the evening I would sprinkle sawdust on the floor and sweep up in preparation for the next day. Walking home along the snow-packed streets I gazed with wonder at the intricate world of frost decorating the branches and tree trunks, fence posts and flower boxes. At my feet lay the powdery snow, as white as silk. From the black sky came tiny ice crystals to sting my face and whiten my hair. As I breathed that pure air, I knew I had done the right thing in coming to this place called Fairbanks.

Right after dinner Mother and I were always in a hurry to be off to rehearsal. Poor Beth was stuck with the dishes.

"Going out again?" Dad would say, looking forlorn and neglected.

"You know we are," Mother would say. "The play opens this weekend."

"Sure, sure," Dad would say, lifting the newspaper to his face.

When he was home, Mother wasn't. When Mother was home, he was gone. It always seemed to work out that way. His work kept him away from home many long hours. No wonder when Mother felt lonely and at loose ends she had set about to fill the long hours. Then Dad got mad when she wasn't home. It didn't make for very smooth sailing around the house.

Already I could see the tension building as it had in the past. Mother didn't say anything about Dad's attitude, and neither did I. We were having a good time together working on the play. I was selfish enough not to want to spoil it, and to be honest, I was content to let Dad stew in his own juices. He always said that

Mother came first; well, that's what we were doing, letting Mother come first.

The play that so engrossed us was called *Sowing the Wind,* and it was put on by the Fraternal Order of Eagles. Rehearsals took place in the Eagles Hall, just off Cushman on Fifth. At that time the lodge members were building an upstairs to be used as a dining room. We had to arrange our comings and goings around the scaffolding.

The cast members were a friendly bunch, and some evenings we all ended up at the Model Cafe for a late snack together. It meant a great deal to me to be accepted by this group, and to be on equal footing with my mother.

On opening night I was a quivering mass of nerves. The performance was put on in the Arctic Brotherhood building, between Second and Third on Wickersham, because they had a fine stage and auditorium. This large frame building, covered with corrugated iron, was two stories high on one end, and heated by steam from the Northern Commercial Company power plant.

My part in the play was a small one, but I worried that I wouldn't be able to maintain the Irish brogue once I was on stage. There was another thing that bothered me—it was nothing new—but I was more conscious of my size than ever before. All my life I had been taunted with jeers, "Fatty, fatty, two-by-four." Mother had dressed me in dark colors to conceal my size, but that never fooled anyone. The thought of walking out on that stage in front of all those people seized me with a fear I had never known before.

"Mother, do I look all right?" I asked her in her dressing room.

"You look fine, Clara," she said routinely. "Just fine."

It was a bad time to talk to her; she was preoccupied with her own make-up and costume. Besides, she had one of the leads with many pages of script to memorize. I couldn't blame her for thinking my fears were unwarranted.

While I waited nervously I watched the crew raise and lower the curtain which was operated with ropes and pulleys by means of a hand crank. Fairbanks was still full of surprises for me. Here the stage was outfitted with a professional curtain in a white silklike material decorated with a large hand-painted swan surrounded by blocks of advertisements from local stores, not the kind of thing I had expected to see in this frontier town.

The auditorium, with its fine stage and orchestra pit, had opera boxes which were reserved by Fairbanks' elite for special events. Victor Durand and his orchestra would provide music between the acts and for the dance that followed the play. Long before curtain time the hall began filling up, mostly with men seated on benches in the center of the hall.

When I peeked around the curtain and saw that full house, I panicked. How could I face all those people? My costume as an Irish maid was a long black skirt, white blouse, and frilly apron; it fit me well. Just pretend you are back in domestic service in Seattle, I told myself. Don't think about the people.

Suddenly the lights in the auditorium went off. A hush settled over the crowd. The orchestra began playing, and slowly, with a few fits and snarls, the curtain went up.

When it was my turn to go on, I managed it without a flaw. No one laughed at me. And, to my amazement, I enjoyed myself.

Of course the play was a big success. Any kind of entertainment was welcome in those days. We did get good reviews in the two dailies and the weekly, but no one was too surprised about that because the cast members had relatives on all three papers.

Monday morning at work Mary said, "I suppose you are going to make a career of the stage after your triumphant debut."

"Oh, no," I answered. "Once a year is enough for me. I get nervous all over again just thinking about it."

"It's good for you," Mary said as if recommending some medicinal prescription. "You should go out more often."

I smiled; it didn't pay to disagree with Mary. She always had an argument ready. I had gone to a few parties, but I wasn't in any hurry to rush into things. Working was a good way to meet people. In this town where the men outnumbered the women two to one, a new girl was a great curiosity. It wasn't long before the men were stopping by the store on some flimsy pretense just to look me over.

At the end of my first month at work I discovered that I owed Mary more money than she owed me. Since my Seattle clothes weren't warm enough, I had to buy long underwear and wool skirts and shirtwaists for work. And, most of all, I needed a heavy coat for walking in the cold weather. I chose a black broadcloth with brown plush lining and a large fur collar. The only time I ever had any decent clothes in my life was when I went to work and bought them myself. Mary was always generous—too generous for my own good—about extending credit so I could buy the things I wanted.

After I worked there awhile, Mary and I became good friends, and I appreciated her many kindnesses to me. There were many things I didn't understand about Mary, especially on those days when she was sharp and critical, but I learned that she had a physical problem that plagued her, and I tried to be more understanding.

With Mary, we never knew what was going to happen next. I remember one afternoon she came storming in the front door, slamming it with such a bang that I thought the glass would fall out. Mrs. Housman and I exchanged worried glances. Had we done something wrong?

"I just came from City Hall," Mary announced, her blue eyes flashing sparks. "I have never been so humiliated in my life."

"What happened?" I asked.

"I went there to pay my taxes, like a law-abiding citizen, and what do I get—insults." She spat out the words like poison.

"What happened?" I asked for the second time.

"There is a new clerk on the desk, and do you know what he said to me?"

"No," Mrs. Housman and I said in unison.

"He said, 'Now don't try and fool me about the taxes. You came here to pay your fine.'"

I gasped. Even though I hadn't been in town very long, I knew what that meant. The girls on the Fourth Avenue Line had to pay a fine to stay in business.

Mary raged on, "I told the clerk that he didn't know what he was saying, and he said, 'Come off your high horse and don't put on an act. Pay up your fine, Fanny.' He called me *Fanny.*"

Fanny! Why, everyone in town knew who Fanny was. Her fame went back to the Dawson days where she was called the "Songbird of the Yukon" when she entertained at the Pantages Theater. After Dawson went downhill, Fanny followed the gold rush to Fairbanks where she became a prostitute on the Line.

"I informed the clerk that he was making a very big mistake," Mary said, yanking off her coat and dumping it on the counter.

"About that time Mr. Pauli, the city clerk, came in. I told him to tell that young man who I was. He told him I was Mary Anderson, owner of Anderson's store. You should have seen the look on his face," Mary said triumphantly. "He turned white, and then red, and then green. I gave him a tongue-lashing he will never forget."

"Did he apologize?" I asked.

"He fell all over himself apologizing. He followed me out the door and halfway down the street telling me how sorry he was."

It wasn't long after that, about a week, perhaps, when Mary came banging in the front door again, madder than a wet hen.

"I have never been so insulted in my life!" she said.

"What happened now?" I asked.

"I was standing in line at the bank when some man came up behind me and swatted me on the rear end!"

My mouth fell open. This was a side of Fairbanks I didn't know about. "What did you do?" I asked.

"I turned around and gave him a shove and asked him what in the hell he thought he was doing. Then he said, 'What have you got your nose up in the air for, Fanny?'"

"Fanny!" I yelped. "Not again!"

"Yes, Fanny," Mary said as she stomped off to her room.

I looked at Mrs. Housman. "Isn't it awful?" I said.

"You'll understand when you meet Fanny," she answered.

"What do you mean?" I asked, but she would not talk about it.

Then one day Fanny came in the store, and I knew. She was wearing a gray squirrel coat, just like Mary's. She had the same pale, creamy skin like Mary's, except her cheeks were puffy-red.

There was a kind of glamor in her, though, in the way she walked into the store, swishing down the aisle leaving a wave of musky perfume. Her blond hair was piled on top of her head with clusters of curls behind each ear. Diamonds flashed on both hands. Her lips, painted red, had difficulty forming the words she wanted to say.

"Hello there, Housy," she said gaily. "What's new?"

"I'll see what Mary has in the back room," Mrs. Housman said.

Fanny pulled off her coat, revealing a good figure going plump. She wore a green checked gingham apron similar to the pinafore that I had worn as a child. The garment was low-necked and sleeveless with a ruffle trim on the neckline and hem, and tied in back with a wide sash of matching material.

Mary came out directly to wait on Fanny. "Come in back," she said, "I have some things you might be interested in." For an hour they laughed and chatted like sisters. As soon as Fanny left, Mary began pulling bolts of checked gingham off the shelves. "Make me three aprons, just like Fanny's," she said to Mrs. Housman.

What was going on? Mrs. Housman seemed to understand, and she went right to work. The apron became Mary's uniform at work, worn over her street dress. To complete the picture, Mary had her hairdresser make up a cluster of blond curls to wear behind each ear. The effect was charming, in a coy kind of way, and the likeness to Fanny was unmistakable. If Mary wanted to dress like Fanny, then why was she insulted when she was mistaken for her? I guess I had a lot to learn about people.

One evening when I got off work earlier than usual, I arrived home in time to hear Mother and Dad engaged in a loud argument. While I stood in the shed sweeping the snow off my boots, I heard Dad say, "I don't like the way she has been acting. As long as she is under my roof, she will do as I say."

"Well, at least give her a chance to explain," Mother said.

I pushed open the door and the talk stopped abruptly. "Clara, is that you?" Mother called.

"Yes."

"Come in here," Dad said. "I want to talk to you."

As I passed through the kitchen, the roast in the oven smelled delicious. I hoped Dad wouldn't delay dinner too long. That was one thing about Mother, no matter how many projects she got involved in, she always had a big meal at dinner time and expected all of us to eat together.

"Yes, Dad," I said, joining him at the dining room table.

"What is this about your trips to the Line?" he asked without mincing any words.

So that was it, I thought.

"I can explain," I said, taking a chair at the table. "It's part of my job at Mary Anderson's."

Dad ran his hand over his bald head and eyed me suspiciously. "I'd like to know what that means."

"It's very simple," I answered patiently. "When the girls on the Line ask to have clothes brought over, Mary has me do it."

"You mean you go in their cabins?" Mother asked.

I nodded.

"I don't like it," Dad said, raising his voice. "I don't like it at all."

How could I explain to them that there wasn't anything wrong with my trips to the Line? They weren't even a bad influence, if that's what they were afraid of.

I didn't tell them, of course, that I had jumped at the chance to go behind the board fence when Mary asked me.

"You're such a green kid," Mary always said.

That first day I entered the zigzag walkway to the Line, I felt a tingle of fear mixed with a strange kind of fascination. Inside the compound were two rows of log cabins facing each other, separated by a wide street. The cabins, or cribs, as they were called, were just like the hundreds of cabins all over town, small, low to the ground and with a smokestack going straight out the top of the pitched roof.

To me the Line was like a quaint village. There were only about 20 cabins, built quite close together. Each crib had a large front window where the girls sat or lounged in loose-fitting kimonos with their legs showing while they smoked cigarettes. At night there was music played on hand-cranked Victrolas.

Most of the cabins had small kitchens where the girls made coffee or scrambled eggs. When they wanted a meal with their gentlemen friends they would order it from the Model Cafe or Carr's Restaurant up the street and someone would bring it down to them.

The girls operated their business with the permission of the city (as long as they paid their fines), but they could not solicit in the saloons or cafes. It was also understood that they would not attend social affairs. Of course many of the girls had men who would hustle for them, drawing trade from the Flora Dora Dance Hall where Ham Grease Jimmy was the floor manager and where music by the Victor Durand orchestra could be heard in the evening with Tommy McSmart on the drums. Tammany Hall had a Madame, and for music, Claud Myrik on the rinky-tink piano. The Fast Track, adjacent to the Line, was another hot spot, with gambling on the side. Many of the cribs were owned by saloon keepers—or by "respectable" businessmen. The girls had their private living quarters in other parts of town.

Although Mary relied on the girls for a good part of her business, she knew that some of her other customers would be upset if they had to shop side by side with a prostitute. For that reason, Mary would take clothes over to the Line or open up the store at night for the girls.

At first I dropped the clothes in the back room of the cabins and returned hurriedly to the store. After the girls got to know me, I was invited into their parlors, if they were alone. We talked while I admired their fancy bedspreads and satin pillows they had embroidered. There were pictures on the walls, gewgaws on the dressers, and bright curtains with flounces at the windows. On the floor were thick rugs and always a double bed enveloped in gauzy curtains. The cabins were spic and span, kept that way by a maid who came in twice a week.

"I just don't like it," Dad said, interrupting my reverie. "You have your reputation to think about, Clara. What will people say when they see you going to that place? You, in a place like that!"

"I don't care what people say," I replied, "I'm not doing anything wrong. My conscience is clear."

Dad still wasn't satisfied. "I want you to tell Mary Anderson that going to those cabins is not part of your job," he said.

"I'll tell her," I said, "but she won't like it."

Lately Dad had been so suspicious, always questioning me about where I went, and who I talked to. Both he and Mother kept bringing up the word "reputation"; that was all I heard, over and over again. I had started dating, but they had no reason to complain. Besides, I figured I was entitled to some life of my own. I worked all day and contributed money to the household; what more did they want, I wondered.

It took me a week to work up enough courage to tell Mary what Dad had said.

"You tell your dad," she said sharply, "that he should mind his business, and I'll mind mine. It isn't going to hurt you to take clothes over to the girls. If such a thing ruins your reputation, you didn't have much to begin with."

I had expected such a reply from Mary, and I thought she was right. So it was business as usual, and I kept my mouth shut. Don't rock the boat seemed to be the safest course to run in those days.

chapter 5

One Sunday afternoon in November, Beth and I were home alone talking and daydreaming in the living room close to the fire. Darkness had already fallen, it came so early on those gray days hastening toward winter. There in the quiet house, with only the pop of dry logs in the fire to rouse us, we felt secure in our happiness at being together.

As I stretched, my eye caught sight of a photograph on the wall that had intrigued me for some time. It was a picture of a young man with bold eyes, fringed with the longest lashes I had ever seen, and an older woman in profile looking lovingly at him. He had a full head of dark hair, parted slightly to one side. There was something about his sharp nose and well-defined jawline that showed a strength of character that attracted me.

I noticed something compelling, almost mystical, about the woman with her black hair pulled into a bun and fastened with an ornate comb. She wore long, gypsylike earrings—which were not in fashion—and at the neck of her tailored dress were numerous strands of small beads.

"Who are those people in that picture?" I asked Beth.

"That is Jess," she said and when she mentioned his name a special quality came into her voice, "and his mother, Mrs. Madole. Jess is my adopted brother, and don't you go trying to take him away from me."

"How could I do that, Beth? I don't even know him," I answered. "Where do they live?"

"Mrs. Madole runs the First Avenue Bathhouse," Beth said, "and Jess works on a mining claim out on Pedro Creek. When he comes into town he stays with his mother."

"You mean he isn't married?" I asked.

"No."

The photograph Clara saw on the wall—Jess Rust and his mother, Cora Madole.

"How did you meet Jess?" I asked.

Then Beth told me that Mother and Mrs. Madole were good friends, and when she and Dad went out in the evenings they left Beth at the bathhouse. "One night I was crying because Mother had been gone so long," Beth said. "Jess came in and took me on his lap and asked me why I was crying. I told him I was lonely and missed my brother. Jess told me he would be my brother and I would be the little sister he had always wanted."

I couldn't help but think that Jess must be a pretty special person to be so kind to Beth.

Later Mother told me that Cora Madole had been a fortuneteller in Dawson. She used the name Madame Renio and set up shop in a small cabin during the gold rush in 1898. She had been divorced twice, first from Jess's father, and then from Ben Madole, whom she had married while in Dawson. Jess was her only son, 25 years old and an eligible bachelor.

On Friday nights Beth and I walked to the bathhouse to take a bath and wash our hair. It was on one of those occasions that I met Mrs. Madole, but not the elusive Jess. He was either coming into town, or he had just left. Mrs. Madole's partner in the bathhouse was Doc Overgaard, a slight man in his fifties, originally from Denmark. He was not a "real" doctor, as Beth said, but he operated the Health Clinic in the bathhouse.

In those days hot water and modern bathroom facilities were hard to come by. As a result, a number of bathhouses were established to serve the needs of the people. Mrs. Madole's First Avenue Bathhouse and Health Clinic, which was down the street from Dad's office, advertised in his newspaper. In exchange she gave him tickets which enabled us to bathe free of charge.

One Friday night Beth and I were at the bathhouse, taking our time, as usual, splashing around in the tubs. The walls separating the individual stalls were open at the floor and ceiling to allow warm air to circulate in the rooms. It also allowed Beth and me to holler back and forth. Suddenly Beth started yelling, "It's Jess! I hear Jess!" She jumped out of the tub and into her clothes.

It wasn't easy for me to make myself presentable before meeting that much talked-about person. I knew I was a sorry sight with my face red from the steamy bath, my hair plastered against my head—and no girdle. There I was bulging in all the wrong places; I felt as big as a barn.

"Jess," Beth said grandly when I finally dragged myself out of the bathtub, "this is my sister, Clara."

His outstretched hand was firm and cool in mine. "Hello," he said. He was taller than I imagined him to be, with broad shoulders and thin hips, and I had to look up to see those harsh, brown eyes staring down at me. His face, clean-shaven, had a ruddy color from the wind and sun.

"Beth talks about you all the time," I said, turning on my brightest smile so my dimples would show.

"She could hardly wait for you to come to Fairbanks," Jess replied. "I think she missed you very much, didn't you, little one?"

"Yes," Beth said shyly, clinging to Jess's hand. "How long will you be in town?" she wanted to know.

"A week or so," he answered. "We will see each other often," he promised.

The longer we stood there in the hallway, the more out of sorts I felt. All I wanted to do was get out of there—the sooner the better. Red-faced and fat, red-faced and fat, I kept thinking over to myself until I could no longer meet those eyes of his.

"Are you still my brother?" Beth asked, pulling on his arm.

"Of course," he answered. "Nothing will ever change that."

"I think we should go now," I said to Beth, taking her by the hand and dragging her away.

"Come see me soon," Beth called to Jess as we went out the door.

The air, colder than when we had left home, stung my face. As we passed the cabins en route, smoke from the chimneys rose straight up like plumed feathers, held intact by the cold, still air. High above our heads the stars were like tiny prick marks in the sky where a sickle-shaped moon glowed waxy white. In the distance I could hear the dogs howling, and that made me more anxious than ever to reach home.

"Guess what, Mother! Guess what!" Beth said even before the door was closed behind us. "Jess is in town."

"Oh, is he?" Mother said. "What did he have to say?"

"Nothing much," Beth said, pouting a little. "He stared at Clara a lot."

"He did not," I protested. "Stop making up stories, Beth. He hardly looked at me."

"He stared at you all the time," Beth repeated. "I knew he would. You will probably take him away from me, too."

"Don't be silly," I said. "He was happy to see you. Jess likes you very much. I could tell."

"Do you really think so," Beth said trying to control the eagerness in her voice.

"I know so," I answered. "He treats you in a special way."

"Well, I think he likes you too, Clara," Beth said.

After listening to our conversation, Mother went to the telephone. "I'm going to call Cora Madole and find out what Jess said. I know he has been waiting to meet you, Clara."

"Oh, don't call," I said, but it was too late.

Mother's call would seem as if we were overanxious to know what Jess thought of me. I was curious about his reaction, but some part of me dreaded to find out.

While Mother was on the telephone I had to leave the room. I couldn't stand to listen to her polite chitchat with Mrs. Madole. In the dark kitchen I sat next to the warmth of the fire. The only light we had was a bulb attached to an extension cord which we carried from room to room and hung on a nail. It was a makeshift arrangement to be sure, but that's all we could afford.

"It's only temporary," Dad had said. "One of these days we'll get the house wired and have more lights."

Sometimes Mother's patience surprised me. Make-do and patch-up, that had been the story of her life. As Mother continued talking on the telephone I grew more apprehensive by the minute. Did Jess like me? What had he said to his Mother? I had met a number of young men since coming to Fairbanks, but none of them had affected me the way Jess did.

At last Mother hung up.

"What did he say? What did he say?" Beth asked, jumping up and down.

"Oh, nothing," Mother said evasively when she saw me enter the room. "He said you were both very nice girls."

"He must have said more than that," I replied. "You were on the telephone half an hour."

"No, no it was nothing," Mother said, avoiding my eyes. "Nothing important."

Beth and I nagged until Mother admitted that Jess had said something more. "But I promised Mrs. Madole that I wouldn't tell you," she said.

We should have left well enough alone, but we didn't.

"I bet he said something awful about me," Beth pouted. "I bet he thinks I'm just a baby."

"He didn't say any such thing," Mother replied.

"Well, what did he say?" Beth demanded.

"I don't like repeating it," Mother said.

"Tell us, please, Mother," Beth said kneeling beside her. "We want to know so badly." Beth could usually get Mother to do anything she wanted; she was the only one who could.

"I promised Mrs. Madole that I wouldn't tell you," Mother said, but her defense was weakening.

That's when I should have left the room.

"Please, Mother, please," Beth pleaded.

"Oh, all right," Mother said. "I will tell you if you both promise not to get mad."

"I promise," I said.

"I promise," Beth echoed.

Mother hesitated a minute, then said, "Jess said he thought Clara was a big, fat slob."

"That's awful," Beth said.

"I hate him," I cried, running from the room.

I had been teased about being fat, even pleasingly plump, but no remark had been so cruel as Jess's. I grabbed my coat and ran out the back door.

The air stung my lungs. I had left the house without a scarf or mittens, and immediately the cold bit my ears and numbed my fingers. Tears were running down my cheeks.

In the darkness the streets were like long, black tunnels and the ground, frozen milky white, was as hard as marble. My flimsy slippers were treacherous for walking, and not one bit warm. I buried my hands deep in my pockets, but the cold air rushed down my neck, causing me to shiver uncontrollably. It wasn't long before my nose and the tips of my ears went numb. I slackened my pace and looked over my shoulder. In the darkness I saw a figure coming up the street.

"Clara, Clara!" a voice called.

It was Mother, and for an instant I was mad at her too. Why had she repeated such a thing to me?

You asked for it, I reminded myself.

"Here, Clara, put these on," Mother said handing me my scarf and mittens.

My teeth were chattering as I wrapped the wool around my head and pulled on the mittens. Mother wiped my cheeks with her handkerchief and took me by the arm. "Let's go home," she said.

I guess Jess's words cut me deeply because I had wanted to make a good impression on him and I knew I had failed. That night the words "big fat slob" reared up in my thoughts, and it hurt all over again.

Late the next afternoon while I was still at work the telephone rang. "It's for you, Clara," Mary said. "I think it's Jess Rust." She winked like one conspirator to the other. She had known Jess and his mother in Dawson.

"Tell him I can't come to the phone," I said, suddenly boiling up inside. How dare he call me after what he said.

"What's wrong with you?" Mary asked. "Jess is a nice guy."

That's what you think, I wanted to say, but instead I mumbled, "I can't talk to him."

Jess called several times after that, but I still refused to speak to him. Why should he want to talk to a fat slob, I thought. Why doesn't he leave me alone? I wished that I had never met him.

Not long after I had arrived in Fairbanks, Dad rented a piano from Peoples Furniture Store. Somehow we found a way to squeeze that somewhat battered upright into our cramped living room. After dinner the family would gather around while I played. Dad had a fine baritone voice and kept the rest of us on key. Some of our happiest moments were spent around that piano on dark winter nights.

One evening—a bitterly cold night it was, too—while we were singing, there was a knock at the door.

"Who can that be on a night like this?" Mother said as she went to the door. "Cora, Jess, come in."

I wanted to run from the room, but there was no place to hide in that small cabin. This better not be one of Mother's methods to get me to make up with Jess, I thought angrily. I remained seated with my back to the company. During the past week I had thought of a number of cutting remarks I would make to Jess when I saw him again, but suddenly I could not think of a single one.

In a few moments Jess was standing beside the piano. "Hello, Clara," he said. "Have you met my mother?"

"Yes," I answered without meeting his eyes. "We met at the bathhouse."

"You look very nice this evening, Clara," Mrs. Madole said. She smiled and I found myself responding.

Jess was as tall and slim and good-looking as I remembered him. "Do you know the song 'Little Bit of Heaven'?" he asked.

"Yes."

"Well, if you'll play it, I'll try to sing it."

He was a fine tenor, and when he finished there was enthusiastic applause.

"Jess," Beth said, "you sing like a bird."

He laughed. "It's been winter too long and you have forgotten what a bird sounds like."

"We haven't seen you at all," Beth said. "Not since that night at the bathhouse."

My hands froze on the piano keys. Surely everyone could hear my heart beating.

"I've been busy," Jess replied.

"I thought maybe you were mad at us," Beth said.

Jess didn't say a word. At last Mother broke the silence. "Let's sing," she said. "Come on everyone, gather around the piano."

We sang until we were hoarse, and when we couldn't sing any more, we sat at the dining room table in the dim light of the overhead bulb and ate a late supper. As I watched Jess I could not help but think: He's not so bad. Maybe Mother was mistaken. Maybe he really hadn't said I was a fat slob. Maybe I didn't want to believe it any more.

When Jess called me at work the following week to invite me to the Thanksgiving ball, I accepted too readily. As soon as I put the receiver down, I regretted what I had done.

"What's wrong?" Mary asked.

"I just told Jess I would go to the ball with him."

"There is no need to be scared," she said.

"But I've never been to a formal dance before. I won't know how to act, and I don't have a thing to wear."

"We can take care of that," Mary said, flipping through the rack of dresses. She eyed them critically. "That won't do. That one is out. No, not that one."

There wasn't anything on the rack I liked, and I was relieved that Mary agreed. She was good at giving me advice about my clothes (how to accent my small waist and detract from my large hips), and I knew I could trust her judgment.

"I know. I have just the thing," she said, disappearing into the back room to return with a gown of black taffeta. "Try this on."

As I pulled the rustling material over my head I knew it was the dress for me. Everything was right about it from the revealing, but not too daring, square-cut neckline to the short, puffed sleeves and full skirt. Adding a touch of simple elegance was the black soutache braid around the neck and sleeve bands.

Mary handed me a pair of elbow-length black gloves. I pulled on the soft kid leather and preened in front of the mirror like an actress.

"And this for a dash of color," Mary said, putting a comb of red roses in my hair.

"It's perfect," I said. "I can hardly wait to show Mother."

My enthusiasm for the dance was not matched by those at home. Mother, who was suffering a bad spell of headaches, did not want to be disturbed. Beth, who thought I had succeeded in taking Jess away from her, eyed me reproachfully.

That week the temperature dropped, and by Saturday it was 55 degrees below zero. Even though stoves were heated to red-hot, the rooms stayed chilly. Forever plaguing us was the fear of fire. Fairbanks, with its wooden buildings and sawdust insulation, was a tinderbox. At our house several buckets of water were kept near the stove.

By evening a dense fog had settled, shrouding the streets and causing an eerie silence to fall over the town. Jess and I had to walk six blocks to the Eagles Hall, but I wasn't going to let the weather stop me from attending the ball.

In my haste to be ready on time, I was half an hour early. There I sat, watching the clock hands creep toward 8:30, while I became more nervous with every passing moment.

"You have two big red spots on your cheeks," Beth informed me as she sailed through the living room.

I rushed to the mirror. She was right. I opened the door to let the air cool my cheeks, and there was Jess coming up the path.

"He's here!" I yelled, slamming the door.

"Get your coat, Clara," Mother said. "I'll let Jess in."

Jess, wearing a heavy coat and fur hat, stood by the stove warming his hands when I entered the room.

"Hello, Clara," he said. "Better dress warm."

"I did," I answered. Beneath my evening gown I had on wool

tights and heavy stockings. Next came a sweater, my coat, two scarves and mittens. I carried my dancing slippers.

The brittle air took my breath away. We walked quickly, heads bowed to the cold. Through the fog we saw the muted light of the street lamps and store windows. Other couples, as heavily bundled as we, mounted the wooden steps of the two-story building that housed the Eagles lodge. Inside there was a welcome warmth and a foyer crowded with people, so many strangers, as elegantly dressed as the Seattle elite I had watched at a distance. When Alaskans did anything, it was first class.

Suddenly I was afraid. Would I know how to act? Would I say or do anything wrong? I didn't want to embarrass Jess in front of his friends.

Jess directed me to the ladies dressing room where a colored maid, wearing a black uniform with a starched white apron, helped me remove my heavy clothes. I changed to my dancing slippers and smoothed my hair. The dress is perfect, I reassured myself, with one last look in the mirror.

When I came out, Jess was waiting for me. My heart nearly burst with pride at the sight of him. Was I really with that good-looking man? What a handsome figure he cut that night in his tuxedo with his diamond stickpin in his starched shirt front.

He took me by the arm and we entered the hall where two wood-burning stoves, one at each end, warmed the room. Electric lights, suspended on long cords, could be seen among the yellow and orange crepe paper festooning the ceiling. There were people seated along the raised platforms that ran the length of the building on both sides. The inlaid floor was ideal for dancing. And how the people loved to dance to Victor Durand's orchestra. The musicians, resplendent in white ties and black tails, assembled on the stage.

But before the ball could begin, there was a certain protocol that had to be observed. That was the filling out of the dance program which all the ladies and gentlemen received along with a tiny gold pencil. The program was like a written guarantee that everyone (especially the ladies) would have a successful evening. There were no wallflowers in this country where women were so comfortably outnumbered.

At midnight dinner was announced. In the upstairs dining room the long tables were spread with white linen and set with gold-edged white china, crystal goblets and gleaming silverware. Waiters in black suits came with steaming platters of food—roast turkey and all the trimmings—followed by pumpkin pie, mince pie and nut cups. There was coffee; nothing stronger than coffee or punch was served. Some of the men (not Jess) would duck out to the foyer for a nip from a bottle, but in those days it was rare that liquor was served at such affairs. After dinner we danced again and again, whirling to the polka, the two-step, the schottische and those lovely Viennese waltzes.

I didn't want the evening to end, but it did. Jess held my arm as we made our way along the deserted streets, our footsteps creaking in the dry snow. The only light at that late hour came through the frosted panes of our kitchen window. Mother was waiting.

"It was a wonderful evening," I said. "Thank you for inviting me." I pulled off my mitten and offered him my hand.

"It was my pleasure," he said, gripping my hand.

"I really must go," I said, pulling away.

Jess took a step closer and bent his head to mine. I backed away.

"What's the matter?" Jess said, those brown eyes flashing. "Aren't you going to kiss me goodnight?"

"No," I said primly. "I am not."

"Well, why not?" he demanded. "Didn't you have a good time?"

"I told you I did, but that doesn't mean I have to kiss you."

"If that's the way you are going to be," he said, "then good-night."

With that he gave me a shove and I fell backwards into a deep drift of snow. Then Jess took off down the path on the run.

I was so astonished I couldn't speak. Neither could I move, bundled so awkwardly in heavy clothing and sinking fast into the soft snow. After struggling desperately, while the tears ran down my cheeks, I finally got to my feet.

I hate him, I hate him, I thought as I groped my way to the door. I never want to see that Jess Rust again. It had been such a wonderful evening. Why did he have to spoil it?

The hinges on the back door squeaked as I pushed it open.

"Clara, is that you?" Mother called.

"Yes."

"How was the dance?" she asked anxiously.

"I don't want to talk about it," I said as I flung myself on the couch.

chapter 6

December came on with a dwindling of light and a sudden warmth that filled the mild, milky days with snow everywhere. I walked to work under trees plump with snow, all curved and gentle and gray-blue. In the yards I passed there were sled tracks and angel wings and children playing in long coats and knitted caps.

Some mornings I met Fred Musgard, the water man, whose sleigh was pulled by two spotted gray horses. White smoke poured out of the stack in the center of the sleigh where a small fire burned to keep the water tank from freezing. Two 5-gallon water buckets swung from the faucet, which was thick with icicles hanging almost to the ground. Colored cards in the frost-framed windows were his stop signs.

Several days after the dance Jess called me, but there was no mention of the snowbank incident. In many ways he reminded me of a child who acts impulsively and then he's sorry, but he doesn't know how to apologize. Still, Jess and I had many happy hours together just walking to town, riding in his dog sled or skating on the river ice. I never knew what he was going to do next, or even when I would see him again. He was a totally unpredictable person. Maybe that's what I liked about him.

When we were together, we talked hour after hour. He told me about his boyhood in Butte, Montana, and how lonely he had been as an only child. After he and his family moved to Seattle, his parents were divorced and Jess and his mother returned to Butte, where she opened a dressmaking shop and told fortunes on the side.

"I don't believe in that fortunetelling business," Jess said, "but I did go to some of her classes and I learned to hypnotize people."

"Could you hypnotize me?" I asked.

"Not unless you were willing," he laughed.

When Jess was 15 he left home, making his way back to Seattle, where he worked for Western Union delivering telegrams. He took on all kinds of jobs—as an apprentice for the Seattle Electric Company, as a troubleshooter and lineman for Bell Telephone Company, as an usher at the Seattle Theater, and a repairman for the White Sewing Machine Company.

While Jess and I were comparing notes about our Seattle days, we discovered that he was a member of the First Christian Church where I had been baptized at the age of 12. And much to our surprise, we concluded that Jess had sung in the choir the night I joined the church. Of course, we hadn't met then, and I was glad of that because I had been a roly-poly girl in those days, and I remembered how ugly I felt when I came out of that submersion tank with the black choir robe flapping around my ankles.

In 1898, when Jess heard about the Klondike strike, he decided to go North.

"I wrote Mother that I was going to Dawson," Jess said, "I took a job as a flunky on a boat and got as far as Wrangell, where I worked all summer in a shingle mill to make enough money to get to the Yukon."

By this time his mother decided she wanted to try her luck up North, so she made her way to Seattle and traveled the Inside Passage to Wrangell, where she joined Jess in 1899. At Skagway they met up with a party of people who had a boat. Since Jess was adept at many skills, boat repairs included, he and his mother were invited to join the group. They carried the boat over the White Pass (2,900 feet) and traveled Lakes Bennett, Tagish, and Marsh, through Miles Canyon and White Horse Rapids on the Yukon.

They still had to cross Lake LaBerge and navigate Five Finger and Rink rapids before entering the main stem of the river for a total of 560 water miles to Dawson—the City of Gold.

There Jess joined 40,000 other men and women in that sawboard metropolis—slightly smaller in population than the Seattle he had left behind—to seek his fortune. Jess went to work as a bellhop in the swanky Regina Hotel, where he was given a room on the top floor. In the meantime, his mother found a small log cabin and hung out her shingle as Madame Renio, Fortune Teller.

Jess didn't strike it rich in Dawson; in fact, he never worked in the mines, but he increased his knowledge and his skills, and he made more money than he would have in Seattle.

He liked to tell the story about the night the miner came to town, his pockets bulging with gold, to visit his girl friend at the Regina Hotel. After several hours of drinking, the miner decided his girl should have a bath in champagne.

"Nothing is too good for my Lil," he said.

The bellhops were ordered to take three cases of champagne to Lil's room. Jess and his buddies couldn't see all that sparkling wine going to waste, so they found some empty champagne bottles, filled them full of water, and took them to the room along with the real thing. Since the miner and his girl were pretty well liquored up, they didn't realize the bath was more water than champagne. From then on the miner's girl was known as Champagne Lil—and Jess and his cronies made a tidy sum selling the full bottles.

That was Jess; I never knew what he was going to do next.

On one of those rare days when Mary let me off work early, I decided to visit Mrs. Madole at the bathhouse. Darkness had already fallen. Yellow lights atop the telephone poles shone down on the snowy streets as I made my way down Cushman Street. At the bridge I turned and walked along the river, passing the Northern Commercial Company's hardware, ready-to-wear and grocery stores. Sandwiched in between was the corrugated metal building that housed the post office.

Before reaching the bathhouse I had to pass the Masonic Temple, a two-story structure with large windows, where Dad's office was located. I saw him inside working, but I did not stop. Somehow I never felt free to walk in and visit. No matter how much I wanted our family to be close, we never were.

The bathhouse was an awkward hulk of a building, two stories high in front, dropping down sharply to one story and then tapering to the low shed at the back where the boiler was installed. It was a narrow building, not more than 20 feet wide, of unpainted boards. From the high front window overlooking the Chena, a light glowed in Mrs. Madole's upstairs parlor.

When I opened the bathhouse door I was assailed by the odor of wet towels and rubbing alcohol, but as soon as I climbed the wooden stairs, the fragrance of coffee took over. Light bulbs suspended from a long cord at the top of the stairs cast harsh shadows on the wallpaper that was somewhat wrinkled from the dampness. From inside the apartment came the murmur of voices. I knocked lightly.

"Clara, hello," Mrs. Madole said, coming from the other room. "What a nice surprise. Won't you come in?"

I followed her through the small dining room to the parlor where a plump, dark-haired woman was seated at the round table in front of the window.

"I would like you to meet Mrs. Ed Williams from Engineer Creek," Mrs. Madole said.

"Hello. I hope I am not interrupting anything."

"Oh, no," Mrs. Williams answered. "I was just leaving." She pronounced it "yust" in her Norwegian accent. She was a pleasant-looking woman with a merry smile and bright green eyes. It did not take her long to gather her belongings and go out the door.

"I hope she did not hurry away because of me," I said.

"No, dear. She has been planning to leave for half an hour," Mrs. Madole answered. "Come, sit at the table and I will give you something hot to drink. Would you like coffee or hot chocolate?"

"Hot chocolate, please. I am not used to drinking coffee the way you Alaskans do."

She removed the deck of cards from the table and took down the poster of the large palm and the sign of the zodiac—the tools of her trade.

"Did you tell Mrs. Williams's fortune?" I asked curiously.

"Yes. She comes here quite often to consult me," Mrs. Madole replied. "I have a number of customers in town who knew me in Dawson, and I tell their fortunes regularly."

"Oh," was all I could think to say. Dad had always made derogatory remarks about fortunetelling, calling it a sham and a cheap trick. I suppose I had unconsciously agreed with him.

"I will be back in a minute with your hot chocolate," Mrs. Madole said.

While she was gone I glanced about the small room, somewhat crowded with furniture, including the large round table where I was sitting as well as a rocking chair and an upholstered armchair near the bookshelves on the far wall. There were two tall windows, one overlooking First Avenue, both with floor-length lace curtains. A number of colorful calendars vied for attention on the gold scroll-design wallpaper. A sewing machine, obviously well used, sat on a table stacked with clothes in various stages of completion. It was not a pretentious room, by any means; it was a room for comfort and work, with a sense of order about it.

When Mrs. Madole returned with my hot drink I said, "Jess told me you take in sewing."

"Yes; I have been doing that for years. In fact, I have some things of Mary Anderson's I am working on now," she said.

Again I was reminded of that gypsy quality in her that I had first noticed in her photograph. Her hair was jet black and glossy, pulled into a neat bun. Her olive skin was smooth, accented by black arched brows and deep brown eyes. Her movements were those of a dancer's, graceful and fluid with shoulders thrust back and head held high.

Mrs. Cora Madole in 1908.

When she joined me at the table with coffee for herself she said, "I have always made my living as best I could. It has not been easy for Jess and me. There were times when I didn't know whether we were going to have enough money to get from one week to the next. But Jess has always been good to me; he is not like some men, he always finds a job."

She went on to tell me that when Jess was in Dawson he worked on the riverboat the *Rock Island* during the summers, returning to his job at the hotel when winter came. On the boat Jess was a cabin boy for Captain La Ballister. They plied up and down the Yukon from Dawson to Saint Michael with trips into Fairbanks after the gold strike.

"When Dawson started going downhill in 1903, I moved here," Mrs. Madole said. "Next year Jess made a trip Outside by way of the White Pass, and in 1905 he returned to Dawson to work for Captain La Ballister until freezeup. Then he joined me in Fairbanks. That first winter he worked as a hoist man for a miner on Goldstream. It was his job to run the steam engine which was used to hoist the men and buckets of pay dirt out of the mine shaft.

"When he wasn't working at the mine, Jess hunted moose, caribou and mountain sheep and sold the meat to Fairbanks restaurants," his mother said. "His real interest is in mining now, and he won't be happy until he makes a good strike."

While Mrs. Madole was talking I realized that Jess's life and mine were similar in many ways. He had moved around as much as we had, and he had been on his own at an early age. There was one thing Jess had that I never had: a strong tie with his mother. I couldn't help but envy him that.

"How long have you been in the bathhouse business?" I asked as I sipped my drink.

"Since last year. I had the building built, and Doc and I opened it during the summer of 1907. Jess doesn't think that Doc has much business sense, and maybe he is right, but Doc is an intelligent person and he helps many people in his clinic downstairs. It is hard work, running a bathhouse, but I am used to such things. You know what it's like to work hard too, don't you, Clara?"

"Yes, I do," I said, grateful for her remark. She was a friend of my mother's, but she accepted me as a person, not as Martha Hickman's daughter.

"Come into the dining room and we can have a little supper while we talk," Mrs. Madole said. "I have some rabbit stew on the stove."

"Thank you. I would like that."

In the dining room the table and chairs and the dresser with an ornate mirror above it took up most of the space, leaving room for a fold-up bed which was concealed behind colorful curtains on one wall. From the table I watched Mrs. Madole work in the small kitchen in the back where the eaves slanted, making it a rather

Jess as hoist man at the Engineer Creek mine.

cramped area. There was a small cookstove with a woodbox nearby, a sink was next to that and on the walls were open shelves to hold her utensils and dishes. In the open area between the two rooms was a small table with plants which were nourished by the sun that came from the skylight. Over the table was a low hanging lamp with a fringed shade that cast a cozy glow throughout the room.

While we ate, I told Mrs. Madole about my experiences in Seattle after Mother and Dad came North with Beth. It wasn't until after we finished eating that I realized how late it was.

"Oh, dear, Mother will be worried about me," I said. "I should be getting home. May I help you with the dishes before I leave?"

"Goodness, no. There are just a few plates. Don't worry about that."

As I was going down the stairs, Mrs. Madole said, "Jess will be in town Saturday."

I smiled appreciatively. That woman did have insight; she knew what had been on my mind all the time.

"Thank you for everything," I said.

The moment I got home and saw Mother's angry face, I knew I was in trouble.

"Where have you been?" she demanded. "I have been calling all over town for you. Mary said you left work at 4:30. I was just about ready to go looking for you."

"I am sorry," I said. "Mrs. Madole and I got to talking, and then she asked me to stay to dinner."

"So that is where you have been," Mother said, almost as if she were jealous. "I don't want you hanging around that bathhouse all the time. It isn't good for your reputation."

"I don't know what you mean," I said, surprised at her remark.

"Everyone knows that drunks and people like that go to the bathhouse to sober up," she said. "Besides, as long as you are under my roof, you will do as I say."

"Well, the bathhouse seemed to be a good enough place to leave Beth when you wanted to go out," I said.

"Don't argue with me, Clara," Mother said, slamming the dishes in the pan. "I know what I am talking about."

After that I stayed off the bathhouse subject, but I didn't stop going there. When it was Saturday and I knew Jess was in town, I could hardly wait for the store to close so I could go see him.

When I reached the bathhouse I rattled the front door in hopes that Jess would hear me and come downstairs. I waited a few seconds, smoothing my hands over my hair and tucking in my blouse, but he didn't come.

I took the stairs slowly, dreading that moment when everyone would turn around and look at me. During those times I felt awkward and heavy. Jess was so well built and slender, I just knew people were saying, "What does he see in her?"

There was laughter coming from Mrs. Madole's room. She had a knack of befriending every stray that came to town, young or old, it didn't matter. They all got an invitation for hot coffee or a meal at her table.

But no matter what Mrs. Madole was doing or who was there, Jess came first. It didn't take me long to learn that I had to share him with her when he came to town. There was a bond between them made of strong links from the past, and that was something I couldn't compete with.

Jess was sitting at the table, with his back to me, talking to Frank Taylor, a bachelor friend of his. I had met Frank at the Thanksgiving Ball where he had worked as a waiter. He worshipped Jess, hung on his every word, and did everything Jess told him to do. Jess was a leader, and I liked that, but his sureness made him cocky and demanding.

Dr. Overgaard saw me at the doorway and said, "I think there is a young lady here to see you, Jess." His words were thickly accented; he had an impeccable air that commanded attention. With his gray hair and neatly clipped moustache, the doctor had an aristocratic look.

When Jess turned I was met by a direct gaze from those penetrating brown eyes. There was something different about him. He had grown a moustache.

"Clara, come in," Jess said, pulling a chair out for me.

"Hello, Jess," I said, sounding too formal, but we were always like that, shy and reserved after an absence.

"I'll fix you some hot chocolate," Mrs. Madole said. "You must be cold."

"Thank you. I would like something hot to drink," I said.

The talk around the table was always the same; it was about mining. Unfortunately, I didn't know the difference between a pay streak and a mother lode, a windlass from a cutlass, or a donkey engine from a trolley car. I could only guess at what they were talking about. Whenever I did venture a comment, it turned out to be wrong. Until I knew what the boys were talking about, I tried to keep my mouth shut. Mary Anderson had said that I was too loud and impulsive, and I guessed she was right.

"I think you have sunk the shaft deep enough," Mrs. Madole was saying. She spoke with a positiveness that I envied, and I wanted to be like her. "You should start tunneling now."

Jess leaned back, stretching his arms and clasping his hands behind his head, tilting in his chair. "I might hit a better vein if I go down another 10 feet," he said.

"How deep is the shaft now?" Frank asked.

"About 80 feet," Jess replied.

"What kind of color are you getting?" Doc asked.

"A little better than $3 to the pan," Jess answered.

Doc nodded as he sipped his coffee, his little finger midair, European style. He wore a white shirt and dark vest to match his trousers, and a tie. I don't think I ever saw him without a tie.

"Pretty good color," he murmured, tapping the ashes off his cigarette.

Jess pushed back his chair. "I'll think about it," he said loudly. "Come on Clara," he said, shaking my chair, "let's go for a ride."

"Yes, let's," I agreed.

In the back yard Jess worked quickly to hitch up the dogs. He had done it so many times that he could almost do it with his eyes closed. His dogs, Diamond, Irish and Murphy, were mixed breeds of malemute and German shepherd with some spaniel thrown in for good measure, and how those dogs could pull. Jess was their lord and master, and they were slavishly obedient to him.

After I got in the sled Jess wrapped me in a wolf robe and tied me in with a wide leather belt so I wouldn't fall out if he made an especially fast turn.

This man I had set my eyes on, and kept running back to again and again, had a volatile temper. When he didn't get his own way, he exploded with some brash and childish gesture. I was easily hurt by these outbursts, sometimes even stunned. There were times when I could sense when he was getting mad and change the subject to avoid an explosion. But there were other times when we disagreed that he would purposely dump me in a snowbank along the trail.

"Now, Jess, be careful," I said. "I don't want to end up in a snowbank this time."

"Just behave yourself," he laughed as we took off with the singing of sled runners on silky snow.

When we went riding Jess often took the trail out towards the Tanana River. It never mattered to me where we went as long as I was with Jess. After we had left the lights of town far behind us, the moon showed us the way, rippling on the snow with a silvery sheen.

There were no signs of habitation out there where the pointed green spruce trees grew close together along the trail. It was just the two of us with the dogs and the solitude of a starry night. That was when we did our best talking, with me deep in the fur robe and Jess on the back runners.

"How long are you going to be in town?" I asked.

"Just a couple of days."

"Is that all?"

"Yes, isn't that enough?"

"It's never enough," I said.

"What do you want?"

"To see you more often."

"You never act very friendly," he said slowing the team to a walk.

"I'm always happy to see you," I said, but I knew what he was referring to. Jess was still trying to get his first kiss. I knew I was being stubborn, but I couldn't help it. Something was holding me back. I couldn't explain it to myself, and I certainly had no success in explaining it to Jess.

It was all mixed up with my parents' constant harping about my reputation and the things that could happen to a young girl if she wasn't careful. The more Jess persuaded, the more I resisted.

"You are going to have to grow up one of these days, Clara," he said.

When we returned to town Jess dropped me off at my house. We stood in the street while the dogs lay at our feet, long tongues unfurled.

"There is something different about you," I said, not wanting to let him go.

"What's that?" he asked.

"This," I said, touching his moustache with my fingers.

"Do you like it?" he asked.

I paused a minute. It did give him a jaunty, rakish air, but it was a different Jess and I wanted him to stay the same. "No," I replied. "When are you going to shave it off?"

"When you kiss me," he bargained.

My cheeks went bright red. Why did he have to say things like that? "Oh, Jess, don't be silly," I said.

"I am serious," he answered.

"All right," I bargained, feeling brave. "I will kiss you when you shave your moustache off."

"That's a deal," he said, and with a wave he was gone.

As the days passed I waited for a call from Jess, but none came.

"Don't sit around waiting for Jess to call," Mary said, always able to pinpoint my problems even before I could. "Go out and have a good time."

There was something to do every night if I wanted it that way, and plenty of escorts, too. I often went dancing with Judge John Dillon, who was the commissioner with a reputation as a ladies' man. Although he was much older than I, we had a fine time together because we both loved to dance. Even to my girlish eyes he was an exceedingly handsome man, so tall and straight with a wonderful head of white bushy hair. When in his full evening dress with a starched white shirt and stand-up collar, he cut a fine figure. I remember he always wore a black bow tie and white gloves.

My mother, and some of my friends cautioned me about the judge, saying I shouldn't be seen with him because it would ruin my reputation. I never listen to such gossip. As long as I knew that I was doing right, I had nothing to worry about.

That winter I joined the Thespian Club, which my mother and father attended. It was run by Anna Caskey, wife of J. Harmon Caskey who owned the *Alaska Citizen*, the weekly newspaper.

Our meetings were held in a small hall over the printing plant across the river in Garden Island, so named because many farmers had their gardens there. On that side of the river was the Tanana Valley Railroad depot, St. Joseph's Hospital, as well as Miller's Saloon, Davis Sash and Door Factory and the Bevin House, a two-story log building with rooms to rent, and a number of warehouses.

Our Thespian Club would hold a short business meeting to discuss plans for a new show, followed by a dance and a light supper. The women took turns furnishing the sandwiches and cakes, and every now and then we had a box social.

Then there were evenings when our group had use of the swimming pool at the Natatorium. Inside that large frame building was a warm-water swimming pool, steam slabs, showers and dressing rooms, and bathing suits for rent. Along one side of the pool and across one end was a balcony which ended with a long slide going down into the water. Oh, the wonderful times we had, all of us together, sliding down that slide with the men trying to push the women to the bottom of the pool.

It wasn't all socializing, our Thespian Club. Anna was a worker and we put on several presentations each season. Her most ambitious effort, by far, was the opera *Erminie*. This required a huge cast of actors, actresses, soloists, dancing girls, and a chorus backed up by the Victor Durand Orchestra. For this special event costumes of satin and silk and high powdered wigs, no less, were ordered from Seattle.

Some evenings, or even during the day when business was slack at the store, I went roller skating at Gordon's indoor rink down the street from Mary Anderson's. It was a huge building with a hardwood floor where many dances were held. Behind the building stood a boiler house which provided electricity and steam for the roller rink. At one time Gordon's had tried to compete with the Northern Commercial Company in providing heat and electricity to the city, but it was not a successful venture.

That winter Jess was in town just enough for me to want to see more of him. He knew I was dating other men, and he urged me to have a good time, "but not too good," he said, and there was a serious note in his playfulness. When Jess came to town, I often broke a date to be with him.

Jess's two dogs, Irish and Murphy, got to know me, and the minute they hit town they would come to the store and stick their noses against the door.

One evening at closing time, Mary said, "Clara, your beau is in town, and your escorts are waiting."

As soon as the store door closed behind me, Irish and Murphy, their masked faces grinning, gave me welcoming yelps as they bounded to my side, taking my mittened hands in their mouths as we made our way home to Jess.

Diamond, the lead dog, considered it beneath his station to meet me at the store with the pups, but he allowed me to pet him when he was in the yard, and so we became friends, too.

When we reached the bathhouse I was surprised to find Jess waiting for me downstairs. In my excitement at seeing him, I almost overlooked the most important thing: he had shaved off his moustache. At that instant Jess looked at me, and he knew what I was thinking. "I'm here to collect your part of the bargain," he said.

"I was only teasing," I stammered. "I didn't mean it." I pressed my palms to my burning cheeks.

"I was serious," he said, "and I kept my word. Don't make promises like that unless you plan to keep them."

"Well, Jess, you can't expect me to kiss you here," I said, gesturing to the open waiting room. "It's so public. Let's wait until we are alone sometime."

"Follow me," he commanded.

He started down the long hallway that led to the back of the building. We passed the doorway to the bathing stalls and the steam rooms. I was strongly tempted to duck into one of these rooms and hide, but I knew Jess would not think that funny. I could just imagine his fury. I hadn't forgotten (and never would) what he had done when I refused to kiss him the night of the Thanksgiving Ball.

Up ahead of me, Jess was leaning nonchalantly against the door frame. "Go in," he said, indicating the open door.

"Who, me?" I said dumbly.

"Yes, you," he answered, forcing me forward while he closed the door.

The small room, finished with tongue and groove wall boards, had one window, up high, that was uncurtained. A single cot was pushed against the wall. There were no chairs, just boxes and those overflowing with books and clothes, tools and cameras, dog harnesses and boots.

"Whose room is this?" I asked.

"Mine," he said, standing behind me with his arms folded across his chest.

"I don't think we should be in here like this," I said.

"Why not?" he asked. "You wanted it private."

"Well, yes, but, well, I don't know," I said nervously. "Oh, look at all the pictures on the wall," I said, trying to change the subject. "Who took them?"

"I did."

"Here's one of your mother, and this is your dog team, and, oh, this one is of a gold mine. I like that one. And this is the bridge over the Chena, I can see Garden Island in the background. I'll bet that's Doc, and this one is Frank. What do you know." My nervousness made me chatter; I just couldn't stop talking. "When did you start taking pictures, Jess, I never knew you took pictures. You never told me."

"I started taking them when I was in Dawson," he said. "I worked for Mrs. Robertson, who had a studio there. She used some of my pictures for post cards."

"That's wonderful, Jess," I said, trying to keep my distance, which wasn't easy with clothes and boxes strewn all over the floor.

Suddenly Jess grabbed my arm and pulled me toward him. "I'm not going to ask you again, Clara," he said.

He kissed me for the longest time, until my head was spinning. He held me close, and I didn't even struggle.

"See, Clara," he said at last. "That wasn't so bad."

"I know," I said with a sigh, my knees wobbling.

He put his mouth to mine and kissed me again. I pulled away. "I have to go home now," I said, backing away from him. "I have to go home."

"Wait, Clara, wait," Jess hollered. "Don't go."

But I was out the door before he could catch me and I ran those slippery streets toward the safety of home.

So that was the beginning.

We had our quarrels, that was for sure, and we had our misunderstandings and hurt feelings. I continued going out with other men (even had a few marriage proposals), but by then I had an idea of who I wanted.

Looking back I can say that winter was the happiest of my life.

chapter 7

Christmas week came, and I was still pondering what to give Jess. I wanted my gift to say what I felt for him, but not everything. Jess was so temperamental. I never knew how he would react. Sometimes I felt as if I were walking on eggs. Besides, this courting business was all new to me.

Mother Madole would have helped me, if only I had asked her, but I couldn't bring myself to say anything. I spent many hours with her in the evenings while she taught me to crochet and embroider. At that time Battenburg lace was popular for edgings. I would watch while she took the delicate little pieces of braid and created an intricate design which was sewn on a dress pocket or handkerchief with a stitch as fine as a spiderweb.

She bought white Irish linen from Mary Anderson's and cut it into handkerchief size and attached a crocheted edging or a deep scallop of lace with a fine hemstitch. I admired the quick way she worked with her hands; she made everything look easy, but when I tried it, it wasn't easy at all.

As Christmas drew near, the most delectable odors came from that wood-burning range, standing sturdy and dependable on cast iron feet. First there were the fattigmans, deep fried and flavored with vanilla; then krumkaka; and a cookie—which we all loved—filled with orange marmalade. At first I sat and watched Mrs. Madole work in that small nook of a kitchen, but soon she gave me jobs to do—shelling the nuts, or sifting the flour, or running to Timmins Store on the corner of First and Wickersham to get groceries.

Then she made doughnuts, hundreds, until every available surface was covered with them. They were fried in rendered-out bear grease. Oh, there is nothing better than doughnuts fried in bear grease! Jess loved them, and his mother kept him well supplied. She also cooked beans for him and froze small portions, wrapped in cheesecloth so all he had to do was cook them, pulling off the cheesecloth after the beans had thawed.

Cora cooked the kinds of things men loved to eat, like headcheese and blood sausage, liver paste and rye bread with crusts crispy and nutty tasting. It seemed magical to me the foods she could prepare with a handful of groceries and a few utensils from her banana crate cupboard. And she never wasted anything. The things I learned from her helped me when I had a family of my own to care for.

On some evenings, when the darkness pressed close against the windows and the steam heat ticked through the pipes, Mrs. Madole and I would sit at the round table in the dining room and she would pull out a deck of playing cards.

"Well, Clara, what will it be tonight?" she would ask.

"It doesn't matter to me," I would answer, preferring that she make the choice. For a while we had a run on solo, then cribbage, and then hearts. She handled the cards crisply, and they made a quick slap, slap noise on the table. I remember so well the fringed lamp overhead casting dark shadows against the walls, a cup of tea near at hand, and sooner or later, the sound of footsteps on the stairs.

Someone was always stopping by to visit, day and night. I wondered when Mrs. Madole had time to get any work done. The hours passed pleasantly in her company; I always felt so at home with her. Still, I couldn't ask her about the gift for Jess. The idea had to come from me.

On one of those gray, woolly mornings when the sun barely managed to get itself above the horizon, I was out running errands for Mary Anderson. The streetlights came on early to illuminate the gloomy, subarctic days before Christmas. I picked up a prescription at McIntosh's Drug Store, and then, on an impulse, I crossed the street to the J. L. Sale Jewelry store.

In a short time I had told the jeweler what I wanted—two small gold shield buckles centered with the initials JWR outlined in gold nuggets. I would make arm bands out of green and pink satin and fasten the jewelry to it. This was a fashionable thing to have; all of Mary Anderson's escorts wore them. Jess took great care when he dressed to go out, and he had a fondness for jewelry, especially his diamond stickpin.

As soon as I started up the street I began having misgivings about the gift. Maybe it is too much, I thought. Maybe it would seem as if I were putting claims on Jess. Maybe he wouldn't like it. Maybe, maybe, maybe. Why couldn't I just make up my mind and stick to it?

On Christmas Eve I worked late at the store, and when I got home Beth was waiting for me to help trim the tree. Earlier in the day she had taken her two dogs and sled into the nearby woods where she chopped down a scrawny spruce. No matter which way we turned it, there was an empty "hole" where no branches grew.

"It's no use, Beth," I said. "It doesn't have a good side."

She shrugged her shoulders and began looping the paper chains she had made in school across the frugal boughs. Mother brought out a small box of decorations—a few glass balls and a length of white cotton to wrap around the skinny trunk. We clipped the candle holders in place; there weren't enough of those either. The handful of tinsel did not hide the tree's imperfections, but we tried. When we were finished the tree had a kind of desperate look.

It rather matched the family feeling at the time, a struggle to make a nice Christmas for Beth, when all the time we had our thoughts on something else—mine on Jess; Dad's on Mother; Mother's on Mother; and Beth was just a 9-year-old girl trying to capture Christmas.

"Oh, let's light the tree now," Beth said excitedly.

"I should say not," Mother said from the table where she was writing letters. "We have to wait until morning."

The glow went out of Beth's eyes. "I don't see what difference it makes," she said.

"That's the way we always do it," Mother answered, gathering up her writing paper. "Besides, it is late and you should be in bed. We have a big day tomorrow."

Mother took the light bulb on the cord to her bedroom while Beth and I undressed in the darkness of the room, brightened only by the firelight flickering from the stove. While Beth settled down on her cot in the dining room, I made my day bed ready in the living room. These two rooms were divided by an open archway which enabled Beth and me to talk back and forth. There were no doors on any of the rooms. Just a curtain covered the doorway to my parents' room. Many nights Beth and I were kept awake by our parents arguing. There was no privacy in our small cabin;

everybody lived their secrets out in the open. I think that was one of the hardest parts of our life. There wasn't any place we could go and shut the door and be alone.

"Is Jess taking you to the Christmas ball?" Beth whispered from her cot.

"Yes," I answered, remembering how hard it was to be Beth's age, not a child and not a woman, and remembering too how Beth met Jess first, and how she thought he belonged to her until I came along.

"Someday I'll get to go," Beth sighed. She was silent for a long time and then said, "I wonder what Jess gave you for Christmas?"

That afternoon Mrs. Madole had come, carrying packages for all of us. Under the tree was a small box for me from Jess. Beth had watched with solemn, dark eyes while I made Jess's arm bands. When I had delivered the gift—and one for his mother too—Jess had not been at home, and for that I was grateful. I still wasn't sure I had given him the right thing.

"It's probably some kind of jewelry," I finally said. My eyes closed and I snuggled deeper under the heavy quilts. The fire burned low, leaving the room cool and sweet, like fresh water.

"Maybe it's a ring," Beth speculated.

"Oh, no," was the last thing I remembered saying.

It wasn't a ring; it was a gold pin in the shape of a bow, covered with gold nuggets. I had seen the very thing at J. L. Sale when I went shopping for Jess's gift.

Christmas Day, while the turkey roasted in the oven and the mince pies cooled on the table, I waited expectantly for Jess to call. I tried to sew, but it was no use; I couldn't sit still that long. Instead, I roamed from one room to the other. When, at last, the phone rang, I yanked it off the hook. It was Jess thanking me for his gift. I could tell by the sound of his voice that he had liked it.

"I will wear my arm bands tonight to the Christmas ball," he said.

The Christmas ball. I shall never forget it, the bitter and the sweet of it. Things seemed to work out that way whenever I went anyplace with Jess.

There was in town a group of German men from the two local breweries who formed the Harmonie Society for the purpose of getting together for songs and a few beers. It started for men only, but the women wanted in, so they came and brought food, and it wasn't long before the dancing began.

Then the society bought a small hall with a kitchen. A piano player was hired and other musicians came too, just for the chance to play. They had such good times that pretty soon the non-Germans were begging to join. Some were invited, including Jess and me, even though I wasn't a singer, but Jess was and he knew all the old country songs. He was a favorite of the German people.

After a songfest we would start dancing about 8 o'clock, and that would go on until sometimes 4 o'clock in the morning. All this time the people enjoyed their beer, but no one got intoxicated.

It became a tradition of the Harmonie Society to give a public dance on Christmas night. Gordon's Roller Rink was reserved for the occasion, where the hardwood floor provided an excellent area for dancing and where there was room enough to accommodate the large crowd. Upstairs on the balcony the orchestra played, and there were tables and chairs where people could sit and watch the dancers.

In the center of the dance floor was a tall, tinseled tree, whose very tip touched the rafters. How it sparkled as we danced around it, and how the glass balls winked, and how the cranberry garlands gleamed from bough to bough. What a magnificent tree it was.

At one end of the room was a large reception table laden with food—those wonderful open-faced sandwiches Germans make—and mugs of beer, courtesy of the breweries. It was there at the reception table, between dances, that Jess did his plotting for the practical jokes he loved to pull. There was nothing he liked better than a laugh at someone else's expense. That was a side of him I discovered Christmas night.

Standing near the refreshment table were two stout Germans with protruding stomachs, Mrs. Gobraugh from Fairbanks Creek and Mr. Barthel who owned the brewery on Clay Street.

"Watch this," Jess said, his dark eyes flashing with mischief. I saw him put some sneezing powder in his hand and make his way toward the German couple. I watched with horror as he very casually blew the sneezing powder at the unsuspecting people.

First Mr. Barthel began sneezing. "Gesundheit," he said, bowing and pouring beer on her stomach.

"Gesundheit," she said, bowing and pouring beer on his stomach.

"Gesundheit," he said, and poured more beer on her.

"Gesundheit," she said, and did the same.

Soon those two portly Germans, gripped by a sneezing fit, were standing in a puddle of beer. A crowd quickly gathered to laugh at their antics. Those fun-loving Germans found humor in Jess's pranks, but I didn't. At that moment I hated Jess, and I was ashamed of him too.

"I don't see why you do such things," I said in a fury when I got Jess over to one side.

"There is no harm done," he laughed as he wiped the perspiration off his face. "Everybody thought it was funny."

"Well, I didn't."

"You don't have to go and spoil everything," he said in a hard tone.

Jess had a way of turning things around so they were my fault, and I usually felt helpless in the face of his arguments.

"I still think it was a mean thing to do," I said as we started dancing, determined to have the last word.

At midnight the music stopped and everyone gathered around the Christmas tree, linking arms German fashion while men on ladders lighted the wax candles clipped to the spicy boughs. When the tree was lit and the house lights extinguished, the tree sprang to life like some magical thing.

The people began singing Christmas carols and I could hear Jess's strong tenor rising above the other voices. I was so proud of him then. Why did he have to be a contradiction of sweetness and devilishness? When he shed his jacket I noted with satisfaction the matching satin arm bands he wore with the gold buckles. Fastened to my black taffeta dress was the gold nugget pin he had given me. They were bonds between us, the first of many.

While we stood admiring the golden glow of the tree in that dark room, mugs of hot grog were passed around. As soon as the candles burned low, spilling wax on the furry needles, they were snuffed out, and the lights came on again. Then the crowd stood back as the main doors were opened, letting in white clouds of fog that swept around our feet, while two men in dark suits with gold watch chains across their chests rolled kegs of beer across the floor. The merrymaking did not stop until well past four o'clock in the morning. Jess and I walked home, my mittened hand in his, and he did not have to persuade me to kiss him that night.

Some weekends when Jess came to town we went walking, even if it was 20 below zero, because we wanted to be alone and there was no privacy at the bathhouse. Arm in arm we would go toward town, stopping often at Friss's Coffee Shop on First Avenue where Jess had once worked as a waiter. There we would warm up on coffee or have a sandwich, especially if they had fresh rye bread that day and thin slices of boiled ham to go on it.

We passed the saloons and pool halls where games of poker and solo and pan were played, and where drinks came fast over the bar any time of the day or night. There was never a shortage of liquor in town. The sternwheelers brought it in, case after case, and it was stored in the warehouses, as valued as the food that was stockpiled against the edge of winter after the supply routes were cut off.

There were times when Jess and I, along with Frank Taylor, went ice-skating on the river rink below the bridge. First the snow was cleared, then it was flooded with water, making a fine rink. On one side there was a large warm-up tent that had a wood-burning fire and benches where we could sit down to put on our skates. In the center of the rink was another tent, this one elevated on a platform, where an orchestra provided music several nights a week. On special occasions there were costume parties on the ice, which were great fun. Children who used the rink during the afternoon could skate free of charge. At the entrance to the rink there was a small admission shack where one could rent skates.

Jess and Frank were excellent skaters. How I loved to watch them skim across the ice, cutting fancy turns, and come swooping toward me, lithe, slim bodies bent forward, hands clasped behind their backs.

Since I was so heavy, plus having weak ankles, I had a hard time skating on those thin blades. But with Jess on one side of me and Frank on the other, I must admit that I became quite good, and thoroughly enjoyed myself.

Downriver from the main rink was another cleaned area where the ice was nicely pebbled for the Scottish game of curling. It was a popular sport for players and spectators. Granite stones, weighing 40 pounds and shaped like shiny teakettles, were slid across the ice toward a ring target painted on the ice. Two teams competed to keep the other's stone knocked out of the ring. Brooms were used to sweep the ice in front of the moving stone to control its travel. The "skip" of the team, like a captain on a ship, would tell the players where he wanted the stone to go. During the winter of 1908, an indoor curling rink was opened on Second Avenue behind the bathhouse. There was a spectators' room with a stove and benches, and a window on the street where people could look in.

All winter long there were parties and dances—any excuse for a dance. My dancing improved with every occasion and there was no want for a partner. Joe Gertz, who had been on the boat north with me, came in from Chatanika and we often dated when Jess wasn't in town.

On New Year's Eve there was a masquerade dance at the Eagles Hall. Mother and I decided to go as twin dolls in short, full skirts, puffy-sleeved blouses and baby bonnets in pink and blue. Dad was kind enough to say he thought we looked cute, but how 200 pounds of anything could look cute was hard for me to buy.

I was still conscious of my size, but Jess never once teased me about my weight. I think he realized how hurt I had been over his remark when we first met at the bathhouse. Jess made me feel as if I was as good as anybody else. It was the first time that had happened to me, and I liked the feeling.

But he was still mercurial in his ways. Just when I thought things were running smoothly, something would go wrong. We never seemed to stay in stride very long. Would it always be like that, I wondered. Why couldn't we get along?

It was in the spring that we had our next big fight. I remember so clearly how the snowbanks began shrinking and wet earth began to show on the sunny sides of the cabins. Icicles ran like rain from the low eaves, making pockmarks in the piles of snow crystals. There was splashing in the streets and soon huge puddles formed that grew and grew, until they finally engulfed the entire street. Mud thickened along the paths where I walked back and forth to work. The days were bursting with oceans of sunlight that blazed off the shimmering water and warmed the peeling logs of the cabins.

"Well, Clara," Mary Anderson said one afternoon when I returned from lunch, "is Jess taking you to the benefit ball?"

Jess had been on Pedro Creek for many weeks. There had been no word from him. I thought perhaps the wet roads kept him away. Every night I expected to see Irish and Murphy waiting for me, but they never came.

"I don't know," I mumbled, as I stood at the door wiping the mud off my feet.

"Everybody in town is going," Mary said, twisting a lock of her blond hair around her finger. "They wouldn't pass up a chance to look at the girls."

I was guilty of the same feeling. The benefit, to raise money for the hospital, was being given by the girls on the Line. Fanny Hall would be there, Diamond Tooth Lil, Dirty Gerty, Bessie, Mary, and the others, all of them dressed in their finery, playing hostess to the town's elite and not-so-elite.

Interest in the ball had reached epidemic proportions. People who had said they would not go under any circumstances had now changed their tune, justifying their actions by saying, "since it's for charity. . . ." It would be hard for people to stay away. Even Jess, I thought deep inside me. Even Jess.

"Oh, you won't be able to keep that Jess away, if I know him," Mary said brightly, tuning in on my thoughts.

"What Jess does is his own business," I said sharply, gathering up my damp skirts and making my way across the room. I didn't see how Mary could say anything. There were plenty of stories about her conduct that weren't too complimentary.

"You don't need to get on your high horse, Clara," Mary said as she swished by me, leaving a trail of perfume I recognized as Fanny Hall's.

I spent half my time making smart remarks, and the other half regretting them. Dad had said something recently about my "high horse." Maybe there was something to it. Lately Mother seemed to disapprove of everything I said or did, but I chalked that up to her own personal unhappiness.

As it turned out, Mother and I persuaded Dad to take us to the benefit ball. We weren't interested so much in dancing as we were in just looking. The roller rink was packed that night. I was on the lookout for that slender young man with the wavy brown hair, those broad shoulders and that proud walk he had inherited from his mother. If he was in that room, I would find him. And I did.

Jess danced by with "one of the girls." She was beautifully gowned in the palest of blue satin. They were talking and laughing like old friends. My heart thudded dismally at the sight of them. I tried not to stare.

"Clara, Clara," Mother said, much too loudly, "isn't that Jess?"

"Where?" I asked dumbly, but she knew I had seen him.

Mother couldn't help but use that as an opportunity to say things against Jess. "He isn't the only man in town, Clara," she said.

"Don't settle for the first one that comes along. I think you are seeing too much of Jess."

As well-meaning as her advice might have been, it didn't ease the sharp pain every time I saw Jess dance by with a different girl. He never came near me, not once.

I couldn't stay there another minute longer. "Mother, please, can't we go home?" I pleaded.

She nodded her assent. "I think we have seen all there is to see."

Out the door I flew, oblivious to the puddles as I raced home, leaving Mother and Dad far behind me. I flung myself on the bed and pulled the covers over my head. I didn't want to see anyone.

The next day Jess called, saying he wanted me to meet him at the bathhouse. I tried to refuse, but Jess insisted, so of course I weakened. I would have to see him sooner or later. Besides, it was Sunday afternoon and I could not stay in the house any longer with everyone looking at me and thinking, "Poor Clara."

When I arrived at the bathhouse, Jess was waiting at the front door.

"Hello, Jess," I said formally, trying to hide my hurt feelings.

"Clara," he said with a curt nod of his head. "I want to talk to you."

I followed him down the hallway to his room. There was no place to sit except on the bed. Jess sat beside me.

"I want to explain about last night," he said, taking my hand. "I went to the dance to dance with the girls. I don't mix company. I could not have danced with one of the girls off the Line and turned around and danced with you. That's just the way I am."

Whenever I was with Jess I was willing to believe anything he said. It was always that way. I would go to him with my mind made up that this time I was right, just let him try and talk me out of it. And here he was—talking me out of it.

"The least you could have done was talk to me," I said, lifting my eyes to his.

"I have explained it the best I can. You just have to understand," he said. "You aren't in the same class with the girls."

My spirits lifted. That put a different light on things. He respected me too much to dance with the girls off the Line, and then with me. That was it, wasn't it? "I don't own you, Jess," I said. "You can do whatever you want to do.

"And you can do whatever you want, Clara," Jess said, after a long silence. "But you had no business on the dance floor with those girls."

"What!" I exploded, jumping to my feet. "What did you say?"

"I said, you had no business on the dance floor with those girls."

"*I* had no business on the dance floor," I shouted. "*You* were the one that was dancing with them."

"I know," he said calmly.

"You always find a way to blame everything on me, don't you?" I yelled. "You act as if I shouldn't have gone to the dance."

"That's right. You shouldn't have. It was bad for your reputation."

There was the word again, and it further inflamed my anger. "I had just as much right to be there as you did," I said, unable to control my shouting.

"No, you didn't," Jess replied.

"And why not? It was a public dance."

"It was bad for your reputation," he repeated.

"And what about your reputation?" I yelled. "You seemed to be pretty friendly with those girls. How do you explain that?"

"I met most of them in Dawson when I was working at the Regina," Jess replied.

"Whatever you do is right, and whatever I do is wrong. I don't want to talk about it anymore," I said, yanking the door open.

In the hallway I bumped into Dr. Overgaard.

"Oh, excuse me, Clara. I didn't see you," he said. "My, where are you going in such a hurry?"

"Home," I snapped.

"I think Jess is looking for you."

"I have seen all of Jess that I want to see," I shouted into his surprised face.

On my way out I slammed the door so hard that the upstairs windows rattled.

chapter 8

The snow had gone. Underfoot the puddles had dried and the mud had turned to dust. Even in the bright sunlight the landscape was brown and drab with only the reddish tinge of the budding willows adding a touch of color beside the olive of the spruce trees. In the hills, where the sun burned on the southern exposure, the snow had started to thaw and run into the streams that fed the Chena.

One day in early May when I was on my way back to work after lunch, the air was ripped apart by the piercing sound of whistles blowing at the mill upriver, and at the Northern Commercial power plant, and the steam laundry downtown. It wasn't long before the bells at the Catholic Church were pealing.

"Breakup! Breakup!" came the shouting in the streets. I joined the throng of people making their way to the river. Work would have to wait.

Along the riverbanks, on both sides, stood hundreds of people. Others were standing on the roof of the Pioneer Hotel and on the roofs of the saloons that lined the Chena.

At Turner Street there was wild excitement. With the use of heavy ropes and a donkey engine, men were removing the center section of the bridge. They must hurry before the ice came crashing downriver to tear out the bridge as it had done many times in the past. The donkey engines whined. The men shouted. The whistles blew. Above it all we could hear the steady grinding and churning of the ice.

Breakup! The rushing ice carried out the bridge pilings at Turner Street.

"Ice jam! Ice jam!" was the next shout that went up. Then came the BOOM! BOOM! BOOM! of the dynamite they set off upriver to dislodge the ice.

By this time the bridge span had been safely removed, and not a moment too soon, either, as tons of ice came hurtling pell-mell down the center of the town with uprooted trees, driftwood, rocks, broken boat hulls, and all manner of river debris taking a free ride.

Slabs of ice, 40 and 50 feet high, would buckle and lift up in the air and then drop into the churning water with a roar and a mighty splash. How the crowd yelled at that.

Snap! Snap! Snap! There went the bridge pilings like so many matchsticks against the powerful push of the river. This spring ritual was as unstoppable as an earthquake as the ice pushed its way out of the Chena into the Tanana, from the Tanana into the Yukon and from the Yukon to the Bering Sea, an immense cleansing process to open the waterways.

I watched as the ice blocks were hurled against the riverbank, rammed into buildings and smashed into beached boats. I'd never seen such a sight in my life. Here it was May 2, 1909, my 19th birthday. What a celebration!

For a week afterward the swollen river ran high, flooding houses in low-lying areas. A ferry transported people across the river to Garden Island until the bridge pilings could be restored.

As soon as the ice went out, folks around town began betting on the arrival of the first steamboat. Interest was keen on this. Only after you have spent a winter in isolation can you appreciate what it means to have the boat come in.

In mid-May before the trees leafed out, it was possible to see all the way across town to the river. It was there among the bare trees we would catch the first glimpse of the smoke from the sternwheeler coming around the bend.

Then the cry, "Steamboat! Steamboat!"

Everyone dropped what they were doing and made straight for the Northern Commercial docks. Women with babies on their hips stood in the bright sunlight; shopkeepers ran into the street wearing their long black aprons; and everywhere there were kids and dogs. There were miners waiting for their partners; husbands waiting for their wives; and Waterfront Brown, the bill collector, waiting for his customers. Nothing ever quite matched the thrill of that first steamboat coming up the river in the spring.

UNIVERSITY OF ALASKA ARCHIVES

In the early days, as many as 11 steamboats, and as many barges, might be seen at the Fairbanks docks at one time.

As the gangplank was lowered and the people streamed forward, they were greeted like voyagers who had just returned from another planet. There was much shouting and handshaking and backslapping.

It was like a holiday. We were all anxious for the mail the boat carried, including the Christmas packages, and the first fresh fruit and vegetables in nine months.

The Northern Commercial Company, which operated the largest general merchandise store in town, owned three of the riverfront docks. Across the street from the docks, on First Avenue, was the Northern Commercial store and post office. Much of the cargo was destined for those two locations. A narrow track was laid from the docks to the warehouses. The goods were loaded on small flatcars and pulled by horses.

On the days when the boats arrived, the post office was packed to the ceiling with letters and packages, with the clerks hard-pressed to sort the mail fast enough to suit the people clamoring at the windows.

In the early days I saw as many as 11 boats tied to the docks at one time, and that many barges. There were docks on the other side of the river that belonged to the smaller navigating companies whose boats worked the Tanana and the Chena. When the boats came in, the boys, 14- and 15-year-olds, hurried to help unload the cargo. It was their chance to earn money and it was their tie with the outside world that seemed so far away.

"I'm glad the boats are running again," Mother said that night at dinner. "I like to know I can get out of here when I want to."

Dad, Beth and I sat in silence. Dad continued eating, his face impassive. Mother's remark was obviously nothing new to him, but it was to me, and I considered it a threat to all the things in Fairbanks I had come to love.

"You aren't planning to leave, are you, Mother?" I blurted out.

"I'm thinking about it, Clara," she said solemnly, "and you should think about it, too."

That was the last thing in the world I wanted to think about. Move again? I couldn't bear it. Leave Fairbanks? How could I? There must be some way I could stay, I thought. But how could I make it on $50 a month from Mary Anderson? It was impossible.

In the weeks that followed life went on as it always had, and I was lulled into thinking that everything was going to stay the same.

Clara, holding a kitten in a hat in front of Mrs. Madole's house on Second Avenue.

Dad got busy and dug a garden plot out back where the yard was fenced in with edgings trimmed from boards at the mill upriver. He bought some plants at the greenhouse, mostly cabbage and cauliflower, and set these out with his carrots, parsnips and little green onions. The lettuce seeds he put in the ground were up in 5 days. I was amazed at how fast everything grew.

After dinner I worked in the garden with Dad. During the early days of June when there was so much sunlight, it was easy to lose track of the time. All of a sudden it would be 1 o'clock in the morning. By then the sun had already set and was getting ready to come up again!

Before the gardens were ready to harvest, the greenhouses began selling fresh lettuce, tomatoes and cucumbers. What a treat that was. Paul Rickert, one of the local gardeners, would load his horse-drawn wagon full of those wonderful vegetables and travel the streets ringing a bell to announce his coming.

In those days there were no garbage collectors, so people disposed of their cans and other rubbish as best they could. Many families, mine included, just tossed the stuff over the back fence to be hauled away come spring. It was a terrible mess to pick up, and we all had to pitch in to clear it out.

There was a honey man, who made the rounds after midnight collecting the buckets from the outhouses. Many homes had a shed attached to the house where gasoline cans with board seats were used as toilets. The seats could be lifted up and the cans removed. One of the sounds I shall always associate with those early days in Fairbanks is the rattling of cans by the honey man late at night.

Our outhouse, however, was not quite so modern. It was down the path in the little building with the half-moon cut in the door. That was a cold walk in the winter. But then, summers weren't much better when the hungry mosquitoes were buzzing everywhere.

There were many things to capture my attention that first long and lovely summer in Fairbanks. I was too busy enjoying myself to dwell on family problems for long. On June 21, the longest day of the year, Fairbanks celebrated the event in its usual grand style with a parade, a dance and a midnight sun baseball game. Jess came to town so we could take in the festivities. About 10 o'clock in the evening we walked across the bridge to Noyes Mill where the baseball diamond was located. Fairbanks had several baseball teams sponsored by local businesses, and competition was keen.

Clara, with Diamond and Irish near the bathhouse. The dogs often announced Jess's arrival in town.

Before the game started there was a preliminary ladies' horse race which was run on a track around the diamond. Jess and I joined the crowd in the bleachers to watch. Mina Bond, a friend of Cora Madole's from Montana, had challenged Blanche Martin, a noted horsewoman, to race. Mina was a nurse in Fairbanks specializing in home care. She rode a wild stallion named Ignatz and won the race easily. It interested me that Mina rode cowboy style, while Blanche was mounted sidesaddle.

How amazing it was to watch the baseball game in the middle of the night while the sun dropped behind the hills, leaving a rosy glow, and then very soon it reappeared, more brilliant than ever.

I think the turning point in my relationship with Jess came the night of the marathon race at the roller rink. Interest ran high on that sporting event because the principal runner was Jujuira Wada, a stocky and stalwart Japanese who had made a name for himself in Alaska as a championship dog musher and runner.

Wada had also made a name for himself in Fairbanks a number of years before, and that name was not a kind one. He was remembered for the part he played in the Fairbanks stampede. During the winter of 1903, under orders from trading post owner Barnette, Wada ran to Dawson to spread the word of the Fairbanks strike.

As a result, a thousand stampeders arrived to find a poorly stocked trading post, and gold buried too deep for quick plundering. Many men left town, but those who stayed nearly starved that winter. Bitter feelings toward Wada and the part he had played in the hoax had not died out even by 1909. There were plenty of men who wanted to see Wada beaten. Six men challenged him and the betting ran high.

Since I did not expect Jess in town that night, I accepted Joe Gertz's invitation to attend the marathon. Joe worked at Chatanika, 25 miles out of town, and was coming in for the big event.

As I left the store the night of the marathon, there were Irish and Murphy waiting for me. Oh, no, I thought, I wish I didn't already have a date.

When I told Jess that Joe was taking me to the marathon, but that I would call it off, he said, "No, don't do that. It's too late to change, and it will make Joe mad. I'll see you there anyway. By the way, who are you going to bet on?"

Courtship days. Jess took the picture by setting up the camera with a remote shutter release and squeezing the rubber bulb to trip the shutter after he was in position.

"I haven't thought about betting," I said. "But it sure wouldn't be for Wada." After thinking for a minute, I said, "I'll tell you what. I will bet myself against you that Wada doesn't win."

"I'm betting on Wada," Jess said, "and I'll take you up on that. If I win, then you are mine."

That night the roller rink was packed. The runners circled the floor, so many laps per mile, and as they neared the end the crowd became wild with excitement. I had never heard such shouting and raving. Even though I hadn't put any money on the race, my interest in it was mighty high because of the deal I had with Jess.

The winner was Wada.

Out of the crowd came Jess, taking me by the arm and saying, "You belong to me now, so I am taking you home." He turned to Joe and explained, "I won her on a bet and now she is my old lady."

"Sure, Jess, sure," Joe said as he turned and walked away. I guess he knew how things were between Jess and me, but he never asked me out again, and I didn't blame him. That was not the first time Jess had spoiled a date for him.

That evening Jess and I walked to the bathhouse where we had a late supper with his mother. From then on I was his old lady and he was my old man. I suspect we knew even then that we belonged together without actually saying it.

In late August when we began harvesting our garden, Dad said I could take vegetables to Cora Madole whenever she needed them. One evening as I walked through the garden I saw an especially fine cabbage I thought Mrs. Madole would enjoy. It was hard to carry, since it was so large, and by the time I reached the bathhouse I was almost ready to collapse. When Cora and Doc saw that huge cabbage, they raved about the size of it.

When I got home that night Dad was raving too, but for a different reason. He was mad. "Some blankety-blank thief stole my prize head of cabbage," he ranted. "I was going to enter it in the fair, and I know I would have gotten first prize. The nerve of some people."

As much as I hated to, I confessed that I was the guilty one. "I'm sorry, Dad," I said, "but you never told me you wanted to enter the cabbage in the fair."

After Cora heard about the mix-up, she invited the family to her apartment for corned beef and cabbage. That put Dad in a better humor, but I still felt guilty about it.

There were times when my family enjoyed being together, but as the days passed, I could no longer ignore the fact that Mother and Dad were drifting farther and farther apart. When September came, Mother had definitely made up her mind to leave Fairbanks.

"Clara," she said, "Beth and I are going out on the boat next week. I would like to have you come with us."

I faced her across the table. "Mother, I can't," I said.

"Why is that?" she wanted to know.

"I just don't want to pull up stakes again," I said. "We don't have a place to live in Seattle, and I would have to look for a job. It is all so uncertain," I trailed off, hoping she would understand.

"Are those the only reasons?" she asked.

I knew what she was thinking. "I am happy here," I said, "and I would miss all my friends."

"You mean you would miss Jess," Beth piped up.

"Yes, I would miss Jess," I admitted, "and Mrs. Madole and

Mary Anderson, and all the people I have come to know. Fairbanks means a lot to me, and I want to stay."

"It would not be good for your reputation," Mother said, starting in on that again. "Dad is gone so much of the time. You would be here alone."

"I would be better off than when I lived in Seattle all alone," I argued. "Besides, I'm 19 and I can take care of myself."

Mother did not protest too much, and I think Dad was pleased that I was staying, although he never said so.

When the day came for Mother and Beth to leave, I was struck with misgivings. Was I doing the right thing? Would I be able to get along with Dad? Would I be lonely? Mother and Beth *were* going away, and I was staying behind. It all seemed so final now, and it was too late for second thoughts.

The morning they were to leave, Jess came to the house to help Dad carry the luggage to the dock. It was a fine September day with the sunlight warming the golden leaves of the birch and, on the air was the musky smell of ripe highbush berries.

We all went on board the steamboat *Tanana* until it was time to pull up the gangplank. It was not a happy farewell, for we did not know when we would see each other again.

As Jess and I were leaving, Beth said, "I'll bet this boat will just get around the bend and you and Jess will get married."

Jess hugged Beth and said, "You have just put an idea in my head, little girl."

It was more than 30 years before I saw my sister again.

I did not realize how lonely the house would be without Mother and Beth. The hardest part was coming home from work—no lights, no dinner cooking on the stove, and no one to talk to. Dad was gone so much, it was as if I was living alone.

One afternoon in September when I was out bill collecting for Mary Anderson—a job I hated—my feet began to hurt. As I continued walking the pain became more severe. I had never had that problem before. Every time I took a step I wanted to scream. If I can make it to the bathhouse, I thought, I will be all right. Just a little farther . . . a little farther.

By the time I reached the bathhouse, the tears were streaming down my face. I had never been in so much pain.

"Clara, Clara, what's wrong?" Mrs. Madole said as I came in the door. She moved toward me, the long, crisp line of her dark skirt swaying above her shoes. Even in my agony I envied her good figure and quick movements. Beside her, I felt heavier than ever.

"It's my feet," I cried, sinking into the nearest chair. "My feet hurt so badly."

"What is this about feet?" Doc Overgaard said as he came into the room wearing a white medical jacket over his dark suit.

"It's Clara's feet," Mother Madole explained. "There's something wrong with them."

"Take off those ridiculous-looking shoes," Doc said, "and let's have a look."

I always prided myself on being able to wear tiny, fashionable shoes, the kind with spool heels and pointed toes.

Doc made a few exploratory probes on the soles of my feet. I flinched at every touch. "Come with me," he said.

I leaned heavily on his arm as we made our way down the hall to the examining room. Doc's practice was somewhat of a mystery to me. Whenever I asked Jess about it, he gave vague answers about electrical treatments and bone adjustments Doc performed.

Mrs. Madole was put out when people preferred the services of Dr. Sutherland, who had an office in the same block, to those of Doc Overgaard. Dad summed up Doc's abilities by saying he was good at "sobering up the boys, but that's about all."

Doc took me into a small examining room. "Sit on the table. I want to take a better look at those feet," he said. "How long have they been bothering you?"

"Never. They have never bothered me."

"Not even in those shoes?" he asked.

"Well, not very much," I admitted. "What is wrong with my feet, Doc?"

"You have fallen arches, and they aren't going to get better unless you stay off your feet for a while."

"But I have to work," I cried.

"You are carrying more weight than your feet can take," Doc explained. "If you don't do something to strengthen your feet, they will give out completely and you won't be able to walk."

"Oh, no," I sobbed. I felt a deep stab of fear. If I couldn't walk, then I couldn't work. What would happen to me then? Tears filled my eyes.

"What's wrong?" Mrs. Madole said as she came into the room.

"It's my feet," I wailed. "Doc says I have fallen arches."

"Dear, dear," Mrs. Madole said, handing me her handkerchief, "don't get so upset. Doc will help you."

"But if I can't walk and if I can't work, what will become of me?" I cried.

"Now, Clara," she said sternly, "don't get so far ahead of yourself. These things work out."

"I will get some towels and a basin," Doc said. "The first thing we need to do is soak those feet."

I looked to Mother Madole for reassurance.

"You must do whatever Doc tells you," she answered. "You must calm yourself. This isn't as bad as you think. You will be all right."

"Are you sure?"

"Yes, I am sure. All things pass. You must not get upset. You will be all right. Doc and I will take care of you here at the bathhouse."

During my week of treatment, Doc devised all manner of exercises to strengthen my feet. The most painful was to walk on a wooden board with cleats. No matter how I cried, Doc did not relent. I had to walk that board every day.

I guess he knew what he was doing because I did not have trouble with my feet again. I never wore fancy shoes, though. Doc bought me a pair of shoes which he described as "decent." They were as unattractive as a pair of shoes could be, complete with insoles, but they did give my feet the support they needed.

While I was confined to the bathhouse, Jess came to town. How I treasured those long hours we spent together; it almost made my fallen arches worthwhile. One day he brought a silver bonbon dish filled with chocolates from Roscoe's candy store. I kept that dish for more than 40 years.

When I returned home, some unhappy news was waiting for me.

"I received a letter from your mother," Dad said. "She wants a divorce."

"Oh, no, Dad. Do you think she is serious?"

"I don't know," he answered, "but I have to go Outside and talk to her and see if I can get her to change her mind."

"When are you leaving?"

"I'm taking the last boat out of here next week. And I think you should come with me."

"Dad, I can't," I answered.

There was no need for an argument. We both knew there was nothing for me in Seattle. Still, I couldn't help admitting to myself that I feared being on my own. No matter how many difficulties we had, my family still offered security and protection.

Already the cabin was showing signs of neglect. The burlap sagged on the walls, the rugs were fraying underfoot, the plants were dying on the window sills. As the weather got colder, there would be more wood to chop, more ashes to haul. Would I be able to take care of myself, and the house too? And what about money? Would I have enough?

There was an aching loneliness inside me that October morning when I stood on the banks of the Chena and watched the steamboat, with Dad on board, move slowly downstream. The smoke from the stack was like a farewell flag against the brilliant blue of the late fall sky.

Dad is gone, Dad is gone, I thought as I made my way up Cushman Street to work. The ground was hard with frost beneath my sturdy shoes. Soon the snow would fall, piling up to the eaves, and there I would be, all alone in the little house.

chapter 9

When I finally heard from Dad, it was bad news. He had not been successful in persuading Mother to stop the divorce. It nearly broke his heart, and mine too. Our family, what there was left of it, was falling apart, and there was nothing any of us could do about it.

Dad, who still thought the grass was greener in the next town, or the next state, or the next country, was headed for Dawson. There he planned to work for his old friend Charlie Settlemeier on the Dawson *News.* Dad had sold his interest in the Fairbanks *Daily News* to W. F. (Wrong Font) Thompson, who combined it with his newspaper, the *Dome Miner,* and named it the Fairbanks *Daily News-Miner.*

Before he left Fairbanks, Dad told me he had asked Mary Anderson to look after me. She told Dad that if things got too rough at the cabin, I could move in with her. I kept that promise in the back of my mind, just in case I couldn't make it on my own. In the meantime, Dad deeded the old house to me in exchange for the money I gave him for the boat ticket.

As each day passed and the temperature dipped lower and lower, the bitter cold seeped in through cracks in the walls and I could not keep the place warm. I tried—I tried very hard—but I had not realized how much work it would be just to keep the fires going. Pretty soon I dreaded going home to that cold house.

One day at work I said to Mary, "I guess I am ready to move in with you now."

She went off like a firecracker. "Oh, Clara, it would never work." She became quite agitated. "It would never work."

Her remarks surprised me, and scared me too, because I had been counting on her help.

"I can't have you here," Mary went on. "I am out all hours of the night and I often have company in. You would have to sleep on a cot in my room, and that would never do."

She was embarrassed, and so was I. Neither one of us mentioned the promise she had made to my father.

"I can't stay in the cabin much longer," I said, feeling helpless and wishing I didn't have to ask for favors.

"Now, don't you worry," she said, going to the telephone. "I will find a place for you to stay."

Before I knew it, Mary had made arrangements with Mrs. Madole for me to get my room and board at the bathhouse for $50 a month.

My heart sank. That didn't leave me any money for clothes or other expenses. The little bit I had managed to save I had given to Dad to help pay for his boat fare Outside.

"There, that is all settled," Mary beamed, rubbing her small white hands together. "And I will raise your wage to $75 a month."

At first I thought that Mary was buying off her promise to Dad, but then I reasoned that after working a year for Mary, I had earned a raise.

My room at the bathhouse, even though sparsely furnished, was warm and all that I needed. Mrs. Madole, generous as always, found colorful curtains for the one small window and a bedspread to help brighten the ground-floor room. Now the cabin on Eighth Avenue was deserted, except for a pitiful collection of dilapidated furniture.

In the evenings, after a fine dinner, Mrs. Madole and I would take up our sewing. She was making me a navy blue princess-style dress with tiny buttons down the front. The dress would have several sets of collars and cuffs. After years of work as a seamstress—at Wanamaker's in Chicago—Mrs. Madole had a professional eye for just the right design and the fabric to carry it out.

In addition to her work at the bathhouse, Mrs. Madole did

sewing for Mary Anderson and other women in town. It wasn't often that she spoke of her finances, but from the few comments she made, I knew she had to watch every penny. Her hands were never idle; there was always work to be done.

Those quiet hours I spent in her cozy sitting room brought us closer together, and I began calling her Mother Madole. It seemed so natural because she was a mother to me in many ways. She is the one who taught me about feminine hygiene, how to dress, how to sew, how to cook. I shall never forget the good advice and training she gave me.

It was in the fall of that year that a young man came knocking at the bathhouse door. He was an English cockney by birth, a waiter by trade, and a would-be gambler who had just lost all his money in a poker game. He was stranded in Fairbanks with winter coming on, no job, no money and no place to stay. Somehow people like that always found their way to Mrs. Madole's. His name was Frank Reynolds and he was hired to do the handy work in exchange for his room and board.

Frank was in his mid-twenties, a tall, rangy fellow with sandy-colored hair and brown eyes as warm and beguiling as a pup. It was his speech that fascinated me. I had never met a cockney before, and when Frank got excited and started talking too fast, no one could understand a word he said. Frank was persistent and faithful, but it took him awhile to catch onto things. I wondered how he managed to make it halfway around the world on his own. When Jess came to town, he and Frank hit it off very well. Frank was almost slavish in his devotion to Jess, and followed his orders to the hilt, just as Frank Taylor did.

That winter of 1909 started out cold, and stayed that way. The air was dry and the snow like dust underfoot. When Frank banked the bathhouse to insulate it against the cold, the snow slipped off his shovel like grains of sand.

Each day dawned with a crack of light in the pearl gray sky that was shuttered a few hours later by a brief slash of vibrant rose melting across the horizon. We lived in almost perpetual darkness, and with a deep cold that seemed more piercing to me than the winter before. At night, in my small bed, I lay and listened to the dogs howl at the moon, to the steam clicking through the pipes, to the building snap and contract in the cold.

One morning when I crawled out of bed, I knew something was

wrong. It was cold, very cold in my room. After dressing quickly, I ran upstairs to Mother Madole's apartment to warm myself beside the kitchen stove.

"What is wrong?" I asked. "The whole building is cold."

"It's the boiler," Mother Madole said. "There is something wrong with the boiler."

"What are you going to do?"

"I have called the repairman," she answered, "and I hope he gets here pretty soon. In this weather it won't take long for the place to freeze up."

When I returned home from work that evening the repairman had come and gone, but the situation was no better. The boiler was putting out very little heat, and the water was beginning to freeze in the pipes.

"I'm sending for Jess," Mother Madole said.

It was a desperate time, with all of us standing by as if watching a sinking ship. There wasn't anything we could do to stop it. By the time Jess got into town, it was too late. Most of the pipes were frozen, and some had already burst.

"There is only one thing to do," Jess said.

"What is that?" his mother asked.

"Close the bathhouse," Jess replied.

Mother Madole was almost in tears. It was a cruel financial blow. She still owed money on the bathhouse equipment, and now there was no income to help pay it off. After working four years in the business, she had lost everything.

There was one bit of good fortune, however. Mother Madole owned a cabin on Second Avenue, directly behind the bathhouse, and it was vacant. At least we would have a roof over our heads.

"Come on," Jess said, trying to rouse his mother. "I will help you move."

We all got busy—Frank, Doc, Jess, Mother Madole and I—and it wasn't long before we settled in the little cabin. There was no running water, but we were on the Northern Commercial steam line, so we were warm and that counted for something. Most of all I missed the flush toilet and the bathtub; it hadn't taken long for me to get spoiled.

The house was small, with a living room, dining room and kitchen on the main floor. Upstairs, beneath the sloping roof, were two small bedrooms, divided by a curtain. There was some

Jess at his Pedro Creek claim. Jess, who was an amateur photographer, took his own picture with a remote shutter release, seen in the foreground.

furniture in the house, and, given time, I was sure Mother Madole would have the place cheerful enough.

That first night in the cabin, after Mother Madole had fixed a hot meal, we all sat around the dining room table to discuss a plan of action. We just couldn't drift on and on, day after day, with Doc and Frank sitting around and no money coming in.

"I need some help out at Pedro Creek," Jess said. "Maybe Doc and Frank and I can go into partnership. If we make good on the prospect hole I am sinking, we can divvy up the profits."

"Sounds all right with me," Doc said. "I could still come into town every week or so to take care of my patients."

"What do you think, Frank?" Jess asked.

"Sure, Jess. It sounds fine to me," he replied.

And so it happened that the three of them became mining partners with Mother Madole as a silent partner, helping with expenses when she could. We knew this mining business was going to mean sacrifices, but in those days we possessed such wonderful optimism. We were so sure we would make it big on that prospect hole, and that the next one would be even better. How we lived on dreams that winter!

Since money was so short, I tried to sell the old house, including the three adjacent lots, for $150 but nobody wanted them. Whether I liked it or not, I was stuck with the old house. At the time, I did not realize there was a mortgage against the place, as well as unpaid taxes.

When the boys came to town for supplies, they stayed at Mother Madole's house, bedding down on the cot in the living room. Out back there was a place for Jess to chain the dogs. I marveled at the strength of those three animals and the heavy loads they could pull.

Diamond and Murphy with Jess at Pedro Creek cache.

Jess was strict with them, and too quick to use the whip, I thought, but Irish, Murphy and Diamond were one-man dogs and they never disobeyed their master.

One day, after Jess had loaded the sled and was ready to head back to the creeks, he could not find Diamond. The other two dogs had run eagerly into harness, and were yelping anxiously to leave. Jess whistled and called; it wasn't like Diamond to take off like that.

Pretty soon we were all in on the search with Jess becoming more and more impatient every minute to hit the trail. It was Doc who finally found Diamond. He was in an old shed, half buried under a pile of boards, with his left leg almost severed.

"Jess! Jess!" Doc hollered. "Give me a hand."

Between the two of them they managed to carry the dog to the house. They laid poor Diamond out on the kitchen table. We thought he was a goner.

"Do you think you can save him, Doc?" Jess asked.

"I'll try. You'll have to hold him down while I sew his leg together."

That was a terrible day with all of us worried about Diamond. Not only were we attached emotionally to the dog, but he was an important part of the mining operation, and it would cost us time and money if we lost him. Then, to make matters worse, the first stitches didn't hold, so Doc had to put them in all over again.

After several days' delay, Jess and Doc finally had to leave without Diamond. Mother Madole and I took care of the dog as best we could, but the only person that could quiet him was Jess. That dog just lay on the floor, whining and crying.

About that time Mother Madole and I decided we would like to see the mine and the new cabin. I would take a week off from work and ride out by dog team with Jess, and Mother Madole would follow the next day by train.

When we were ready to leave, Diamond was well enough to go along. The wound had healed nicely, but Jess didn't want to take any chances, so he put the dog in the sled with me. From the very start we had trouble. Diamond jumped out of that sled, again and again. He trotted ahead of Irish and Murphy, barking sharply. Then he would come back to the sled and bark at Jess, pleading with those bright blue eyes.

"That dog will wear himself out running back and forth like

that," Jess said. "I think I'll try him in the harness. If he starts to limp, I will have to tie him in the sled."

Diamond was so excited to pull the sled that he quivered with delight. Up went his beautiful brown tail, curling proudly over his back. The sled was heavily loaded, so on the steep grades I would get off and walk while Jess ran behind the sled, hopping off and on the runners to steady the load or to catch his breath, as the need would be.

As we traveled the white ribbon of road that made its way out of town, over the top of Birch Hill and across the frozen creeks and hills to the gold fields, the sun soared into the blue sky and shimmered on the snow-laden trees. The bells on the dogs' harnesses, tied with colored pompons Mother Madole had made, jingled merrily in the quiet, crisp air. I leaned back in the fur robe and I thought I had one foot in heaven.

It was 3:00 in the afternoon by the time we reached Gilmore Creek, where we stopped long enough to have a hot lunch at the roadhouse. Since Diamond showed no sign of limping, Jess let him lead us the rest of the way.

After we left the main road we branched off to the west, skirting the base of the 2,000-foot Cleary Summit, until we reached Eight Above on Pedro Creek. There on a rise, outlined against the starry sky, was Jess' new cabin. A light shone in the window, and on the air I caught a whiff of the wood smoke coming out of the chimney. The dogs yapped at their pleasure at being home and quickened their pace. Then the cabin door opened, and there stood Frank Reynolds waving his arms to welcome us.

We had a fine supper that night, the four of us, around the table. There within the clean, white light of the gasoline lamp that hung from a ceiling beam, we played cards and drank coffee. The good wood stove warmed us; I felt very much at home.

Jess said, "Well, Clara, it is time for you to leave."

"Leave?" I said. "What do you mean, leave?"

"It is time for you to get down to the roadhouse, or they will think you aren't coming."

"To the roadhouse," I said. "Why do I have to go there?"

"You can't stay here with us men," Jess replied. "You have your reputation to protect."

I wanted to say, "You sound like my mother," but I didn't. I was learning to hold my tongue.

"Fairbanks is a small town," Jess was saying, "and a lot of people know you came out here tonight. It is better for you to stay at the Costa House."

"Oh, I don't want to go, Jess," I said. "I don't see any need for it."

"I will pick you up in the morning so we can meet Mother at the train," he said, as if that settled the argument, and it did.

How I hated to leave the warmth of that cabin. Reluctantly I pulled on my heavy clothes and said good-by to Doc and Frank. Out in the cold night, with the moon as bright as lamplight on the snow, Jess and I walked hand in hand. It was 2 miles through the quiet woods to the Costa House, but by matching my stride to Jess's, we covered the distance quickly. The two-story log roadhouse, angular and black against the white hills, did not look very inviting.

My small cot in the dormitory upstairs was partitioned from the other beds by calico curtains. A wooden crate, covered with a flour sack, held a candle in a dish for light.

Under the eaves was a curtained cubicle with a five-gallon oil can with a board toilet seat with an old catalog hanging on a string nearby. Fortunately I was the only occupant in the dormitory, which was usually shared by men and women. As I tried to get comfortable on that rickety old cot, I couldn't help but think I would have been a lot better off at Jess's cozy cabin among friends. Well, with everyone looking out for my reputation, I thought, I guess I don't need to.

The next thing I knew, Jess's dogs were barking beneath my window, and it was time to meet Mother Madole's train at the Gilmore station. Diamond's leg was a little stiff, but he was in harness and barking furiously for us to get going.

Soon we were off with a swish of the runners over the crusted snow. In that part of the country the vegetation was stunted by permafrost. The willows and small spruce trees only reach a height of about 2 feet due to the permanently frozen condition of the soil. As Jess pushed the sled uphill and rode the runners on the way down, he would suddenly burst into song. A great feeling of contentment came over me gliding along in the yellow sunlight, safe in Jess's capable hands.

At Gilmore, Mother Madole stepped down from the train wearing her long black coat with the fur collar and a hat of sheared beaver. It is true that she loved good clothes and expensive fabrics.

That day she looked as well dressed as any woman alighting from a train in New York or Chicago, even though she was in the Alaskan hinterlands.

During the ride to Pedro Creek I sat in the front of the sled so I could get off easily and help Jess over the bad places. The trail was glaciered in some parts, and that was where Diamond balked. He had a fear of glare ice. Then Jess would lead the dogs across while I stood on the brake, taking care so the sled would not slide off the trail.

As soon as we were settled at the cabin, the first thing Mother Madole did was start cooking. Like many Norwegian women, she was the happiest when she was turning out a batch of cookies, or cutting a pie crust, or simmering a rabbit stew. All week she kept Frank and Doc busy carrying in wood and filling the barrel with snow to melt for water. Next to cooking, she loved to scrub, and it wasn't long before the teakettle was polished, the windows shining, and the table rubbed within an inch of its life.

During those lovely sun-filled days, Jess and I took every opportunity to be outdoors. For the first time in my life I put on a pair of snowshoes. I plodded behind Jess, following him where he had put out snare lines for the rabbits. We hunted for grouse and ptarmigan, which he kept frozen in the woodcutter's cache. Some of that meat he would bring into town when Mother Madole ran low on food.

One day Jess suggested that we climb to the top of Pedro Dome. Since it didn't look too steep, or particularly far, I agreed. It was from the top of that dome in 1901 that Felix Pedro sighted smoke from the *La Velle Young* and so began the first act of the gold rush that brought Fairbanks, and the surrounding creek towns, into being.

Since there was a lot of heavy brush on the dome, we could not use our snowshoes, but had to break trail as best we could. Jess was light enough to walk on top of the hard-crusted snow, but for me with all my weight, it was a different story. With every step or two I broke through and plunged into snow above my knees. The long skirt I was wearing didn't help matters any. It was soon wet, matted with snow, and it felt as if it weighed a ton. Jess had outfitted me with leggings, a short fur jacket and a pair of bear-hide mittens, but still I was cold. The wool stocking cap pulled over my ears was warm enough, but it did lack something when it came to style.

By the time we reached the top of the dome, I was thoroughly exhausted and chilled to the bone. We sat on a pile of rocks to catch our breath, but soon an icy wind began blowing and we had to start moving again.

Down the dome we went, in a zigzag course around the clumps of bushes, with the wind coming at us all the while. My skirt was frozen stiff and stood out from my legs like a cage. There I was, stumbling through the snow, trying to keep up with Jess, who seemed to be having a fine time for himself. I was too proud to tell him how tired I was.

"This is the life," he said, striding ahead.

"Oh, yes," I panted.

"This is the way to live, out in nature's wonderland. Don't you think so, Clara?"

"Yes, Jess, it sure is," I gasped.

"I wish we could do this every day," he said.

"Every day," I echoed.

In spite of my discomfort, I never complained, not once. If I wanted to follow Jess, I knew I would have to do the things he enjoyed doing. And, as tired as I was, I did love the outdoors too.

When, at last, we reached the cabin, it looked like heaven to me. As soon as we were inside, I fell into the nearest chair while my teeth chattered uncontrollably.

"You should have seen her," Jess bragged to Doc. "She climbed all the way to the top of the dome."

"Well, Clara, that makes you a sourdough," Doc said, bringing me hot tea along with towels to dry my feet.

"She sure is," Jess said proudly. "You wouldn't have known she was a city girl a short time ago."

With compliments like those I was ready to climb the dome all over again. It was during that week on Pedro Creek that I began to notice a change in Jess's attitude toward me. He was kinder, he treated me in a gentler way, as if I was someone special.

Jess was not outwardly affectionate, so I had to read the signs as best I could. At night when the gasoline lamp was turned off, the afterglow lent a romantic intimacy. Jess would first kiss his mother good-night, and then me. It wasn't my imagination, was it, I wondered, but didn't Jess linger longer over our kiss than ever before? And didn't he take every opportunity he could to hold my hand, to touch my hair, to lean against my shoulder?

Those were the thoughts I hugged close to me as I burrowed deep beneath the blankets on the bunk bed while Jess climbed the ladder to the loft where he and Doc and Frank slept in their bedrolls.

Jess was changing. He had changed from that brash young man who had pushed me in the snowbank that Thanksgiving night to a thoughtful, more mature suitor.

Too soon our week on Eight Above was over. After Jess and I took Mother Madole to the train depot, we started home by dog team, taking our time and letting the dogs pad along as they would while the harness bells made music on the trail.

Why is the trip home always faster? As we neared town, I thought, no, not yet. I'm not ready to go home; give me a little more time. I could have gone on riding until dawn.

In my attic bedroom, as I undressed for bed, I thought: Just let that Jess Rust try and get away from me. ◀■▶

chapter 10

On the outside of the cabin on Second Avenue, where we lived, Mother Madole hung a black sign that was bordered in gold and hung from a post. It read:

MADAME RENIO

Palmistry   Card Reading   Astrology

It was the same sign she had used in Dawson when she told fortunes for a living. There she gained fame when the Redmond brothers—on her advice—struck it rich.

It was also in Dawson that Madame Renio was tried for witchcraft. There was a miner in town who would not make a business move without first consulting her, much to the frustration of a couple of quick-buck artists who were trying to involve him in a wild goose scheme. Madame Renio advised him to grubstake another group of men, and as a result, they made a fortune. This infuriated the sharpshooters, so they swore out a warrant for her arrest for witchcraft.

At the Dawson trial Madame Renio was cleared of all charges, and after the public exposure, she had more business than she could handle. She made enough money to enable her to buy some real estate in Seattle and go into business when she reached Fairbanks.

Jess rarely talked of his mother's clairvoyance. Whenever I questioned him about it, he became defensive, although he did not appear to put much faith in it himself.

During the time Mother Madole and I lived together in the little cabin on Second Avenue, she used the living room for an office. When she had a customer, she would pin up the sign of the zodiac and the poster of the palm on the curtains. While she gave her reading she sat at the heavy round table, with claw and ball feet, placed in the middle of the room.

At these times I would stay in the dining room, but in such close quarters, I could not help but overhear some of her conversations. The things she said sounded strange to me, as if they were coming from a person I had never met.

"Astrology explains the effects of certain planetary conditions and teaches us what we should do in order to control our natural tendencies in order that we may progress, be healthy, happy and prosperous," she would say.

It sounded like a lot of wishful thinking to me, and because I was young and in love there was no need for astrology in my life. Both my parents attended the Christian Science Church, and I had gone with them on a number of occasions, but formal religion never satisfied me. I preferred to find my own answers about God and the universe.

There was an occurrence at the cabin, involving hypnotism, that made me uneasy. It happened one evening when Mother Madole held a public lecture on astrology and hypnotism. A group of people crowded into our living room where Madame Renio presided, dressed in a long black skirt and wearing a red and white checked blouse. Her dark hair was swept into a full pompadour. Her voice was deep and eloquent, and her dark eyes urged the people to understand. She considered astrology an art, and she never belittled it by dressing like a gypsy or using a crystal ball.

After she finished speaking, she offered to hypnotize someone in the room. A young Negro man, who worked around town as a messenger, volunteered. Within a few minutes we could see that the fellow was under her influence.

"Now, I am going to tell him that he is fishing and he must pull the fish out of the water," Madame Renio explained.

Sure enough, the man began going through the motions of pulling a fish out of the water, using a broom handle as a fishing pole.

"Oops! Got one," he said. "Oops! Here's another one."

Then suddenly he did a turnabout and said, "Bang! Bang! I got a gun. Bang! Bang!" and he used the broom handle as a gun.

Madame Renio was startled; something had gone wrong. The young man should not have disobeyed her command.

"You are fishing," she said sharply. "You are fishing."

"Bang! Bang! Got him," the man said over and over.

Then we heard the sound of laughter and everyone turned around to see Jess standing at the back of the room. "No, he is not fishing, mother. He is hunting. I hypnotized him too."

Madame Renio controlled herself until the people left. Then she said, "Jess, don't you ever do that again. I do not use hypnotism as a cheap parlor trick. You know how dangerous that can be."

The look that passed between them made me afraid. It was the first time I had seen Mother Madole mad at Jess. That evening left me with a strange feeling, and it did not encourage me to explore the occult in which Mother Madole put her faith.

At last the dull, dry days of May gave way to the sudden bursting and budding of June. The tender green of the trees and bushes had a glossiness that shimmered in the long hours of sunlight. There was a great awakening of earth and sky. Weeds popped out of the ground, robins nested and warbled, and white butterflies hovered over the dandelions.

I put cheesecloth over my bedroom window to keep out the mosquitoes that hatched and hummed, eager for fresh blood. By lifting out the glass window, some small breeze found its way into my hot attic room.

It was one noon when I hurried home for lunch that I found Jess waiting for me.

"Oh," I said, "I didn't expect you in town today."

"Well, I don't have to tell you everything I am going to do," he said. "Come with me."

He took me by the hand and led me up the stairs to my room. With the bed pushed against the wall under the eaves, the only furniture that could fit in there was a small dresser. There were no chairs, so we sat on the bed.

Jess was quiet for the longest time. Then he said, "Hold out your left hand."

I did as I was told. He slipped a ring on my finger.

"What is this for?" I asked.

"If you don't know, I'm sure as hell not going to tell you," he said, and down the stairs he went. The front door banged shut.

I sat dazed. I was under the impression that I had just become engaged to Jesse Worthington Rust, accomplished in a matter of seconds, and without a single kiss.

It was true; I never knew what Jess was going to do next. He was 9 years older than I, and he had resisted marriage for a long time. Now he was ready, and so was I. My heart filled with joy.

The ring he slipped so easily on my finger had two rubies and a diamond in a Tiffany setting. It was, without a doubt, the most beautiful ring I had ever seen. I went to the window and looked up the dusty road toward town. How I hated to go back to work that day.

It was slow in the store that afternoon, so Mary and I sat on the counter, swinging our legs and talking, the way we always did when we were alone. Suddenly she grabbed my hand.

"What is this?" she asked.

"My engagement ring," I said. "Jess gave it to me today."

"Jess Rust," she said loudly. "You are engaged to Jess Rust?"

Jess, left, and prospecting partner Frank Reynolds at Little Eldorado in 1910.

I nodded my head.

She jumped off the counter and began pacing back and forth in front of me. "Jess Rust," she said, "well, he is a nice fellow, but he will never set the world on fire."

"I don't want him to," I said.

"But, Clara, you could have done so much better."

Her words cut me deeply. No doubt she had my best interests at heart, but she had no right to say the things she did. I knew what I wanted. I loved Jess and I wanted to marry him. Mary's words cast a dark cloud over a day that should have been so happy. Things were never the same between us again.

That week after the engagement announcement came out in the paper, my friends came to congratulate me and to see my ring. From that time on, Mary never made another derogatory remark about Jess.

Our future depended on Jess's prospecting. In the spring of 1910, Jess and the boys—Frank and Doc—had given up the Pedro Creek claim (and the new cabin). They made a deal to work Five Above on Little Eldorado Creek where testing indicated a rich lode. They agreed to pay a royalty on the gold they mined, and to pay rent for the equipment and buildings which were owned by Fairbanks outfitters Brumbough, Hamilton and Kellog. On the property there was a boiler house with a hoist, a bunkhouse, two small cabins and another large building for the cookhouse.

Mother Madole mortgaged a large piece of property—the house on Queen Anne Hill in Seattle—to launch this new venture. Everybody's future hung in the balance. The stakes were high, but we figured it was worth a risk for a big gain. Little Eldorado had already produced fortunes for a number of miners. We were next.

There was one flaw. Right next to the block of pay dirt where the men would sink their mine shaft was an old shaft full of water. Jess and the boys decided that the best method would be to drain the shaft by digging an open cut to the tunnel outlet so the water could come out through the bedrock drain. The measuring, the deliberating and the arguing that went on over that business I shall never forget. There were weeks and weeks of preliminary work, clearing the ground for the cut, digging for the drain, more measuring and then consulting with our neighbors Fraker and Nelson, who worked the property adjacent to ours. It seemed to me that weeks were wasted in talking and getting ready. Would they ever get the gold out; that's what I wanted to know. What was taking so long?

Mother Madole and I were both curious about the mine operation, so in mid-July we decided to pay the boys a visit. We planned to take the auto stage instead of the train since the auto would drop us off within a mile of the mine, rather than a 5-mile walk from Eldorado siding.

Seven passengers crowded into the old Ford touring car that left town late one afternoon. We sat on each other's laps while two men perched on the running board. Whenever we hit a muddy spot, they got off and pushed. On the steep grades, especially going up Cleary Summit, everybody got out and pushed. For this we paid $5 apiece for a 20-mile ride which took 6 hours.

By the time Mother Madole and I started walking down the winding road to Five Above, it was almost midnight. It was cool in the hills, but as bright as day now that we were getting 20 hours of sunlight. As we walked, my heavy satchel bumping against my leg, I heard the sound of Little Eldorado Creek nearby as it splashed and sprinted over the rocky creekbed.

There is on the air at that time of year a spicy aroma from the birch and willow, from the spruce and tamarack, and from the wild flowers—the pale pink moss rose, the gleaming white dogwood, the pink-fringed bluebells—that is as sweet as nectar. There is at that time of the night a stillness that is like music to my ears. As soon as we reached the cookhouse the boys, who had been waiting up for us, gave us coffee and pie before we went to bed.

That week on Little Eldorado started out hot and stayed that way. The days dawned early, about 2 o'clock in the morning, with a blue and cloudless sky, and by midafternoon the temperature was almost 90, scorching and dry, as only July can be. These were working days for Jess and his crew. There was no time to play like last winter on Pedro Creek. In summer, every day counts double.

Jess had hired two extra men to help with the work. Already they had spent more than a month digging the bedrock drain in their attempt to reach the flooded mine shaft. It was Jess' plan to reach the base of the flooded shaft from the top of the ground by undercutting below the shaft. Once they hit the shaft, the water would come flooding into the drain ditch.

Somehow their measurements were off, and they never did reach the shaft. Now they were working underground in the Fraker and

Nelson mine. The plan was to tunnel until they reached the bedrock drain. Once they made that connection, the tunnel would be boarded up, and then they could break through to the flooded shaft.

While Jess and the boys put in 8- and 10-hour shifts underground, Mother Madole and I cooked for the crew. On those sweltering days the heat from the cookstove was unbearable. As soon as we finished one meal, it was time to start on the next one. How those men could eat. In the morning the stacks of pancakes vanished into thin air. The pies and doughnuts, the cookies and homemade bread disappeared as soon as they reached the table. There was always a pot of coffee boiling on the stove.

Doc worked with us in the kitchen, hauling in the water, hauling out the slop buckets. There was wood to be cut and ashes to dump. When Doc helped slice the meat or peel the potatoes, the job was done to perfection, but he was "slower than molasses in January," as Jess would say.

During the afternoon, Mother Madole and I headed for the blueberry patch to get berries for fresh pies. As soon as we settled down to serious picking, the mosquitoes descended in a ferocious horde. Unfortunately, Mother Madole was allergic to them. All it took was one bite and her skin became red and swollen. To protect herself she wrapped newspapers around her legs before pulling on her stockings, and put papers across her back and arms before pulling on her sweater. To top it off, she had an old wide-brimmed hat with mosquito netting fastened to the brim and then tied under her chin.

The mosquitoes were so thick that I watched little brown birds light on Mother Madole's hat and carry off a beak full of bugs. Since I could not stand to be wrapped in newspaper on those hot days, I made up my mind that the mosquitoes would not bother me. It worked, too. All afternoon, side by side with Mother Madole, I picked berries, wearing a sleeveless dress, and escaped with only one or two bites.

One day Jess surprised me by handing me a pair of overalls and some old boots. "Put these on," he said. "I am taking you down in the Faker and Nelson mine. You ask more questions about mining than any darn woman Ⓓever met. Now I am going to show you what a mine is all about."

"That sounds like fun," I said, but that was before I knew what I was getting in for. The Fraker and Nelson mine was 135 feet underground.

Down into the dark earth we went, swaying to and fro in the iron bucket that was fastened by a hook to the hoist cable. The cable was wound around a large drum which was run by a donkey engine. As we sank deeper beneath the ground, the clackety-clack of the engine became fainter and fainter.

I crouched in the bottom of the bucket; I was so scared I couldn't talk. The shaft was cribbed with 8-foot poles, all dovetailed like the corners of a log cabin. Water oozed through the cribbing, giving off an incredibly dank and musty smell.

At last the bucket hit the bottom of the shaft with a loud clatter. When my eyes became accustomed to the dark I saw two lights moving toward us.

"What is that?" I asked.

"It's the carbide lamps on the miners' helmets," Jess said. "The men are coming to load their wheelbarrows full of pay dirt into the bucket."

With Jess leading the way, we took slow and careful steps along the spooky tunnel, lighted by wax candles. The flickering shadows loomed against the dirt walls. The air, damp and evil smelling, was heavy to breathe. My hands were icy cold, and my feet, in boots too big, stumbled over the debris on the tunnel floor.

It wasn't long before we reached the Fraker and Nelson crew where they were hacking away at the bedrock with picks and shovels and loading the dirt in wheelbarrows. In the dim light I could see the sweat on the men's faces; their shirts were blotted to their backs. It was muscle-stretching, backbreaking work under miserable conditions. What men won't do for gold, I thought.

As Jess explained the mining operation to me, I tried to grasp the things he was saying, but he was an impatient teacher, expecting me to understand in a few minutes what had taken him years to learn.

Farther along the tunnel, beyond the work crew, there was an opening just big enough for a man to crawl through.

"My crew is back in there," Jess said. "You'll have to get down on all fours."

"What?" I cried. "What did you say?"

"You heard me," Jess said. "Get going."

"But, Jess, I can't crawl through there," I protested.

"You wanted to see where we were working, now you are going to see it," he said.

He was serious. He *did* want me to crawl through that hole. I got down on my hands and knees and started through. There was one thing wrong. I was bigger than the hole.

"Jess! Jess!" I screamed. "I'm stuck!"

"I know. I can see that," he said, and he gave me a hard shove on the rear and I went sprawling face first in the dirt.

I started bawling. "Oh, Jess! How could you do this to me," I cried. "I want to go back."

"Come on, Clara," Jess said, gently wiping my tears with his handkerchief. "Don't be a baby. I want to show you where my boys are working."

"But, Jess, I am covered with dirt."

"Don't worry about that. You always look good to me."

There was nothing like a little of Jess's charm to get me moving. I picked myself up.

Soon we came upon a wooden tram car that the boys used to carry dirt out of the tunnel.

"Get in," Jess said, pointing to the tram.

"Oh, no! What if I get stuck again?"

"You won't," he assured me.

I settled into it as carefully as I could, and Jess pushed the tram car along the boards they had put down for a track. Up ahead in the flickering candlelight I saw the headlamps of Jess's crew. Frank and the hired men were digging the tunnel in the hopes of connecting with the bedrock drain. In exchange for using the Fraker and Nelson mine, Jess supplied them with cut wood.

Even though the boys worked long hours, the work was going too slow to suit Jess. Here it was the middle of June, and they hadn't even started digging for gold yet.

"If we don't reach the drain pretty soon," Jess said as we started back, "we will have to give it up and sink our new shaft alongside the flooded one. It's a risky business to work close to a shaft like that."

"How deep will you have to dig for the new mine?" I asked.

"At least a hundred feet."

"That will take months, won't it?" I asked.

"I know," he answered. "The summer is going fast, and we aren't any closer to the gold than when we started."

Jess was disappointed with all the delays, and I was too. Why did our dreams have a way of going sour? Why couldn't we have some good luck for a change? All we ever did was work, work, work and we never got ahead. Would it always be like that?

Even though I dreaded going back through the hole, it had to be done, and I did it. From the bottom of the shaft the small patch of sky looked a million miles away. Jess rang the bell to indicate to the hoistman that two passengers were coming up.

As the bucket was pulled out of that black hole, swaying this way and that, it bumped against the cribbing and caused my stomach to lurch.

"It's all right," Jess said.

It wasn't all right with me until I was in the sunshine with both feet on the ground.

"I am proud of you, Clara. You did fine," Jess said, putting his arm around my shoulders. "There are a lot of men who won't go down in a mine shaft like that."

"Now you tell me," I said.

He hugged me close. My Jess, so brusque, so shy, and afraid to show his true feelings. Sometimes I thought I was the only person who understood him, and I often had doubts about that.

One evening just before I left Little Eldorado, Jess and I were out walking. He said he realized that he wanted me, and needed me now and forever. After talking it over with Mrs. Madole, we decided to get married in October, the exact date to be settled later. By then Jess and the boys would have finished the cleanup, and they would still have time to fix up the cookhouse where Jess and I would live. Mother Madole would move out to the mine too, taking the small room attached to the bunkhouse.

After Mother Madole and I returned to town, it was hard to settle down to the old routine when the future beckoned so appealingly. I daydreamed the hours away, thinking about my wedding and what it would be like married to Jess. Even though Mother Madole didn't say it in so many words, I thought she was waiting for Doc to ask her to marry him, and we would have a double wedding.

But if he was going to ask her, he sure was taking his time about doing it.

chapter 11

While I was preparing for my wedding, I received word that my parents were divorced. The news did not surprise me, but I was taken aback when I heard that Dad had remarried right away to a friend of my mother's in Seattle. Dad and his new wife settled, for the time being, in Vancouver, British Columbia, while Mother and Beth made their way to California, where they lived for a number of years.

It was idle daydreaming on my part to suppose that anyone from my family would be at the wedding, but I had hoped for at least a word, some small gift, perhaps, but there was nothing.

In early October Jess wrote that he was washing down the remains of an old dump that was paying off pretty good. They had abandoned the idea of trying to drain the flooded shaft and had begun sinking a new one. In order to scrape together enough money to carry us through the winter, Jess was working the old pile of pay dirt on the property.

"I will send some gold in with Doc to help pay for the wedding," Jess promised.

Since we had not set the wedding date, I wrote Jess and told him that we would be married Saturday night, October 25.

"If this is not all right, let me know. Otherwise, we will go ahead with our plans," I wrote.

It just so happened that there was a man in Mary's store who worked the claim above Jess's and was going out to Little Eldorado that day. He agreed to deliver the letter to Jess.

We had no direct word from Jess, but a few days before the wedding, Doc came to town. Mother Madole and I waited expectantly, hoping he would say, "Oh, by the way, here is the money from Jess." But he didn't say a word about it.

By this time Mother Madole and I were getting frantic. We had guests coming for the wedding dinner, there were groceries to buy, and the colored maid to pay. We just did not know where the money would come from.

My wedding day dawned with a stony kind of coldness, hard and unyielding. The cold seeped in the cracks beside my bed, and the blankets froze to the wall. Frost, thick and furry, formed on the inside of the window.

It was early when I awoke; darkness enveloped the house. I lay in bed under the eaves, my heart pounding heavily, and I thought, "Tomorrow morning at this time I will be Jess's wife. Tomorrow. Tomorrow."

By noon the little house on Second Avenue was thrown open to the wedding guests, who had already started arriving from the creeks. Mr. and Mrs. David Roy from Gilmore got there before lunch. While Mother Madole put the finishing touches on the wedding cake, I entertained the Roys as best I could. Doc, nervous as a cat, puffed on one cigarette after another.

"What's wrong with Doc?" I asked Mother Madole as I fixed another pot of coffee.

"I don't know. He has been acting strangely."

There would not be a double wedding this day. Doc had not asked Mother Madole to marry him. Just for a moment—standing there in that cramped kitchen—I resented the fact that Mother Madole had planned everything for my wedding as if it were her own. She put the wedding announcement in the paper; she invited the guests; she had made out the dinner menu; she had arranged for the minister; she had even arranged for the dressmaker to make my dress.

My dress. Whenever I thought about it, I shuddered. If only it hadn't been gray taffeta; it made me feel old and heavy. The material was from a dress Mother Madole had torn apart and saved from her Dawson days. Since Jess and I were having a quiet wedding at home, the fabric seemed appropriate enough. Besides, it cut down on expenses and Mother Madole was paying for everything, so what could I say?

The design, a princess style with a long skirt and yoke and collar of Viennese lace, was fine, if we had only left it at that. But we kept adding things like the pleated flounce and bows above the knees, and the white lace medallions, outlined with blue embroidery thread, tacked across the front and on both shoulders. It was too much.

Fortunately I had an hourglass figure—thanks to a tightly cinched corset—but I still weighed 200 pounds and with all those bows, and pleats, and lace medallions, I looked it.

By early afternoon Frank Taylor arrived, with several other guests, bringing wedding gifts that were placed on the big living room table. There were packages from Mary Anderson, although she had not delivered them herself. I was being stubborn, I realized it even then, but I did not ask Mary to the wedding because of the remarks she had made about Jess. Later I regretted that I had shut her out that way.

Whenever the back door opened I looked anxiously, expecting it was Jess and Frank Reynolds. But it wasn't them. Even though the splashy sun brightened the day, the temperature had not budged any higher than 35 degrees below zero. On these days, heading into winter, the sun faded fast, and in a few short hours it would be dark.

"Where is Jess?" I asked Mother Madole. "It's after 1 o'clock. He should have been here by now."

"I don't know what to think," she said. "He had better get here pretty soon. We still don't have any money, and there are things I need to buy."

"I have a little money saved," I said. "Please let me give it to you."

"No," she said firmly, "Jess and I will take care of everything. That is the way I planned it."

With each passing minute I became more edgy and nervous. Everybody was there except the bridegroom. Had Jess been in an accident? Or had he decided he didn't want to get married? Where could he be?

"I think I will go over to Mrs. Wilson's and take my bath now," I said to Mother Madole; "maybe by the time I get back, Jess will be here."

Mrs. Wilson ran a rooming house next door where we could take a bath for a small charge. I took my time soaking in the hot tub, trying to forget the nagging fear that something might have happened to Jess.

I took extra care with my nails and hair, sweeping it into a high pompadour the way Jess liked it. My cheeks glowed rosy-red in the mirror; there was little need for make-up.

As I hurried along the snowy path to our cabin, my black coat with the plush lining held close around me, the sun was beginning to slip lower in the sky. I checked the shed, thinking Jess might try to fool me by putting the dogs in there, but there was no sign of them.

"If this is another one of Jess's tricks, it's the last one he will ever play on me," I said as I pushed open the kitchen door.

"Now, dear, don't get excited," Mother Madole said. "I am sure he will be here any minute."

No sooner were the words out of her mouth than we heard the dogs yelping and suddenly the back door flew open.

"What in the hell is going on around here?" Jess demanded.

"What do you mean?" I asked, stunned by his remark.

"Why didn't you tell me we were getting married today?" he shouted. "If some guy hadn't told me this morning that he read it in the paper, I never would have known."

"Didn't you get my letter? I sent it more than a week ago."

"No, I didn't get your letter," he ranted. "I had to find out from some stranger when I was getting married."

"It isn't my fault," I said. "I sent the letter with that man who works the claim above you. He said he was going right by your place, and he would deliver it."

"Well, he didn't do it," Jess replied, cooling down a little. "What time is this big wedding coming off anyhow?"

"At 7 o'clock," I answered.

"That doesn't leave me much time," Jess said. "I guess I better get ready."

"Wait a minute, Jess," Mother Madole said. "Where is the money?"

"What money?" he asked.

"The money you said you would send to help pay for the wedding."

"I sent it," Jess replied. "I sent it in with Doc."

"With Doc," Mother Madole said.

"With Doc," I echoed, and my heart sank.

"Yes, with Doc," Jess shouted. "I gave him $150 worth of gold."

"Shh, Jess," I said, pointing to the living room. "We have guests."

"I don't care. I just want to know where my money went. Where is he? Where is Doc?"

"Right here," Doc said, appearing in the doorway.

"Where is the money?" Jess demanded.

Doc took a nervous puff on his cigarette. "It's gone," he said quietly.

For a moment the only sound in the room was the snuffling of the fire in the stove.

Finally I said, "Where did it go?"

"I wanted to buy you a big wedding present," Doc said, meeting my eyes. "I thought I could double the money in a poker game, but I lost it all."

Just then Frank Reynolds came bursting in the back door. "Ow, it's cold out th'air," he said rubbing his hands. "I tied up the dogs, Jess," and then after one look at our solemn faces he asked, "What's wrong? Somebody die?"

"Doc lost all the money in a poker game," I said. I was all for booting him out, but it hadn't been my money.

"Ow, my god," Frank said.

A deadly silence followed.

I said, "I have about $50."

"No," Mother Madole answered. "You will need your money later, Clara."

Jess made his way across the room to the telephone.

"What are you going to do, Jess?" I asked.

He gave the number of the Cascade Laundry to the operator. "Mrs. Shinkle," he said into the mouthpiece, "this is Jess Rust. Are you still interested in buying my dog?"

"Oh, no," I gasped, pulling at Jess's arm. "Don't do it."

Jess ignored me while he talked. "I am in kind of a bind. I need some cash. How about $50? Fine. I'll be right over." He slammed down the receiver. "Go untie Irish," he said to Frank.

"Not Irish," I cried. "Oh, Jess, please don't do it." The tears were streaming down my face; I loved those dogs as much as he did. "There is no other way," Jess said as he stalked out the door. While I stood in the open doorway, with the cold air streaming around my feet, I saw Jess heading toward town with the trusting Irish by his side.

When Jess returned, with the money and without the dog, there was no time to dwell on the fate of Irish. There was much to be done before the minister arrived. Jess and Frank still had to take their baths and get haircuts. Since Jess could not decide whether to have Frank Taylor or Frank Reynolds as best man, they flipped a coin. Reynolds was it.

Wearing her elegant gown of red velvet and lace, Mother Madole stood by my side as matron of honor while the Reverend Condit of the First Presbyterian Church read the wedding ceremony. I wore no veil, nor carried flowers—an item impossible to buy in town those days. I did have the white Battenburg lace handkerchief Mother Madole had made for me, and I have it to this day. Jess and Frank, solemn in dark suits and stiff, white shirts, looked as nervous as I felt.

Even though Jess took pictures on all other occasions, he never thought to take a single picture that day, and no one else did either. I suppose it is just as well. When I think about my wedding dress and how I must have looked, I am glad that no photographic record exists.

Our guests joined us around the table in the dining room where the maid served a dinner of roast breasts of grouse (from birds Jess had supplied), mashed potatoes and gravy, canned corn on the cob and canned peas. And the champagne, how it flowed that night.

The tiered wedding cake, spicy-sweet with candied fruit, was frosted and topped with a miniature bride and bridegroom. In the glow of my happiness I could not help but be grateful to Mother Madole for all she had done. My generosity even extended to Doc, even though he had come close to ruining my wedding day.

At midnight, amid a shower of rice, Jess and I left the warmth of Mother Madole's cabin and walked the 10 blocks to my family's old house. It was bitterly cold with patches of ice fog hovering above the ground. The moon, hard and round, swayed overhead. Our footsteps squeaked loudly in those hushed, hollow streets as we walked, my mittened hand held tightly by Jess.

As we approached the little house, I thought of all the things that had happened in the two years since I first saw my mother standing in the doorway that morning I arrived in Fairbanks. Now, here I was, crossing the threshold with Jess, my husband.

Earlier in the week I had cleaned the cabin in preparation for our wedding night. The floors had been swept and dusted, and fresh linen put on the big bed that folded down from the wall. There was kindling and water, and some hours before the wedding Frank had started the fire.

Jess lighted a lamp, since the electricity had been turned off, and put more wood in the stove. I shall never forget how cold it was in that cabin; it never did warm up. By morning, the bucket of water next to the stove was frozen.

I undressed as quickly as I could and got into bed, my skin prickled with goose bumps. Soon Jess slipped in between the blankets beside me, and we forgot all the frustrations and worries of our wedding day. When he put his arms around me and held me close, I loved that man so much I thought my heart would burst.

chapter 12

Whitey. Was there ever a horse like him? He was as shaggy as a mountain goat and as sway-backed as an old mule. To make matters worse, he had only one eye. When he got tired he sat down on his haunches and stayed there until he was ready to get up, whenever that might be.

It was Whitey we were dependent on to get Jess and me and all our belongings out to Little Eldorado. Jess borrowed a sleigh, a double-ender with handlebars, and we piled it high with clothes, bedding, wedding gifts, food and a mattress—where I perched, wrapped in Jess's wolf robe.

We started out one cold and misty morning the end of October with Jess on the back runners, or running alongside to encourage Whitey to move faster—but that was useless. There was no need of reins either, because no amount of urging would speed him up.

By the time we reached the Roys' cabin at Gilmore Creek, Jess and I were frozen to the bone and utterly exhausted. It didn't take much persuasion to convince us to stay the night. After we put Whitey in the warm barn nearby, Jess threw the wolf robe and mattress on the Roys' cabin floor and there we stayed until morning.

The next day was beautiful with the sky as blue as the ocean from horizon to horizon. A blazing sun set fire to the ice crystals on the little bushes and across the shimmering expanses of snow. Since the Roys were in a traveling mood, they decided to accompany us the 11 miles to Little Eldorado. When they offered to take Whitey and the sleigh back to Fairbanks, we readily accepted.

On the steep grades Jess and Judge Roy had to push the sleigh up the hill. Madge and I walked alongside, trying to coax Whitey to move faster. Halfway up the hill he sat down in his traces, panting heavily. His bony sides heaved in and out like an accordion. The sight of him sent Madge and me into a giggling fit. The men gave us disgusted stares. For some reason, they couldn't find a lick of humor in the situation.

Cleary Summit was the last, and longest, hill to climb. I didn't see how that knock-kneed, one-eyed nag was going to make it. "This is where I wish I hadn't come," Judge Roy said, eyeing the steep slope ahead of us.

"Me too," Jess agreed.

We all put our shoulders to the load and started up. We pushed and we shoved, and we hollered and threatened that dumb beast. Nothing made any difference; Whitey would make it in his own sweet time.

How we shouted for joy when, at last, we reached the top! I gave Whitey a few lumps of sugar, and with that he perked up his ears and began trotting down the hill. Madge and I grabbed the mattress and hung on for dear life.

As soon as our sleigh was spotted coming down the hill, one of the miners in the valley blew his steam whistle, and soon all the whistles were blowing up and down the creek. Never was a wedding party greeted so royally. At that moment, coasting down the snowy hillside with the whistles ringing in my ears, I knew that my wedding was unique and complete.

When we arrived at the cookhouse, Doc and Frank were waiting for us with a full-course meal steaming on the back of the stove. They had come ahead a few days earlier with a load on the sled. With them were the two hired men, Qually and Charlie.

"That damn Diamond," Doc said when we were having supper; "I had a heck of a time with him. He balked all the way."

"He misses Irish," Jess said. "We broke up a winning combination."

"We had to lead Diamond by the collar almost all the way," Frank said.

"Then when we got to the top of the summit, Diamond broke away and ran off with the sled," Doc added. "We had to walk the rest of the way home."

Serves you right, I felt like saying. I couldn't forget that it was Doc's fault that we didn't have Irish.

"If you think the dogs are bad, you should take a trip with Whitey," Jess said.

"I am not looking forward to that trip back to town with that old nag," Judge Roy added. "How do I get myself into these things?"

After the Roys left darkness came quickly, bringing with it a deeper and more penetrating cold that caused the frost to creep farther up the window panes and the cookhouse logs to pop. Frank lit the gasoline lamp, filling the room with white light.

When the dishes were done, I sat on Jess's lap in the rocking chair next to the stove and we surveyed out new home. Thanks to Mother Madole the walls were covered with flower-sprigged calico that gave the room a feeling of warmth and cheer. On the wall next to the wood-burning stove were wooden crates that held dishes and utensils, cooking spices, tea, coffee, flour and such. Beneath an uncurtained window was a workbench, and nearby were two buckets and a wooden barrel that held the snow we melted for our water supply.

In the middle of the room was a long table with benches where our crew would join us for meals. The floor—rough wooden planks—was bleached white from many scrubbings with lye water.

Across the back of the cookhouse was an area partitioned by a heavy gray canvas curtain tacked to the rough wood ceiling. On one side was the room for our winter's supply of food which required warm storage; on the other side was a small, windowless cubbyhole which was our bedroom. It was big enough for a fold-up bed, a dresser and a chair. The bed, which Jess made, was constructed of two-by-fours with holes bored in them and ropes woven back and forth for springs. With the mattress we had brought from Fairbanks, and the wolf robe, it offered some measure of comfort.

Just as we were getting ready for bed that first night, we heard a terrible commotion outside the cookhouse door.

"What is that?" I said.

"I don't know," Jess answered. "Let's find out."

He opened the door and in the darkness we could see shadowy figures carrying bug lamps—Log Cabin syrup cans with candles inside—banging spoons on pans, ringing sleigh bells and rattling a cook's triangle.

"Hey! What is going on here?" Jess shouted.

"Who are you?" I yelled.

Before we knew what was happening, the crowd pushed forward and we were surrounded by a dozen or more miners from nearby claims. They came, with jugs of whiskey and pans of cake and bread, to shivaree the bride and bridegroom. There had not been a bride on Little Eldorado in a long time, and they wanted to give me a reception I would never forget. They hugged me and kissed me and slapped Jess on the back.

"You old son-of-a-gun," one miner said to Jess, "you got yourself a damn pretty wife."

Some of the miners, strangely enough, were wearing women's clothes. One had on a lady's wrapper with grouse feathers in his hat, while another fellow had two cook's aprons pinned together with nails. Still another man had a hat draped in mosquito netting topped with paper flowers.

"Why are you wearing dresses?" I asked.

"We didn't want you to get lonesome," one of the miners said. "It was too cold for the women to come out tonight, so some of us dressed up to keep you company."

That prompted a fresh round of laughter, and some risque remarks. Pretty soon someone pulled a harmonica out of his pocket, another man played the comb with a piece of tissue paper, and Jess began whistling. There I was, the only woman among all those men, and they all wanted to dance.

Doc and Frank pushed the table against the wall, and I danced until my feet were sore and my head was spinning and I begged our guests to let me rest. On and on, until the small hours of the morning, the party continued. When the food was gone, the bottles empty and we were too tired to talk, the miners plunged into the cold while Jess and I bedded down under the wolf robe in our cubbyhole in the cookhouse.

Those days on Little Eldorado hold some of my finest memories of my life with Jess. There I knew great happiness, and later—heartbreak. Each day I arose early to accomplish my tasks. There was nothing I wouldn't do for Jess. I even learned to cook!

It was Jess who taught me how to mix and set the sourdough batter for the hot cakes, and how to make bread and doughnuts out of sourdough starter.

One morning when Jess was on his way to work he said, "Some applesauce would be nice in place of canned fruit."

"Fine," I said. "How do you make it?"

"Just put some dried apples in a kettle, add water, and let them cook until they are soft. Then add sugar to taste."

That sounded simple enough, so I did as I was told. Pretty soon the apple slices were overflowing the kettle, and even though I tried to poke them back in, they wouldn't stay. I got another kettle and put some of the extra apples in it. It wasn't long before that kettle was full too, and I began working on the third pot. When Jess came there were apples all over the stove, and I was in tears. Jess thought it was the funniest thing he had ever seen, and he couldn't wait to tell everyone about it. People up and down the creek laughed about it for weeks. And we ate applesauce until it ran out our ears, and apple pie and apple tapioca.

When I wasn't turning out culinary masterpieces, I helped Jess and the boys cut wood. In preparation for the new shaft, they had to cut spruce poles for lagging. These 10-foot poles would be driven into the ground inside the mine shaft to prevent it from sloughing in. Additional logs would be needed to crib the shaft to hold back the dirt. With an ax swung over my shoulder and a warm cap pulled over my ears, I tried to match the boys pole for pole—rarely succeeding.

If Jess and his partners had seen the futility of trying to drain the mine shaft sooner, they could have spent the summer digging a new one. As it was, they didn't start digging until after the snow fell. By then the ground was frozen.

The two hired men, Qually and Charlie, had been with the Fraker and Nelson mine during the summer. When they were laid off, they agreed to work for us in exchange for room and board, plus tobacco money. If we hit pay dirt—and everyone knew we would—they would be paid for the hours they had put in. In the meantime, they had a warm place to stay, plenty of home-cooked food (the quality of which fluctuated with the experience of the cook), and the guarantee of a job with Fraker and Nelson in the spring. Qually and Charlie, along with Doc and Frank, lived in the bunkhouse adjacent to the cookhouse, which had a small apartment partitioned off for Mother Madole.

From the cookhouse window I could watch the two hired men digging the new mine shaft. It was tough work to pick and shovel that ground at 15 and 20 below. It was Jess's job to keep the steam up in the boiler house and to sharpen the steam points used in thawing the ground. The steam points are hollow bars about 6 feet long with a four-sided rounded point at one end. Steam flows through the holes in the head, which is attached to a hose. At night Jess pounded the points into the ground and turned the steam on. In the morning Qually and Charlie began shoveling dirt.

When the shaft was down 5 or 6 feet, a windlass was mounted

over it. The men took turns digging and turning the windlass to bring up the buckets of dirt, which were dumped on the ground. After the cribbing was started, Jess, Frank and Doc had to erect a 25-foot gin pole, braced upright in the ground 30 feet from the mine shaft. Guy wires and a large pulley at the top would allow the iron bucket to be hoisted out of the mine by a donkey engine. Jess nailed crossbars to the top of the gin pole, like a ladder, so he could get to the pulley when it needed repairs.

The gin pole would also come into use to remove dirt from the mine shaft as Qually and Charlie continued to dig. Later, it would be used to hoist the pay dirt that would be dumped in tailing piles, ready for sluicing in the spring.

One afternoon, on a cold day in November, I heard two sharp blasts from the Fraker and Nelson whistle. I grabbed my coat and hurried out the door to join the men who were running up the hill. At the top of the rise, we stopped. From there we could look down on the trail from town. Coming along the white ribbon of a road was a large sleigh drawn by four horses, followed by a cutter driven by a woman in a black coat.

"It's Mother," Jess sang out.

"With the grub," Frank shouted.

"Boy, do we ever need it," I chimed in.

Fortunately Mother Madole had been successful in raising the money we needed to buy our winter's supply of food. As soon as she arrived, we all pitched in and helped unload the sleigh while she gave instructions where everything should be stacked in the storage area.

"Where do you want the petrified spuds?" Jess asked, hauling in the case of dehydrated potatoes. He had his own name for things, like "condemned milk" for canned milk, and "putrid pullets" for dried eggs. He kept us laughing all day at his wisecracks.

How would we ever eat all that food, I wondered as we stashed away cans of dried onions and gunnysacks of yellow ones. We had cases of fresh eggs and 300 pounds of potatoes. There were several kinds of dried beans—lima, pinto, navy and kidney—and lots of sugar for baking, both white and brown. Then came the barrels of butter in brine, and the cases of canned fruits and vegetables. On the shelves we put the boxes of raisins and dried prunes and figs for stewing, and the exquisite little apricots, the pale miniature pear halves, and the slices of dried peaches and apples.

There was a frozen food cache in the entryway of the cookhouse where Jess hung the side of beef and found room for the hams and slabs of bacon alongside the wild game he had shot—caribou, porcupines, rabbits and grouse. Storing the food was just part of it. Every few days we had to turn the cases of eggs so the yolks wouldn't stick to the shells. Once a week we had to empty the sacks of potatoes and rub off the sprouts so the spuds would stay firm. We had to do the same thing to the onions.

Jess and I helped his mother get settled in her apartment, where he had installed a small heater and built shelves as she instructed. With bright calico on the walls and fresh curtains on the windows, Mother Madole settled in.

In the evenings, after dinner, we gathered around the cookhouse table for a game of hearts or black lady. Sometimes Jess and I went walking, just to be alone, or visited a miner up the creek for a game of poker or penny ante. I was happy that Mother Madole had come, for we had good times together, but I felt her pulling Jess in a way that I could not explain. It was just there—a certain feeling—a tiny wrinkle on the surface of my much longed-for happiness.

 **chapter 13**

One afternoon, shortly before Thanksgiving, a woman from a nearby mine stopped to visit. It wasn't often that I had someone new to talk with, and I was enjoying myself, chattering away a mile a minute. Here I was a married woman entertaining a friend in my kitchen, serving her coffee and fresh doughnuts I had made myself. I was mistress of my domain; I had found my place in life, and now when I voiced my opinions, people listened. It was wonderful, this feeling of confidence.

After the woman left, I was pleased with myself in a smug way. When Jess came in, I greeted him with a big hug and kiss. I was bubbling over with happiness; I didn't know life could be so good.

"Clara," he said, "I heard you talking to that woman."

"Oh, that's all right," I said breezily, "I didn't say anything I wouldn't want you to hear."

"Oh, yes you did."

"What's that?" I asked defensively.

"I was shocked to hear your language."

"My language? What about my language?"

"Not only was I surprised, but I could see that Mrs. Thompson was shocked too."

"What in hell do you mean?" I demanded. "Just tell me, dammit."

"That's what I mean," Jess said. "All that swearing. You can't say a single sentence without a cuss word in it."

I couldn't have been more surprised if Jess had slapped my face.

"I never pay any attention to your language when we are alone," he said, "but by golly, kid, we are going to have to stop you from swearing. I am ashamed of you."

I started bawling. Jess was right and I knew it, but it hurt so much to have him tell me.

"Well, whose fault is it? I blubbered through my tears. "You and the other men swear all the time. That is all I ever hear. What can I do?"

Jess put his arms around me and hugged me tight. "Now, Clara, don't cry," he said. "I will tell you what we can do. We will both try to stop swearing. Every time I use a swear word, you can pinch me, and every time you swear, I will pinch you."

I raised my head from his shoulder. "Do you mean it?" I said. "Do you think it will work?"

"Sure it will," he assured me. "By the time we have our Thanksgiving party, we will have the problem licked."

We had invited a big gang for Thanksgiving dinner. Sherman Fraker and Otto Nelson, our good neighbors, were coming. So were Frank Taylor and Al Wooden from Fairbanks and the Roys from Gilmore Creek. With our crew of seven, we would have a full house that day. In preparation, Mother Madole and I spent hours at the cookstove.

"What are you doing with all the wood?" Frank Reynolds wanted to know as he carried in armload after armload. "Nobody could burn this much."

We had proof of our endeavors. From out of the dark cave of an oven came the fruitcakes studded with candied cherries and then dampened with brandy and stored in a cool place. We made batches of cookies, some frosted, others filled with jam; some fried and then sprinkled with sugar. There were breads, too—sweet bread glistening with citron and glaze, dark rye with caraway seeds, and white bread and dinner rolls as fine and as delicate as cake.

For the main course Mother Madole prepared a young pig's head and a beef roast that weighed 15 pounds.

Early Thanksgiving Day I placed the candleholders we had made from tin cans in the center of the table with the arrangement of spruce boughs, cut fresh that morning. At each place setting I put the nut and candy cups made from egg cartons covered with crepe paper. Our dishes were everyday white enamel tin plates and chipped cups to go with them, but no one seemed to mind.

"I say, Clara," Judge Roy said, "you look mighty pretty today. Married life seems to agree with you."

"Jess must know how to make her happy," Madge added.

I turned to hide my embarrassment. It was difficult for me to handle such personal conversations. There were times when Jess kissed me in public, and it made me feel ill at ease. I hoped in time I would get over my sensitivity.

"The table looks fit for a king," Doc said.

"It reminds me of the first dinner Madge served at the mine," the judge said.

"Now, David, you don't have to tell about that," Madge protested.

"I certainly do, too," he said, patting her on the arm. "My wife worked so hard to fix a beautiful table. You should have seen it. There were little bouquets of flowers at each place setting with a fancy tablecloth and napkins. Only trouble was, there wasn't enough food to feed those hungry boys."

"So they ate the flowers," Madge said. "I was so mad I cried. I told the judge I would never cook for those cannibals again."

"I learned a long time ago," Mother Madole said as she carried a bowl of steaming mashed potatoes to the table, "that with men the food comes first, and plenty of it. They never miss the fancy decorations, but they want their grub."

"Hear, hear," said the two Franks and Al Wooden, pounding on the table.

All went well until we started eating.

"Please pass the butter," I said.

Everyone was busy talking, and they didn't hear me.

"Please pass the butter," I said again.

When that didn't get any results, I let loose with, "God damn, what do I have to do to get some butter around here?"

The room was suddenly silent.

Jess reached under the table and pinched me hard on the leg.

"Jesus Christ," I yelled, "what did you do that for?"

Then he pinched me again. At that moment I realized what I had said. I started crying and laughing at the same time until I was almost hysterical. Jess started laughing too until the tears ran down his cheeks. Our guests watched, dumfounded.

Judge Roy said, "What was that all about?"

"Well," Jess said, wiping his eyes, "Clara and I are trying to stop swearing. So when I hear her swear I give her a hard pinch, and she does the same thing to me."

"And he just pinched me twice under the table," I admitted. Our friends got a big laugh out of it, but more than that, the trick worked. I never swore again.

At night when Jess and I had the cookhouse to ourselves, we would turn off the lamps and leave the room dark, and watch the firelight shadows on the ceiling. I would sit on Jess's lap in the rocking chair and he would sing "Little Bit of Heaven," "My Wild Irish Rose," "Mother Machree" and others. Sometimes when he played his mandolin, I sang with him. We found such joy in the simple things.

In the corner of the cookhouse was the barrel we used for melting snow. On bath night Jess filled it to the top, and once it melted we heated the water on the stove. When it was hot, Jess and I took our baths, late at night, using the washtub which was placed on the floor near the stove. I would take my bath first, sitting cross-legged in the tub while Jess sat on the edge to scrub my back.

We were young and we loved playing games like the high kick, using the clothesline strung up in the kitchen as our guide. Jess marveled at how limber I was for such a large person. Those were the days when I could bend over and put my hands flat on the floor without flexing my knees.

"That's amazing," Jess said. "How did you do it?"

"Oh, that's nothing," I answered. "Watch this." To show off I sat on the bed and put my right foot behind my head. It was a trick I had been doing since I was a child—in preparation for my career as a circus performer (how I craved attention).

"I bet I can do that," Jess said, climbing on the bed beside me.

"Let's see you try," I teased.

By sheer force Jess managed to get his foot behind his head, but then something went wrong. He couldn't get it down again. He struggled and groaned, but his foot would not budge.

"Clara, I'm stuck!' he howled. "What should I do?"

"I don't know," I said, wringing my hands. "That never happened to me."

I was scared. Jess looked very strange sitting there on the bed with one leg behind his head and unable to move.

"I'm locked in this position, and it hurts," he moaned.

"I'll go get Mother Madole," I said, jumping off the bed and gathering up my robe.

"No!' Jess shouted. "Don't do that."

"Why not? Maybe she can help us. I don't know what else to do."

"No," came Jess's strangled reply.

"Well, what about Doc?" I said anxiously.

"No!' Jess wailed again. "I feel like a damn fool. We have to get out of this one ourselves."

"But how?" I cried.

"Try moving my leg."

When I touched him he let out a howl of pain. "Don't do that again," he roared.

That made me afraid to touch him again. The thought of hurting Jess sent a jolt to my stomach. "What should I do? I don't want to hurt you."

"Help me roll over."

He managed to roll over on his side, and by rocking back and forth, his leg finally popped out of its locked position.

"Oh, I'll never do that again," Jess said, stretching out.

"Me either," I agreed.

By then we were both sweating and completely worn out, but we had solved the problem ourselves, and we were proud of that much. Poor Jess. He was stiff and sore for days, but we didn't mention our stunt to anyone; Jess would have been the laughing stock of Little Eldorado.

There were evenings when Jess hitched up the dogs and we'd ride to Cleary or Chatanika to attend a dance. I will never forget those nights, especially coming home, when the moon hung breathless like some living thing in the black sky and the northern lights danced overhead. First a wavering wisp of silvery light would appear, and then more lights gathered until it was like a huge banner of rose and green and purple waving in a windstorm.

Jess would stop the team while we watched the lights moving, faster and faster, and we could hear the crackle and swishing noise they made. Sometimes the sky would be lighted with a fiery red electric curtain, sweeping almost to the ground.

That was the winter Jess taught me how to ski. More often than not, I found myself sitting on the skis and sliding downhill. Since there were no sport clothes for women in those days, I had to wear my long blue serge skirt that faded when it was wet.

"You can always tell when my wife tries to ski," Jess said. "She leaves blue streaks on the hillsides."

I was better at snowshoeing than skiing, and I could keep up with Jess, mile after mile, when he checked his trap lines. It wasn't long before I could spot the rabbit trails, and I learned how to set out the slipnoose on the low-hanging branches. Whenever we went out

Jess carried his .22 and I carried the single 12-gauge shotgun that Frank Taylor had given me for a wedding present. The first time I shot it, I was standing on a fence taking aim on a rabbit. When I pulled the trigger, that gun really kicked and knocked me off the fence and into the snow. My shoulder was black and blue for days.

Christmas came on with a flurry of fresh snow that fell like sifted sugar over the glazed white hills and frosted treetops. By that time of the year the daylight hours were a precious few, and in early afternoon the blue shadows of twilight spread across the snowy banks of the silent Little Eldorado Creek.

To announce the holiday season I hung the sleigh bells and a swag of greenery on the cookhouse door. It was time for the cooking and baking to begin again, with Mother Madole and me outdoing ourselves with cookies and candies and little frosted cakes.

On Christmas Eve, Jess and Frank brought in the tree, a tall, full spruce we had spotted in the hills while hunting. I got busy and popped a big batch of popcorn and we all sat around stringing—and eating—the corn to deck the tree. Mother Madole had waxy red cranberries for stringing, too. Walnuts in the shell, covered with tinfoil saved from tobacco cans, were hung on the spruce boughs. Charlie and Qually made candleholders out of tin cans.

There were no gifts that year because no one had any money, but we had a feeling of joy and companionship and a sharing of ourselves—the real gifts of Christmas. The provident Mother Madole had hidden a turkey in our winter food cache. We had a traditional meal that Christmas of 1910. After dinner, while the woods filled up with snow and the candles flickered on the tree, we listened to Jess strum his mandolin.

During the dark days of January, when the temperature took a nose-dive down to 50 below, work on the mine shaft came to a halt. Jess kept just enough steam in the boiler house to keep it from freezing. The men used this slack time to wash their heavy work clothes, using the hot water at the boiler house and stringing a line across the room. Usually there was a card game in progress while all this laundering was going on. I liked to join the boys in the lull of the afternoon, when I was caught up with my chores.

One day in late winter Mother Madole and I got in a big fight that threatened to break up the entire camp. We had had a few skirmishes during the winter—I resented the way she bossed me around the kitchen—but they had not been serious.

"Now, Clara, I am going over to my room," Mother Madole said. "I want you to watch the pot roast so it doesn't run out of water."

"All right," I agreed. I had cooked a pot roast before, and I didn't consider it a difficult task. After puttering around the kitchen awhile, I decided to run over to the boiler house.

About an hour later, Mother Madole came storming through the door, "I thought I would find you here," she shouted. "What is wrong with you, Clara? I give you a simple job, and you can't even do that right."

"What is it?" I asked anxiously. "What did I do wrong?"

"You let the pot roast burn, you stupid girl. I could smell it burning all the way over to my room."

"Oh, I am sorry," I said, running out the door after her.

"Being sorry isn't good enough," she said angrily. "You have ruined the dinner. We don't have meat to throw away like that. You have some lessons to learn, you dumb girl. You are so selfish; you only think of yourself."

"But Mother Madole, I did not mean to burn the meat," I said as we entered the cookhouse where the air hung heavy with the smell of burned food.

"You had no business going over to the boiler house. You should have stayed here and done as you were told." She dumped the meat on the cutting board. "Look at this! Just look at it."

The meat was hopelessly burned.

"I didn't think the fire was that hot," I said.

"That is no excuse," she snapped. "I have tried to teach you, but you can't seem to do anything right."

"I am sorry. It won't happen again."

"I know it won't happen again. We don't have another pot roast. That's why it won't happen again."

Never before had Mother Madole yelled at me like that. I had been wrong, I knew that, but when she continued to rave, I got mad.

"I know I never should have left the cookhouse," I said, "but there is no use crying over spilt milk. I would be happy to help you fix something else for dinner if you will tell me what to do."

"You can figure that out for yourself," she said, pulling off her apron. "I am going to my room."

The door banged behind her and I was left alone to prepare dinner for five hungry men. It wasn't much of a meal that night, just canned vegetables, fried ham and biscuits. When Jess went to get his mother, she refused to join us at the table.

"I will take Mother something on a tray," Jess said.

I gave him a dirty look and didn't lift a finger to help. It made me madder than ever that Jess was siding with his mother.

When we were alone that night Jess said, "You better go over and apologize to Mother."

"No," I said stubbornly. "I have already told her I was sorry. She didn't have to yell at me and call me names. I don't see why you always have to take her side." I started crying. "Your mother always comes first with you. You think more of her than you do of me."

I stomped into our bedroom, expecting that Jess would follow and say he was sorry. Instead, he slammed out the door and I was left alone with my tears.

Four days went by, and Mother Madole still refused to come out of her cabin. Jess or Doc carried her a tray, three times a day. I was sure she had plenty of critical remarks to make about my food, but Jess had sense enough not to pass them along to me.

The atmosphere in the cookhouse was tense. We got through each meal with a minimum of words. Every day it got worse, and I was miserable. I wouldn't talk to Jess, he wouldn't talk to me, and Mother Madole wouldn't come out of the cabin. Whenever Doc or Frank tried to joke us out of our bad mood, Jess would get mad and I would start crying.

One evening Jess took me into our room and said, "This fighting has got to stop. We are both too stubborn. We can't have these quarrels if we are going to have a happy life together. I realize the situation is as much my fault as it is yours."

I started crying, and Jess took me in his arms. "Let's promise we will never go to bed mad at each other," he said.

"Never again," I sobbed. "I have felt just terrible."

"Being mad and holding a grudge like that can develop into something bigger," he said.

"I know."

Jess wiped my tears. "You know, Mother has been very good to us. It isn't easy for her, living out of town away from her friends. We have each other, but she doesn't have anyone."

"That's right," I agreed. "I know she has been good to us, and I never wanted to fight with her."

"It would please me very much if you would go over and make up with her," Jess said.

Jess was my lord and master; I could not refuse him anything. As much as I hated to give in, I went over to Mother Madole's cabin and apologized. We put our arms around each other and had a good cry. Even though I was still a kid in many ways, I could see that the issue had not been the pot roast alone. When I had lived in town with Mother Madole, it had been her home. She was boss, and we got along fine. But now that I was Jess's wife—and doing my share of the work—I felt that I was entitled to my say. As a result, Mother and I clashed often. Even though she had encouraged Jess to marry me, it was hard for her to share him.

There were other times that winter when she shut herself up in her cabin, harboring wounded feelings, and I would not see her for several days. Jess always went over to kiss her good-night, and if she started complaining about me, he left. We maintained our pact of never going to bed mad, and that one thing prevented little problems from becoming big ones. Jess never asked me to apologize to his mother unless I was in the wrong. I trusted Jess implicitly. He was older; he was wiser. And he was my husband. Even though it hurt my dignity to say I was sorry, for Jess I would do it.

As soon as the sun began appearing again for long hours in the days of late February, Jess and I went to the spring, about a mile down the creek, to get our drinking water. There the water flowed pure and icy cold. We hauled the water in a 50-pound butter barrel fastened to the sled. Once it was filled with water Diamond and Murphy had to give their all to pull that heavy load over the trail.

One day Jess came in the cookhouse and said, "I have too much work to do at the boiler house, and I can't take time out to get water. It is time you took the dogs out by yourself. Diamond is used to you now, and you shouldn't have any trouble."

It was one thing going to the creek with Jess, but quite another to take those two dogs out by myself. I didn't argue (that never did any good), but bravely set about hitching up the team. The trail to the creek was downhill and extremely bumpy. Once those dogs started pulling, we went so fast that I had to ride the brake most of the way. The skinny shadows of the tall birch and cottonwood trees fell across the trail and blinked like shutters as I passed. The patches of sunlight on the snow looked like yellow water sparkling and flashing.

At the spring I had a heck of a time getting those dogs stopped, but once they settled down they seemed content to wait, red tongues hanging down, while I broke the ice crust on the water with an old ax Jess kept there for just that purpose. I dipped that lovely water into the barrel and put a canvas cover on it with a barrel ring to hold it tight. I poured water on the canvas, as I had seen Jess do so many times, so it would freeze around the edges and the water wouldn't spill out.

I mushed the dogs to their feet and off we went. There was no need for "gee" or "haw" as those dogs knew their way home better than I did. When we reached the first rise I did not ride, but walked behind to steady the sled on the bumpy, uphill climb. When we got to the next rise, much steeper than the last, those dogs balked, just stood there stiff-legged and refused to budge.

When I grabbed Diamond by the collar and tried to pull him forward, he looked nonchalantly over his shoulder to Murphy as if to say, "I wonder who she thinks she is?" No matter how much I hollered and pulled, it was no use. Those dogs had me beat. The only thing I could do was dump out the water to lighten the load, and then how those blasted dogs did run. I had to hang on to the handlebars with both hands to keep from falling off.

By the time I got back to the cookhouse I was blazing mad. "You can get your own darn water," I said to Jess.

"Oh, no, I'm not," he said. "You get back on that sled and try again. You can't let those dogs get the best of you."

"Jess, do I have to?"

"Yes," was his firm reply. "Those dogs have to know who's boss."

He gave me a chain to rattle when the dogs balked. Jess sometimes used the chain on them, and they were afraid of it and knew what it meant.

Down the trail I went for the second time. At the spring I dipped the water as before. We started home and we made it over the first rise, but when we reached the next one, the dogs balked again. No matter how much I shook that chain and hollered at them, they held their ground, grinning from ear to ear. Again I had to dump the water. But just as I was getting back on the sled, those dogs took off like a streak of lightning and I fell into a snowbank while the dogs sped on, the empty sled bumping along behind them. I shouted a few choice cuss words at them, for all the good that did, and picked myself up and started walking home.

When I was within sight of the camp, I met Jess coming along the trail. By then the tears had frozen to my cheeks, but I was still madder than a hornet. Jess got the water that day, but he was determined that I would do it the next time.

Two days later Jess told me to hitch up the team.

"What's the use?" I said. "They are going to balk again, I just know it."

"I am going to fix them this time," Jess said. "You go ahead with the team, and I will cut across the hills and wait in the bushes on the second rise. When they balk, you start rattling the chain, and I will use the bullwhip on them."

"Oh, Jess. That seems so cruel."

"They have to learn to mind you," he said.

My heart wasn't in it, but I did as I was told. After going through the whole procedure of filling the barrels we started back. Sure enough, when we got to the second rise those dogs stopped dead in their tracks. I shook the chain, but I was afraid to use it on them for fear they might turn on me. While I stood rattling the chain, Jess jumped out on the trail and really laid it into those dogs with the whip. I truly felt sorry for them, even though I was still mad at them for their stubbornness. But that did the trick. When I got back on the sled they pulled for all their worth and over the rise and home we went without pause.

At camp Jess said, "When you unharness the dogs, tell them they were good boys, and pat them before you chain them to their houses."

After that I didn't have any more trouble with Diamond and Murphy, and I looked forward to those trips to the spring. How we would fly over the trail! Whenever we came to that second rise, Diamond would look back at me with his ears flattened and his grin on as if to say, "Now we are the best of friends."

Soon the liquid days of spring came on, smooth as honey, with the constant dripping and ticking of the melted snow off the eaves of the cookhouse. From the window I watched the snow on the tarpaper roof of the bunkhouse shrink each day under the glare of 13 hours of sunlight. In the morning the chickadees fluttered across the yard in search of seeds, while high in the spruce tree the black raven—that had hung around all winter—cawed loudly before swooping down to scavenge in the garbage dump out back.

With the warm weather and the thawing, there came a new problem. The trail to the spring was too soft for the sled, so we could no longer haul our drinking water. We had to use the runoff water from the hillside that drained into a ditch nearby. It was dark, brackish water and every drop had to be boiled for cooking or drinking. Even then it tasted vile and left a miserable stain on the dishes.

Mother Madole especially did not like the drinking water, so she set about to find a substitute. She enlisted the help of Frank, Charlie and Qually. They went into the hills gathering the tender willow shoots, the new spruce tips, the birch buds, and the stalks of the wild rhubarb. All this greenery was dumped into a wash boiler, covered with water, and boiled several hours before the hops and sugar were added.

After that, the brew was strained into a barrel, yeast added, and placed behind the stove to ferment. The boys scoured the countryside for old bottles, picking through the dump where the winter's collection of garbage had been tossed, and begging bottles from our neighbors up and down the creek.

Mother Madole let the brew work a few days before bottling and storing it in a cool corner of the cookhouse cache. Every day or so Charlie and Qually had to shake a bottle to see how the beer was doing.

"Not yet," Mother Madole would say. "Not yet."

When she did give the go-ahead, those boys guzzled that beer in less time than it had taken to make it. Even Doc said that you couldn't buy beer that good. Soon the word got out and the miners came visiting to sample the beer and take home the recipe. All spring the bottles were recycled from camp to camp.

While there was still snow on the ground, Mother Madole and I began planning our garden. First we gathered tin cans and punched holes in the bottom, and filled them with thawed dirt from the boiler house. Mother Madole, always the practical one, started cabbage, cauliflower and tomatos in her cans, but I wanted flowers so I started flats of pansies, phlox and stock. Soon every window in the cookhouse and bunkhouse was filled with containers that very quickly sprouted little seedlings.

136

In late May the plants were set out in the garden plots we had prepared. Mother Madole put her vegetables in the dirt embankment around the cookhouse, saving the south side for my flowers. Down by the spring there was an old barn with a sod roof—the moss mixed with the dirt held the moisture and served as fertilizer. We couldn't see that go to waste. There we scattered leaf lettuce seeds, carrots, chives and started a clump of parsley. In no time at all we were eating fresh vegetables. How good they tasted after a long winter of dried fruit and canned food. When it came time to water our "roof garden," Mother Madole climbed up and I dipped water from the barrel we kept filled from the spring. The water bucket was hoisted to the roof by a rope.

The turnip seeds we planted down by the old dump grew to an incredible size. That was organic gardening at its best. Along the warm embankment of the cookhouse, my sweet peas grew so tall they topped the roof. In that same bed the stock, the nasturtiums, the phlox and bachelor buttons bloomed profusely in colors more vibrant than I had ever seen in Seattle. The perfume was so heavy and sweet that the honeybees hung in swarms over the flowers all summer.

It was nothing new, but that summer money was so short that I rarely had any to spend. Since I had been used to earning my own, I hated to ask Jess for every penny.

"Jess, I have to find some way to earn money," I said one day.

"Why don't you work that old dump we worked last summer?" he said. "I will make a rocker for you, and you can keep all the gold you get."

I watched while Jess built the rocker. It was a small contraption with two boxes—one on top of the other—set on rockers, like a cradle. It was operated with a handle I could push back and forth. Nearby there was a small gravel pit where I got water for sluicing. After I shoveled the dirt into the top box, which had a tin bottom with holes in it, I poured water over it, and then began to wash the gold from the gravel. The fine particles of gold sifted through to the bottom box where they got caught in the riffles—the trough which was built with cleats and covered with canvas. When I was ready to start the operation again, I removed the top box, dumped out the rocks and shoveled in more dirt from the dump.

Whenever I could sneak a spare minute away from the cookhouse, I spent it working the rocker. It wasn't long before I was gold feverish about the whole thing. I couldn't wait to see how much gold was caught in the riffles; I was frantic to pile more gold in my poke. Patience was required, though, and that I had in short supply. Rocking for gold is a slow, backbreaking business and there were those disappointing days when I made less than a dollar, but it was better than nothing. I was like the donkey with the carrot in front of his nose—something big, I thought, was just within my reach. I guess we cannot live without hope.

Now that the weather was warm, the boys went 10 and 12 hours a day digging in the mine shaft. We still had not reached bedrock. The donkey engine was in constant use, hauling the buckets of dirt out of the mine, hour after hour.

Then we hit a snag. Our wood supply for the boiler ran out. There was no time for the boys to stop work and cut wood, but fortunately, there were a hundred cords cut and stacked on the property. It belonged to August Bostrom, who owned the mining claim.

Since Doc was spokesman for the partners, he went into Fairbanks to negotiate with Gus. We didn't have much money, but we could give him a small payment and then pay off the rest at cleanup time.

When Doc returned to Little Eldorado a few days later he said, "Go ahead and use the wood. All the arrangements have been made."

A week later Sam Wise, the marshal from Chatanika, came into camp. I was outdoors hanging clothes on the line when I saw him ride up.

"I have a warrant for the arrest of Jess Rust, Frank Reynolds and Doc Overgaard," he said.

"There must be some mistake," I told him.

"No, ma'am, there isn't. Those three men have been stealing wood that belongs to Gus Bostrom."

About that time Jess joined us. "What is going on here?" he asked.

"I have a warrant for your arrest," Sam said.

"What the hell for?"

"You have been stealing Bostrom's wood," the marshal told him.

"I have not," Jess said. "I made arrangements with Gus to pay for that wood after cleanup."

138

"Well, Gus doesn't know anything about it," Sam said. "He swore out the warrant, and until this thing is settled, I am going to have to take you and Doc and Frank to jail."

"Jail!' I cried. "You can't do that."

"Yes I can, ma'am," he said.

What a disgrace to have our men in jail. What a blow to have the work shut down. Mother Madole and I stood by helplessly; I couldn't stop crying.

It was three days before Jess and the boys were released from Chatanika jail. When they returned to camp the story came out. Doc had never talked to Bostrom about the wood. As soon as he got into town he lost all the money in a poker game. Doc was too ashamed to tell us what he had done, so he made up the story that we could use the wood.

With the help of Judge Roy, arrangements were made with Gus and the boys were released from jail without a fine. Mother Madole had to mortgage the house in Fairbanks to pay for the wood we had already used. The partners had to sign a promissory note to pay for the rest of it after cleanup.

After that I was so disgusted with Doc that I could hardly talk to him. That was the second time he had pulled a dirty trick on us; I could never trust him again. Jess and Frank laughed about the time they spent in jail, but it was no laughing matter as far as I was concerned.

From then on nothing seemed to go right. We had trouble with the donkey engine, we were low on food, and everyone was tense and edgy. We were farther in debt than ever, and our future depended on a good cleanup. The harder we tried, the more desperate we became.

At last we hit bedrock! The loads we brought up now had gold mixed with the rocks and dirt. As soon as the sluice boxes thawed and we had enough water, we started washing a few loads in the evening. We were getting color, not much, but it would get better as we continued to tunnel the new mine shaft.

Sometimes I would wake up in the middle of the night and think: What if something went wrong? What if we didn't make it? How would we pay back all the money we owed?

It would take a lifetime.

chapter 14

In early June, just as the wild roses were spreading their color against the boiler house wall and the bluebells were blooming down by the spring, we had our first big cleanup.

That afternoon August Bostrom, the owner of the property, came from town dressed in his fine black suit and his black fedora, in interest of his royalty. James Barrack, representing his father's company, Brumbough, Hamilton and Kellog, was also there. We owed them money for the use of the boiler house equipment. These two men stood beside the sluice box taking note of the weight of the gold cleaned up so they could collect their percentage at the bank.

As soon as Jess and the boys let the water flow in the sluice boxes, I was right beside them shoveling the heavy rocks as fast as I could. The water poured down the elevated wooden troughs and pretty soon I could see the glitter of gold flakes and the dull gold of heavy nuggets collecting in the riffles. What a thrill after all our hard work!

I was so excited that I ran up and down the sluice boxes shouting, "Look at the gold! Look at the gold!" It seemed like a million dollars to me.

It wasn't a million, of course, but it was a good cleanup. If our luck held, we would have a nice stake by the end of summer. Since we had started our venture on borrowed money, by the time we paid off some of our debts there wasn't much left. Fortunately, the next two cleanups were good ones too and netted us enough money to pay Charlie and Qually. The big cleanup was yet to come, and that one would be for us.

Then we ran into problems. It had to do with the tunneling. Doc and Frank thought we should spread out the tunneling and develop the richer vein. Jess took the opposite and more cautious approach.

"It's too risky to spread out the tunnel," he argued. "We still have that old shaft full of water to contend with. I think we should do our cleanup as far as the tunnels go, making sure we get everything as we go along."

"But Jess, why waste our time on that when we can work the richer pay dirt?" Frank asked.

"I say let's get all we can as fast as we can. Now we have a chance to really make some money," Doc put in.

"I'd be all for it," Jess answered, "if we didn't have that old mine shaft to worry about. Our measurements are still off on that thing, and we don't know how close we are getting to it with our tunneling."

"You worry too much, Jess," his mother said.

"I have a reason to worry," Jess said, "and you do, too. All it would take is one mistake and we would lose everything."

The arguing continued, but both sides stood firm. It was the three partners against Jess. It didn't seem to matter to the others that Jess was the only experienced miner among them; they still wouldn't give in. Fraker and Nelson agreed with Jess that further tunneling along the rich vein was dangerous, but they were not partners and Doc and Frank would not listen to them.

When the arguing reached an impasse, Jess said, "Let's close down for a few days and think this over."

The more Jess thought about it, the madder he got. He was right; he knew he was right. Why didn't the others listen to him?

"I can't stand staying around here any longer," Jess said to me one night. "Let's pack our duds and go into Fairbanks for the Fourth of July and have a little fun for ourselves."

Jess and I hadn't been to town together since we were married. It would be like a honeymoon to go on a trip with him. The only money we had was the gold I had rocked. It wasn't much, but it was enough for one bang-up time during the biggest holiday of the year. This was the only time the mines closed down in the summer. Everyone boarded the train for Fairbanks and a celebration that would last two glorious days.

On the morning of the third Jess and I walked the 5 miles to Little Eldorado siding to catch the narrow-gauge Tanana Valley Railroad. What a sight it was to see that engine coming up the track—wheels screeching, bells clanging, whistles blowing, and the passengers hanging out the windows shouting greetings. Everyone was in a party mood that day. Several flatcars with benches had been hooked behind the coach cars to accommodate the overflow crowd. Some of the women, dressed in gowns of white batiste, wore flower-decked hats and carried parasols. The men, in dark suits and celluloid collars, just went wild after being cooped up in camp for so many months.

After picking up passengers at Chatanika, the train headed back toward Fairbanks with stops at Olnes, Vault, Ridgetop, Dome, Fox, Gilmore, Engineer Creek, Goldstream and Ester Siding, as well as at the smaller camps en route, or wherever a miner flagged them down.

When Jess and I reached town we walked up to the old house on Eighth Avenue. There I rested while Jess went uptown to Frank Taylor's pool parlor and shooting gallery to tell him we would be in town for a few days. Frank and his friends, Al Wooden and Sid Stuart, had been living in our house since we moved out to Little Eldorado, with the understanding that Jess and I could use it whenever we came into town.

While we were in town Jess's friends treated us royally. We danced half the night at the Eagles Hall and spent the other half at Frank's shooting gallery. When we were hungry we ate in restaurants, and when we were tired we went to the cabin for a nap.

There was an atmosphere of excitement in that town; you could feel it everywhere. The crowds on the street, at the dances and in the cafes were hellbent on having a good time. Jess and I were like two kids who had skipped school. Our thoughts of the mine, the tunneling and the arguments were far behind us.

On the Fourth of July—a sun-spangled day it was—the grandstands along the riverfront were packed with people who had paid their dime for the chance to sit down and watch the festivities. Red, white and blue bunting draped the stands and the storefronts in a burst of patriotic pride. American flags, posted along the main thoroughfares, flapped lazily in the breeze.

I sat in the grandstand while the parade went by. There were floats, preceded by the Fairbanks City Band and the Eagles Color

Guard, which included my Jess wearing a white shirt and straw hat. As the parade passed, the sun blazed and the clouds on the horizon piled up like plump pillows while my face slowly turned red.

Contests were held in front of the grandstands, so convenient to the First Avenue saloons where the men could duck in for a glass of beer between games. The Italian man's ice cream stand attracted all the kids in town. Jess and I watched the three-legged race, the sack race, the wheelbarrow race and the tug-of-war between the two rival mining camps.

That day I won the fat woman's race (much to the disgust of my husband) and the nail pounding race (which redeemed me in Jess's eyes). When it came time for the horse races, First Avenue was cleared and the races began. The betting ran high on the street corners and in the saloons. There was another dance that night at the Eagles Hall with Victor Durand and his orchestra. Jess and I danced until dawn.

The next day no one wanted to go home. It was a puffy-eyed, foot-dragging, worn-out bunch of miners that boarded the train in the morning. The party was over.

When Jess and I got off the train at Eldorado siding, we were not looking forward to that five-mile walk to camp. The trail seemed longer than usual as we sweated under the hot sun and battled the mosquitoes. Jess carried a heavy load on his back with gifts for Mother Madole and purchases for the crew. We were about halfway home when an enormous black cloud moved across the sun, followed by lightning and the rattle of thunder. The heavens let loose with a downpour. Jess and I were drenched to the skin.

Up ahead, through the mist, we spotted an abandoned shack where we took shelter. We didn't stay there long! Just inside the door there was a hornet's nest. We were immediately surrounded by those fierce insects. Both Jess and I were stung several times as we ran, flailing our arms and hollering loudly. It was still raining hard, but that was better than being stung by hornets. What a sorry, sodden sight we were when we finally reached the mine.

That night at the dinner table Jess brought up the subject that was on everyone's mind. "What are we going to do about the tunneling?" he asked.

At first no one spoke. Finally Doc said, "We have decided to put in another thaw and tunnel farther. You will need to fire up the boiler tonight so we can have some steam."

"I am still against it," Jess said, trying to control his voice.

"Well, Jess, you can certainly see that it is to our advantage to thaw more ground and wash the high yield first," Doc said.

"That's not the point," Jess exploded. "The point is we could tunnel right into the old mine shaft full of water. Why do all of you ignore the most important thing? Mother, please," Jess pleaded, "can't you stop this?"

"Now, Jess," she said, "you are just being stubborn. We need to make money now, or we will never get through the winter."

"But don't you see?" Jess said. "We could lose everything this way."

"I don't think there is much chance of that," Doc said. "We haven't hit that old mine shaft yet."

"But we are getting closer to it all the time," Jess said.

"Well, in this business there is always a risk, and I say, let's take it," Doc said.

"Me too," Frank added without looking Jess in the eye.

"It's three against one," Mother Madole said.

I had no voice in the matter, but I trusted Jess's opinion more than the others. He was the only experienced miner among them, but they would not listen to reason. It was a sad and quiet Jess that crawled into bed that night.

The next morning I felt a great sense of unease. While I was doing my chores I continually glanced out the window to watch the activity at the mine. I listened intently to the sounds coming from the boiler house. It was a cloudy, overcast day, but without rain. The warm, muggy air added to my feeling of oppression. In the still air every sound—the dumping of the mine shaft bucket, the scrape of the shovel on the rocks—could be heard distinctly in the cookhouse. Mother Madole and I exchanged few words while we prepared lunch.

I had just stepped outside the cookhouse to gather a bouquet of flowers for the table when I heard the bell at the boiler house clanging furiously. I ran to the mine with Mother Madole right behind me. Jess was at the hoist pulling the men up as fast as he could.

"It's flooded!" Jess shouted. "The mine is flooded! They tunneled into the old shaft!"

When Doc, Charlie, Qually and Frank reached the top their faces were white with fear.

"The water was following us up the shaft! It was that bloody close," Frank said.

"I thought we were goners," Doc said. "When that water started pouring through we ran like hell."

"By the time we reached the bucket, I was standing in water," Qually said. "My feet are wet," he added, as if he couldn't believe he got out alive.

The men were lucky, and they knew it. They escaped with their lives, but everything else was lost. All our equipment, the pumps that could have been used to pump out the shaft, the points needed for thawing, the shovels, picks, wheelbarrows—all underwater at the bottom of the mine.

There was nothing to be said. Jess turned and walked away. I followed him to the cookhouse. He was packing his clothes.

"I can't stay here. I am so mad I'm afraid I will kill somebody," he said. "I have to get away and think these things over."

"Oh, Jess," I sobbed, "let me come with you. I don't want to stay here alone."

"I have to go alone, Clara. Try to understand. I hate leaving you here like this, but it is best for now. When I find a job and a place to live, I will send for you."

As I packed a lunch for Jess, the tears rolled down my cheeks. I was sick at heart to be left behind, but I knew it had to be that way. If I traveled with him, I would only hold him back. I stood in the cookhouse doorway until Jess disappeared down the leafy trail. When would I see him again, I wondered. My worst fears had come true. We were in debt, we had lost our chance to make it big, and Jess was gone, too.

When Mother Madole came to the cookhouse, I couldn't help feeling resentment toward her. Wasn't she partly responsible for the disaster? Why hadn't she listened to Jess's advice? And what good had her so-called clairvoyance ever done us?

"Where is Jess?" she asked.

"He is gone."

"Gone? Where did he go?"

"He went to look for a job," I answered. "He said that Doc and Frank had gotten us into the mess, and they could clean it up."

"It was a bad thing that happened," Mother Madole said.

"Why couldn't you have seen it was going to happen?" I said, starting to cry again. "You are supposed to know such things."

"Clara, you don't understand," she said. "I have never been able to see into the future for anyone close to me. There is too much interference, too many emotions. I can only do it for strangers."

It was 3 days before Jess sent word that he was working for the Fairbanks Telephone Company on a line crew between Olnes and Chatanika. Later when his letter arrived, Jess said that he had met Paul Rickert of the telephone company at Little Eldorado siding and he was offered a job right away. "Our luck isn't all bad," Jess wrote. "I hope it won't be too long before we are together again."

Within a week we had cleaned up the camp and moved off the mining property. Mother Madole, who had lost her house in Fairbanks, took a job at the lunch counter at Little Eldorado siding. There was nowhere else for her to go.

Frank went into Fairbanks, where he got a job as a waiter on a riverboat. When Doc left, he didn't have any plans, but we later heard that he went to work at the quartz mine on Cleary Hill.

Just as I was beginning to worry about where I would live, Otto Nelson asked me to cook for the Fraker and Nelson crew of 10 men, which included our old hands Qually and Charlie. I wasn't sure I could handle such a big job, but I had no other choice. I took it.

My day began at 5 o'clock in the morning. I would build up the fire in the cookstove and start a large pot of rolled oats. While that was cooking, I mixed the sourdough hot cake batter and put the coffee on to boil. The boys always wanted stewed fruit, either apples or prunes. I started that the day before. As soon as the crew came to the table, it was time to fry the bacon and eggs.

In addition to cooking three meals a day, it was my job to scrub the cookhouse floor and wash the kitchen towels. The rough floor, with wide cracks between each board, was difficult to keep clean. I would go over the whole area with suds, and then lye water to whiten the wood. Next I sloshed clear rinse water over the floor, sweeping the excess water into the cracks. Of course, all the water had to be heated on top of the stove.

To whiten the towels, I boiled them in a copper boiler on the stove. Then they were rinsed, wrung out by hand and hung outdoors on the lines strung between the tall, gray-barked aspen trees with their small leaves clustered high overhead like a green umbrella.

Whenever I had spare time I walked over to the old mine to gather the firm, shiny heads of cabbage that thrived despite the weeds, and the carrots and onions on the sod rooftop. There were days when I couldn't make myself go there. It hurt too much to see the hoist standing idle, the cookhouse windows blank, and the boiler house empty. My memories as a bride on Little Eldorado crowded my mind, and the tears fell.

Diamond and Murphy kept me company. However, not long after I moved over to Fraker and Nelson, Murphy got into a man's yard down by the creek and killed a piglet. The man took off after Murphy and shot him. That was one more heartache I had to bear. After that, Diamond became so lonesome he wouldn't let me out of his sight. When I hung clothes on the line, Diamond walked back and forth with me, his morose expression matching the feeling in my heart.

There were many nights I cried myself to sleep. When would I see Jess again? When would we have a home of our own? I was beginning to feel very tired, and the long days stretched ahead endlessly.

chapter 15

Yellow leaves, curled and dried, rattled across the wooden platform at Little Eldorado siding. September had come, leaving the small trees bereft and buffeted.

I sat alone on the train. As it began to move Mother Madole waved to me from the platform, a lonely figure against the painted fall landscape. I leaned my head against the back of the horsehair seat. In 6 months my first child would be born.

Jess was working in Fairbanks and wrote that I should join him. I went gladly, turning my back on mining life forever. Diamond, deposited in the baggage car, was as eager as I to be with Jess again. He seemed to sense what was happening. We would live, the three of us, in the cabin on Eighth. Thank goodness for the old house; I do not know what we would have done without it.

As the train clacked along the tracks I remembered the big dreams we had dreamed of striking it rich. In reality, all we had received was bitter disappointment. I would not look back with regrets, I vowed; that was useless. There came over me this feeling that nothing would ever come easy for us, that we would have to work hard for everything we got. At the same time, I knew that wouldn't matter as long as I was with Jess.

When the train pulled into the Fairbanks depot, Jess was the first person I saw. My heart lurched at the sight of him. How different he looked, his face weathered and creased with lines I had never seen before.

"Jess! Jess!" I cried, stepping down from the train.

As soon as he hugged me, I knew everything was going to be all right.

"Clara, I missed you very much. This has been a lonesome 2 months," he said.

The minute Jess opened the baggage car, Diamond shot out like a bullet, nearly knocking Jess to the ground in his excitement to be with his master again.

It was a wonderful feeling to walk up the path to the old house. Jess and I had a place of our own. I was discouraged at first at the rundown condition of the cabin, but with a broom in one hand and a scrub brush in the other, I set about putting the house in order. It wasn't long before I had geraniums blooming on the window sills, the good china showing on the dining room shelves and pictures brightening the burlap walls.

In late September when work at the telephone company slacked off, Jess got a job cutting and delivering wood for August Bjerrmark. Almost everyone in town used wood for heating, except those served by the Nothern Commercial steam line. Woodcutters were kept busy all winter. It was rough work and I worried about Jess going out in the bitter cold and returning, sometimes late at night, with his clothes frozen stiff and caked with sawdust.

It took two men to run the huge saws, which were mounted on runners and pulled by a horse along the snowy streets, stopping where there was an order to cut wood. About this time Frank Reynolds was out of work, so he joined Jess on the saws. Since he didn't have any place to stay, he moved in with us, much to my displeasure. Frank slept on the couch in the living room and took all his meals with us. Gone was our precious privacy.

As soon as Mary Anderson found out I was in town, she called and asked me to work part-time. We needed the money so I could not refuse, although I was having frequent sick spells. When I told Mary I was pregnant, she gave me outing flannel and satin ribbons to make nightgowns and blankets. Jess and I were both excited about the baby, but he was counting on a boy so much that it worried me. Would he be too terribly disappointed, I wondered, if it was a girl?

When Mother Madole came into town from Little Eldorado in November, she stayed with us a few days while she looked for a place to live. She had lost the mortgaged house, but that had paid off some of the mining expenses, which eased the financial burden. She decided to rent the Whitney house on First Avenue near the old bathhouse. It wasn't long before her Madame Renio sign was hanging out front, and she was taking in sewing.

One evening in late November Jess came home from work and

Fairbanks in the winter of 1910, showing the Fairbanks Brewing Co.

said, "I think Mother bit off more than she can chew with that big house she rented."

"What do you mean?" I asked.

"The rent is too high for her to handle alone, so she asked if we would move in and share expenses with her."

"Oh, Jess, I don't think it's a good idea. I think we should stay in the old house."

"But this place is cold, and it needs so much work done to it, and I don't have time to fix it up," he said. "Besides, with the baby coming, Mother would be a lot of help to you."

"Would Frank move over there too?"

"Of course."

There was no use arguing. Mother Madole needed our help, so we must go. From the very start I had reservations about the move. The Whitney house had a large living room, bedroom and kitchen with an attached lean-to that was used as a bedroom. One area of the living room was curtained off for use as a sitting room for Madame Renio, with Frank's cot set up on the other side.

Jess and I had the big bedroom, which gave us some privacy, but it was not the same as having a place of our own. Mother Madole's bedroom was in the lean-to off the kitchen. When a friend of hers from Dawson came to town, she moved in with Mother Madole. Pretty soon, wouldn't you know it, Doc showed up, and he moved in too, sleeping on a cot in the living room.

There was always someone coming or going, and the confusion and noise was sometimes more than I could bear. It just wasn't good for all of us to be living under the same roof. Somehow we got through Christmas, but it wasn't the special occasion we had all shared a year before at Little Eldorado. My happiest memory of that holiday was the gift Jess gave me. He had saved the money, a dollar at a time, to buy me a gold lapel watch.

Since Jess and I had not discussed the arrangements he had with his mother about paying our share of the rent, lights and food, I had no idea what our obligations were each month. It seemed to me that our bills kept mounting, and we never had any money.

One evening in late January Jess and his mother got into an argument about the bills. I was resting in the bedroom, and I could hear their voices getting louder and louder. Pretty soon they were shouting.

"You aren't bringing in enough money," Mother Madole said. "You are not paying your share."

"What in the hell are you talking about?" Jess yelled. "All I ever do is pay bills around here. It costs me twice as much as it did at the old house."

"You have no idea what it costs to run a house," Mother Madole said.

"That's where you are wrong. I will show you how much I know." He stormed into the bedroom and yanked open the dresser drawers. "Where is our account book?" he yelled.

I jumped up and got the book for him. Ever since we had moved into town we had kept an itemized account of our expenditures. Jess was more thorough about keeping it current than I, and as a result, everything we had paid out was written down.

Jess waved the account book in his mother's face. "Look at this. I have more than paid our way. You seem to forget that Frank and Clara and I are the only ones working around here. I am tired of keeping freeloaders like Doc and your lady friend. As long as you think we aren't paying our way, then we will move out."

"Now, Jess, there is no need to do that," his mother said.

"I have made up my mind. We are leaving."

When Jess was pushed too far, there was no turning back. Before I knew what was happening, Jess and Frank were out the door to start the stoves in the old house, and I was ordered to start packing. Within a few hours we were moved. Here is my childhood all over again, I thought. Moving, always moving. Will we ever settle down?

In a way I felt badly about leaving Mother Madole; I knew it would be difficult for her to manage financially without us. Not long after that she had to give up the house and move back out to Little Eldorado where she worked again at the lunch counter for Fred Meyers and Hugh Polson. As soon as she left town, Doc married a young Norwegian girl, Karen Knudtson. That was a great shock to Mother Madole. She was so bitter about it that she tried to sue Doc for the room and board she said he owed her, but that was useless. Jess and I knew his mother was lonely, and we tried to visit her when we could.

Although I was happy to be back in the old house, it was difficult with Frank there all the time. He and Jess were inseparable that

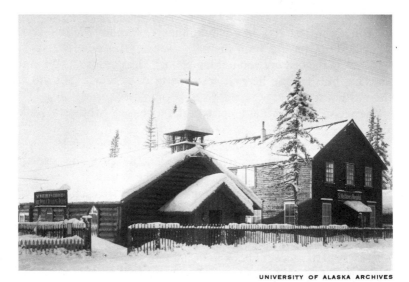

UNIVERSITY OF ALASKA ARCHIVES

St. Matthew's Episcopal Church and Hospital on Front Street.

winter. When Jess stayed home in the evenings to play cards with me, Frank stayed too. When Jess went to the pool parlor, Frank went too. When Jess and I went to the movies (silent films shown on a screen in an old store building), Frank went too. He didn't seem to have any desire for a life of his own. Then, to make matters worse, I wasn't feeling too well, and I had to quit my job.

As my confinement drew near, I rarely left the house. There were no maternity clothes in those days, so I wore a long Mother Hubbard dress that was not very attractive. Even though I had never been around anyone when they were having a baby—and I didn't know very much about what was happening to me—still, I was not afraid. It seemed like the most natural thing in the world. At that time there were two hospitals in town, St. Joseph's, run by the Catholics, and St. Matthew's Episcopal Hospital. Since money was short, we decided it would be less expensive to have the baby at home.

About this time Mr. Bjerrmark became ill and had to give up his wood business, which meant Jess and Frank had to look for another job. They were fortunate to start right away cutting wood for a man named Carney. Jess kept Carney's horse, Old Sal, in the back shed so he could get the saws out in the morning. That Sal must have been related to Whitey; they were two of a kind, slow-moving and contrary, and likely to spend more time sitting on their haunches than working.

In the evenings when Jess wasn't too tired, he worked on the baby cutter "for his son." It was a lovely little sleigh, painted green, with curved runners and high sideboards. There was room in it for the rabbitskin robe Mother Madole had made. It was the custom in those days for women to take their babies to town in cutters, well wrapped and bedded down, and leave them sleeping outside the stores while they did their shopping.

March of 1912 was a month of hard winds. They raged the length of the Tanana Valley, stripping the trees of every vestige of snow and polishing the snowbanks to a razorlike sharpness. The snowstorms followed, stirred by the winds, hissing around the window frames and dumping piles of snow on our doorstep. It took Jess an hour every morning to shovel out to get to the saws.

One night while a blizzard raged, I began to feel cramps in my stomach. Was the baby coming, on that of all nights? I wasn't sure. At first I lay quietly, without waking Jess, listening to the howling

Clara and Cora de Lila, born in March.

of the wind and feeling the walls shudder with each blast. There were moments when I thought the little house would surely collapse under the next onslaught.

By midnight my pains were more intense and coming with greater regularity.

"Jess, Jess, wake up. I think you better call the doctor."

Jess jumped out of bed and pulled on his clothes. Outside the storm still howled. "I hate to leave you, Clara," he said, "but I have to go get Dr. McCollum and the nurse. They would never make it in this storm. I'll hitch up Old Sal and make a run for it."

Jess threw more wood on the fire and woke Frank up. "The baby is coming," he said. "Get some water on to boil. I am going for the doctor."

"Hurry, Jess," I called.

I knew I would have to hang on a little while longer. Jess had to drive across town in those snow-clogged streets. It might take him an hour, maybe more, but he would get through. I always felt safe with Jess; even though I worried and fretted, he never failed me.

Just when I was beginning to think the baby would be born without the doctor or Jess, I heard them coming in the back door—and not a moment too soon, either. Within a short time I delivered our first child—a 12-pound girl. Jess was disappointed, I knew he was, even though he tried to hide his feelings. He had been so sure it would be a boy.

"Next time we will have a boy," I said.

"Yes, next time," he agreed.

To please Jess's mother and mine, we named the baby Cora de Lila. She was a good girl, sleeping quietly in the basket beside our bed. Mina Bond, a practical nurse and friend of Mother Madole's, stayed with me several days. From the first day Jess was good about helping with the baby, never complaining about changing diapers or rocking her when she cried.

It changed our life to have a little one in the house; all our activities revolved around her. Now we were more crowded than ever, and I was hoping Frank would take the hint and find another place to live, but he didn't. I began resenting his intrusion more than ever. Every time I walked through a room I was falling over Frank's boots, or picking up his clothes or sweeping up his tobacco. Jess did not mind having Frank with us. Whenever I complained about Frank, Jess got mad.

"Frank is no trouble," Jess would say. "We work well together and it helps us financially to have him here."

"But we don't have any time alone," I argued. "He is always here."

"It is something you are going to have to put up with."

It was then I realized that if anything was going to be done about Frank, I would have to do it myself. Jess ruled our household, there was no doubt about that, and it scared me to think of going against him. But if I had to, I would.

Fortunately the boats started running in mid-May and Frank got a job as a waiter. I was visibly pleased, and everyone knew why. Frank lived on the boat. At last Jess and I had the house to ourselves. Frank's belongings were stored with us in anticipation of his return in the fall.

When the woodcutting business slacked off, Jess went to work for the telephone company again. On warm days we took the baby and boarded the train for Little Eldorado siding to visit Mother Madole. She had married Fred Meyers, one of the cafe owners where she worked. Jess had his doubts about the marriage, mainly because mother was quite a bit older than Fred, but we hoped she would find the happiness she deserved.

In those days we were still buying water from the man who delivered it in 5-gallon cans in a horse-drawn sleigh. With the baby in the house, we needed more water than before, and it became an expensive item.

"I think it is time we dug a well," Jess said when summer came. "We can't go on buying water like this."

Since we did not have any tools, Jess had to borrow a pick and shovel and scrounge around to buy a secondhand pump and materials for the well.

From my kitchen window I could watch Jess digging, and it was reminiscent of the days at Little Eldorado when the boys were sinking the mine shaft. It was ironic that this time we hoped to strike water. When Jess hit a frozen spot in the ground, he had to wait until it thawed in the summer sunlight. There was no boiler house with steam points this time.

When the hole was deep enough Jess built a windlass over it, and I helped haul up the buckets of dirt. It was a hard and miserable job. When it rained, the hole filled with water, and for days we pulled up nothing but mud. Jess dug down 15 feet, and still we did not hit water. There were times during the summer when Jess worked out of town, and when that happened the well digging came to a halt.

For all our efforts that summer, we did not hit water. The well was not a total loss, however. We used it for cold storage, placing butter, eggs and other perishables in the bucket, where they stayed cool even on the hottest days.

The sound of the ducks and geese honking overhead in those late days of September reminded me that soon the ice would thicken in the rivers, the boats would stop running, and Frank would be on our doorstep once again. I did not mention my feelings to Jess. I only hoped he would be out of town when Frank came so I could settle the matter alone.

As it happened, I was home alone with the baby when Frank came knocking at the back door.

"Oh, you are back," I said, standing in the doorway.

"Yes; I thought I would put a few of my things inside."

It is now or never, I thought. If I don't tell him now, it will be too late. "I was hoping you would get another place to stay for the winter," I blurted out before I lost my courage.

"Is that what Jess wants me to do?" Frank asked.

"No, I haven't talked to Jess about it. That's the way I feel. We are too crowded for you to stay here." My heart beat frantically. I had never done anything behind Jess's back before.

"If that's the way you want it," Frank said, "I will leave, then."

He took his belongings and walked out. What a relief it was to see him go down the path, suitcase in hand. I almost shouted for joy.

We never saw or heard from Frank again.

Several times during the winter Jess said, "It sure does seem strange that we haven't heard from Frank. I wonder what happened to him?"

At times like those, I kept very quiet. I was sorry Frank had to end his friendship with Jess that way, but I was not sorry for what I had done. My instincts to protect the old house were becoming stronger and stronger. That cabin of logs and tarpaper with the birdhouse on the roof, the garden plot out back and the laundry lines hung with diapers was the house I had always wanted for my own family. No one was going to take it away from me now.

chapter 16

One day in the fall of 1913, I got a telephone call that sent me racing (as fast as I dared—I was pregnant) downtown to see George Bellows, who owned the Bijou, a tobacco and magazine store on Turner Street. George, an old family friend, had helped finance my father's venture in the Fairbanks *News*.

"I have some bad news for you, Clara," George said. "When your dad left, he did not pay off the house mortgage, nor the back taxes. When Captain Barnette's bank went bankrupt, I paid off the mortgage so you would not lose the house."

"I had no idea Dad left things in such a mess," I said. "George, I just don't know what to do. We don't have any money right now, and I can't pay you."

"I don't want you to worry yourself about it, Clara," George said. "I know that you and Jess are having a hard time. Pay me a little bit whenever you can. Just give me a dollar or five dollars at a time, and I will not charge you interest."

We were fortunate to have a friend like George, but still, Jess and I worried about the debt and began paying it off as we could. We had always said, "At least we have a roof over our heads," but even that had almost been snatched away. Several years earlier I had tried to sell the house for $150, but no one would buy it. Now we owed $500 in mortgages and back taxes. It was a staggering sum.

Before the cold weather set in that fall, Jess and I began winterizing the house to make it warmer for Lila and the new baby. We repaired the chinking between the logs and Jess installed storm doors. Up went the storm windows with cotton stuffed in around the edges to make them airtight.

The thing we needed most was a heater under the house. There was no basement, just a small, dug-out space under the kitchen where I stored my barrel of berries and put the root vegetables in the sand. A trapdoor in the floor led down a rickety few steps to the hole. Jess decided to enlarge the area in order to install a heater. He had to cut away the foundation log before he could start digging. He hauled the dirt out by the bucketful until he could run a wheelbarrow under the house. I helped when I could, but even at that, we did not get finished before winter. We had to board it up until spring and make do with the old heating system that sent the hot air to the ceiling while our feet froze.

We lived in the midst of unfinished projects. The pile of dirt from the well was still in the back yard, a reminder of another job undone. Of course we were still buying water. Would we ever get ahead, I often wondered. Would our lives ever be easier? Would I ever have a decent house?

Before our second child was due, we made arrangements with Dr. McCollum and Mina Bond to assist with the birth at home. Again Jess was counting on a boy. This time he was so sure he was going to get his hunting partner. From the moment labor began, I knew the birth was not going to be an easy one. And it wasn't.

One time during the long ordeal, I heard the doctor say to Jess, "Which one do you want me to save, your wife or the baby?"

"My God, my wife," Jess said.

"I don't think I can save them both."

But he did. On September 16, 1913, our second daughter was born, slightly battered from the doctor's instruments, but a healthy baby just the same. As a breech birth she had tested the skill of the doctor and nurse who had to turn her so she would come out headfirst. Although Jess was relieved that the baby and I were doing well, he still had not gotten his boy.

"Jess, I am sorry. I hope you aren't too disappointed."

"I can't understand it," he said. "Why can't we have a boy?"

Now there was the big problem of what to name the baby. Mother Madole Meyers was hurt because we had named our first baby Cora but called her Lila (because I didn't like the name Cora). It was time to do something about that. In order to avoid confusion, we changed Cora de Lila's name to Clara de Lila, and we named the new baby Cora Lorraine. As Cora grew older she looked enough like her grandmother to be her daughter. At last everyone was happy.

It took me a long time to recover from Cora's birth. When Mina

Bond went on another nursing case, Jess took off from work to help with the two babies. The thing he disliked most about the household chores was washing the diapers on the scrubboard. How he cursed that job. The minute he heard there was a used washing machine for sale, he ran right out and bought it, without even trying it.

"Why did you buy that contraption? It isn't any good," I complained. "The women I have talked to say it doesn't get the clothes clean, and it leaves lint on everything."

"I don't care. I am using it," Jess said stubbornly. "As long as I am doing the washing, I am keeping it."

As soon as I was on my feet again, I tried that newfangled machine. The wooden tub, corrugated inside like a washboard, stood on wooden legs. The agitator, looking like a four-legged milk stool, was inside the lid that fit over the tub, and the gears were on top of the lid. There was a large wheel on the side of the tub that was connected by a belt to the electric motor, which sat on a shelf under the tub. The wringer (what a blessing that was after wringing by hand) was run by these same gears.

Early in the morning on washday, while I was fixing Jess's breakfast, I filled the copper boiler with water, put it on the back of the stove and let it heat. When the water was hot, I added the Fels Naptha soap and the white clothes I wanted to boil clean. When the water was hot enough, I dumped it in the washtub along with the other dirty clothes. I can still remember the joy of plugging in the motor and listening to the machine do my work for me. No more bending over the scrubboard.

After the wash was done, the water had to be drained into a bucket and carried outdoors. Later Jess drilled a hole in the wall close to the floor so the water could run through a hose into the back yard. To dry the clothes in the wintertime meant hanging the wet things on lines strung across the kitchen and on the special drying rack Jess had made. In the springtime I could hardly wait to hang the clothes outdoors, and I usually rushed the season by putting them out before the snow was gone. What lovely, fragrant clothes we had, wind-whipped and sunshined on.

One day when Jess came home from work, he announced, "I have a buyer for the washing machine."

"Oh, no. You can't sell it," I said.

"Why not?"

"Because—because I like it," I finally admitted.

Jess never did stop teasing me about the washing machine I didn't want and wouldn't let him sell. Even though the machine took up a lot of room in my kitchen, it was worth it. I soon learned to leave a little water in the bottom of the tub so it wouldn't dry out and leak.

That winter Jess had his fill of working outdoors sawing wood and walking the lines for the telephone company. When he heard there was an opening for a fireman in the boiler room at Northern Commercial, he asked for and got the job. Now, instead of 10-hour shifts, he worked 12, firing the boiler with four-foot lengths of native spruce, birch and tamarac.

Jess worked nights one week and days the next week, and for that he was paid $150 a month—good wages at that time. As an added benefit, we got our lights and telephone free, and a discount on everything we bought at the company store.

All the N.C. power plant employees were on the volunteer fire department; it was part of their job. There were some disastrous fires in Fairbanks in those days that threatened, more than once, to destroy the entire town. Most of the hotels, saloons, banks and shops were built of flimsy wood, stuffed with sawdust and covered with tarpaper. Tinderboxes all.

Of course the worst fires came in the winter when it was 40 below. Whenever the sirens sounded—always in the middle of the night—Jess jumped in his clothes and made a run for the power plant. It was wonderful the way the townspeople rallied around whenever there was a fire—or any disaster, for that matter—we were all neighbors and the Golden Rule prevailed.

One winter, a fire threatened the entire downtown area. Jess, manning the power house boiler, was hard-pressed to keep up pressure for the pumps because the wood he had was green and wouldn't burn. It was desperate, so the store manager, Mr. Richmond, gave the order to throw on cases of ham and bacon. That got the boiler going and saved the town.

By 1914 the economy of Fairbanks was in worse shape than it had been the year before. Gold production was down, and many of the men who worked the mines left town. The mines, which had produced more than $9 million in gold the first year I arrived, were down to about $3.5 million. There was no other industry to keep the town going. As a result, businesses closed and the buildings along Second Avenue and Cushman remained vacant. There were empty cabins all over town, inhabited only by mud swallows nesting under the eaves. In those days Fairbanks was resting on past laurels without any new direction or impetus for progress. There was talk that Fairbanks would be like so many other boom towns—Dawson, for example—that had its heyday and then died.

Despite the negative predictions about the future, Jess and I never considered leaving Fairbanks. We both maintained that Fairbanks was here to stay. Fortunately, about that time a small gold strike at Chatanika, 20 miles from town, sparked a revival of mining activity. There was one problem, however: fuel. In the past years the woodcutters had chopped down the easily accessible supply. Now they had to drive to wooded areas farther from town, which increased the cost to $24 a cord.

One small, bright star on the horizon was the promise of a railroad from Seward to Fairbanks. Due to the efforts of Alaska's delegate to Congress, Judge James Wickersham, a bill allocating money for the railroad construction was passed in 1914 and work started the following year. This did not mean an immediate upsurge in Fairbanks, but it did mean there was cheaper and year-round transportation on the way, which was needed badly. The railroad would make it possible to ship coal from the mines at Healy, 100 miles south of Fairbanks.

In the meantime, the town was in a slump, and our life was still a struggle. We were always short of money, but that was nothing new. Whenever we got a spare dollar, which wasn't often, we put it into the house. After five years of marriage and two children, I was discouraged with the many inconveniences. So much of my time was spent heating water, carrying it out, chopping wood and dumping ashes. At last we did have heat under our house. Jess had finished digging the basement and put in a wood-burning stove made out of an oil drum. Since we could not afford hot-air pipes, Jess cut holes in the floor for registers and the heat came up that way.

The day Jess came home and told me he and Carney had salvaged a riverboat with an inboard motor that he was going to fix up, I was more discouraged than ever.

"Oh, Jess, there are a lot of things we need more than a boat," I said. "Here we are with two babies in the house, and we still don't have any water."

"I know, Clara, but it won't take me very long to fix up the boat."

I knew all about that—the hours it would take, the parts he would have to buy, the tools, the paint and who knows what all.

"How much did it cost?" I asked.

"I got it for practically nothing," Jess said evasively. "It even has a 50-horsepower engine."

"We live in the house all year long," I said, "but we can only use the boat a few months out of the year. I don't understand it. You always seem to find the time and money for the things you want."

"You will enjoy the boat too, Clara. You will see."

I lost count of the hours Jess spent on the boat. Every night after work, no matter how tired he was, Jess was in the back yard tinkering with the motor or refurbishing the 35-foot boat that had been swamped for nearly a year in the Tanana. There were many times I wished he would direct his energy toward finishing the well. We were still buying water.

Cora, 2, and Lila, 3, on a visit to Mother Madole's cabin at Little Eldorado.

To pacify me Jess painted *Clara I* on the side of the red boat. I wasn't sure whether I should feel honored, or whether it was fair warning that a *Clara II* might be along in the future. In those days of few roads—and even fewer cars—everyone traveled the waterways. Jess's experiences on the sternwheeler with Captain LaBallister had taught him to respect the swift and tricky currents of the Chena and Tanana rivers. He could read the channels like the back of his hand.

After we had taken a few trips in the boat, I had to admit I enjoyed those outings as much as Jess did. It was wonderful to get out of town for a change of scene. Somehow carrying water from the river and heating it over a campfire was not an inconvenience when we were outdoors like that.

When Jess got off work on Friday night he would load our camping gear in the wheelbarrow and walk it the eight blocks to the river where we kept the boat tied. Then he came back for little Lila and Cora, whom he deposited in the wheelbarrow while I followed, dragging the baby buggy along the soft, sandy streets so the children would have a safe place to ride in the boat.

The long summer hours of golden sunlight allowed us to travel all night on the water if that was our pleasure. Sometimes we had a destination in mind; a high sunny bank, perhaps, where the spruce trees grew tall and cushioned the ground with fragrant needles, or we just traveled until some place struck our fancy. There we pitched our tent, surrounded by a cathedral of silence, and pass the blissful days. Each morning we woke to the sound of squirrels in the food box, the rabbits thumping the forest floor, or the birds atwitter because the sun barely gave them a chance to sleep the way it bobbed up a scant few hours after it set.

It wasn't long after we had launched the boat that Jess came home with a canvas canoe.

"What is that for?" I asked.

"We are going to take it with us upriver so we can explore the small streams along the way," Jess said. One thing always led to another.

We would meander up the Chena, the outboard motor making a comfortable putt-putt sound, with the canoe tied behind. After we made camp, Jess would take the canoe and drift along a narrow, unnamed stream where the trees leaned sideways into the water and drop in his fishing line. In no time at all he would have a fine mess of grayling. While Jess built up the fire, I got out the cast-iron skillets—one for the fish and one for the fried potatoes—and we had a feast. Some of our happiest times were spent together in the woods like that with the blue smoke rising like an arrow toward the top of the blue-green spruce, while the children played happily and the river at our feet slipped seaward. Jess and I had so much—yet so little—but we were happy.

Not long after my outburst about Jess's boating extravagances, he came home with a point and lengths of pipe. Before I knew what was happening, he cut a hole in the kitchen floor and rigged up a tripod. He had given up digging the well from the outside and would launch the battle from the inside.

The thump, thump of the weight pounding the point into the ground was like music to my ears. At last I was going to have running water! When Jess got tired of pulling the weights on the pulley, then I took over. A week or so later when we hit water, I was so excited that I put aside everything to wash clothes. Oh, what a joy it was to fill the copper boiler full of that sparkling clear water and put the diapers in to boil.

After a few hours I lifted the boiler lid to see how the diapers were doing. What a mess! Everything had turned red.

"Jess, come quick!"

"What is it?"

"Look what happened."

"I was afraid of that," he said. "There is too much iron in the water."

"What are we going to do?" By that time I was practically in tears.

"You will have to boil the water for tea and coffee, or else it will stain the cups and they will never come clean. I will see what I can do about the wash water."

While I did the ranting and raving, Jess sat down and figured out a solution. He installed a hand pump, and then he got a 50-gallon oil drum, which he painted inside and out with white enamel. This barrel sat in the kitchen under the pump so we could fill it easily. We added lye and chloride of lime to the water, gave it a good stir and allowed the sediment to settle before using it. That made the water soft and pure for washing and bathing.

When the girls got older it was their chore to work the pump handle. The barrel had to be filled once a week. I can still see Lila standing on a chair pumping the handle and complaining, "Mama, my arm is tired."

Even though we still had to carry out the water and dump it in the back yard, I did have running water, and for that I was grateful.

It would be 15 years before I had indoor plumbing. In the meantime, we made use of the outhouse in the back yard with the fur-lined seat. As the years passed Jess had to move the house seven times, leaving behind a well-fertilized garden plot. That was the only advantage there was.

Jess's long shifts at the power house, along with the many projects at home, were beginning to take their toll. I watched with concern as his face became pinched with fatigue and marked with deep furrows. That lovely auburn hair I loved so was thinning. It lay lightly on his scalp, forever receding. His clothes hung on his wiry frame like a scarecrow. Months passed before Jess picked up his mandolin or harmonica. There didn't seem to be time for music in our life anymore.

One night when I was sick in bed (I was pregnant for the third time), Jess came home bearing a mysterious looking package. He

Lila in front of the old house, 1915.

166

acted a little sheepish about it, as if he knew I would suspect the gift was more for him than it was for me.

"I thought you might like a little entertainment while you are in bed," Jess said.

He had bought a small Victrola, one of the first of its kind, with a turntable on top and a handle on the side to wind the spring. To this day I can remember the first three records we owned because we played them over and over—the Hawaiian medley, the Irish songs, and one called "Uncle Josh at the Circus." Jess was so proud of his purchase that I didn't have the heart to scold him.

"Thank you, Jess. I am sure we will all enjoy it."

And we did, even though there were other things we needed more than a Victrola. From then on Jess bought a new record every payday, and once again there was music in our house.

Sometimes Jess arranged surprises that were more practical. I happened to look out the window one day to see a drayman pull up and begin to unload timber.

"What is that for?" I asked the driver.

"I dunno, ma'am," he said. "Jess told me to unload it here."

When Jess came home that night he explained that he had bought the lumber at cost from Northern Commercial. There was enough to put new floors in all three rooms—and how they needed it. I got down on my hands and knees with Jess, despite my pregnant condition, and we tore out the old floor and put down the new one. After that we spent several weeks sanding the floors and painting them. Even though refurbishing the house meant a lot of work, as well as living in a mess, there was always a sense of satisfaction when we were finished. Also, the old house was beginning to look more respectable.

When President Wilson declared war on Germany in April 1917, a large number of Fairbanks people volunteered for service. We gave them a patriotic send-off complete with a parade down to the docks where they boarded the *General Jacobs* for Fort Gibbon on the Yukon River for indoctrination. Gold stars appeared in windows where family members in their country's service never returned. Everyone in town was involved in the war effort. Jess worked with the Red Cross, and I knit socks for the boys overseas while I waited for the birth of our third child.

This time Jess and I were so sure we were going to have a boy that we picked out a name for him. We would call him George, after

Jess's father. As we had done in the past, we made arrangements for Dr. McCollum to deliver the baby at home. On June 24, before Jess even had time to summon the doctor or the nurse, the baby was on the way. Jess quickly sent 5-year-old Lila and 4-year-old Cora to a neighbor's while he delivered our third child.

A girl; another girl. Jess, now resigned to his lot in life, didn't seem as disappointed as he had been with the first two girls. Our George became Georgia June. Once again we had a baby basket beside our bed.

The same day June was born, Mother Madole Meyers returned from Seattle, where she had undergone a successful cataract operation. She stayed with us a few days to help with the children. She was wonderful to the girls, and it was thanks to her that our children were outfitted regularly with new clothes. All her life she sewed for them. At Eastertime, Christmas and birthdays Mother Madole made new dresses—complete with matching hair ribbons—and in the winter she fashioned long wool coats with fur collars and cuffs and knitted caps and scarves and mittens by the dozens.

Little by little we had whittled away the debt we owed George Bellows on the house, but it still was not paid off and we did not have a title.

One afternoon Jess came hurrying up the path. I could tell by the look on his face that something was wrong. Besides, he never left work early unless it was something serious.

"What's wrong?" I asked, even before he had a chance to get in the door.

"We need $50 right away."

"Fifty dollars! We don't have that kind of money."

"I know we don't, but we are going to have to get it."

"What for?"

Jess slumped into a chair. "It's George Bellows. He is in the hospital."

"Is it serious?"

"Yes. We have to get the money somewhere," Jess said. "If George should die while holding the mortgage, we could lose the house. No one would understand our payment system."

George's bookkeeping was casual, to say the least. Whenever we paid him, he would make a notation on a scrap of paper, on the back of a used envelope or on the calendar. Rarely did he give us a receipt, but Jess kept the account itemized in his book. Jess, George and I were the only ones who knew we owed him only $50 on that longstanding debt, but if it ever had to go to court, we would be sunk.

"Where are we going to get that kind of money?" I asked. A feeling of helplessness surged over me at times like those. There was never any way I could help Jess. He had to go out and fight our battles alone.

Jess left the room abruptly and returned with his diamond ring. No matter how tough things got, Jess had always managed to hang on to that ring he had bought during his single days. To him a diamond was a symbol of success, and as long as he had that ring he felt he was somebody.

"I am going to hock it," he said, slipping the ring on his finger for the last time.

"Jess, isn't there another way?" I cried.

"No. There is no other way."

As I stood in the doorway and watched Jess disappear among the leafy trees up the path, my thoughts rushed back to our wedding day when Jess had to sell Irish to pay the expenses. The tears started coming, and I couldn't stop them. It isn't fair, I cried out loud. It isn't fair.

Jess hocked his $600 diamond ring for $100.

"I got the extra fifty to help with the expenses of the baby," he said. "We should be able to redeem the ring in a year."

"Sure, Jess," I said, but we both knew it was impossible.

He never did get the ring back, but we did get the title to the old house, witnessed by one of the Catholic sisters at St. Joseph's Hospital.

Two days later George Bellows died.

chapter 17

One afternoon in the fall of 1919 Jess called from work to say our friends Sig and Margaret Magnusson wanted to go upriver and pick cranberries.

"Why don't you get a lunch together and meet us at the boat when I get off work?" he said.

Jess didn't have to ask me twice; I was always ready when he said "Let's go." We enjoyed the same things, whether it be music, dancing, working on the house or just being outdoors. We often laughed about my first hiking expedition up Pedro Dome. I had come a long way since then. Now I could set up camp, cook over a fire, catch fish and paddle a canoe as well as Jess.

Sometimes I looked back on those early days and thought how young and naive I had been. Someone was certainly watching over me. It is my belief that certain things are meant to be, and Jess and I getting together was one of them.

I hummed happily to myself as I made sandwiches and a Thermos of hot coffee for our supper on the boat. While we were gone our young neighbor, Mardy, would watch the children. I was looking forward to this unexpected outing and the cranberries we would get. Surely there would be enough to boil and strain for jelly, and from the pulp I would make cranberry butter, our favorite.

On that crisp September evening we set out with Jess at the helm, steering a course upriver. The yellow trees, like lighted lampposts, were reflected in the muddy Chena water. Against the bronzed ground the salmonberry and the cranberry leaves flamed red while the new growth of spruce held a steady green. As we cut through the dark water, the golden birch and cottonwood leaves drifted down like huge flakes to float on the brown surface. Before long

Jess spotted the cranberry patch which he had staked out on an earlier trip.

"Let's pull into the shore and eat in the boat before we stir up the mosquitoes," Jess suggested.

Sig jumped out with the rope and pulled the boat into the bank while Jess stopped the engine and pulled the prop.

We had become the owners of a new boat, the *Clara II,* a sleek new river craft built by our friend Sam Jensen and outfitted with a new 75-horsepower Ferro engine which Jess was buying on time from Northern Commercial Company. The boat was 35 feet long with a removable canvas cover that could be attached to a wire frame when needed. Since the weather was clear, we had traveled this night without the canvas cover. Our picnic basket rode safely beneath the wooden decking at the bow. While I got out the sandwiches, Margaret poured the coffee.

We were chilled from our ride on the river, and we were looking forward to that hot coffee and something to eat. With my sandwich in one hand and my coffee cup in the other, I sat on the outer edge of the boat as I had done many times before. But suddenly the cup went one way, the sandwich another, and I somersaulted feet over head into the river. When I plunged into that icy water it took the breath right out of me. It was a frightening, helpless feeling.

"Oh my God!" I heard Jess yell. "Oh my God!"

The current was so swift that it almost pulled me downriver before I could grab the outer rigging of the propeller. I clung frantically to the iron bar while the current pulled at me with all its force. I knew if I let go, I'd be a goner. The water there was more than 15 feet deep.

"Hang on, Clara, hang on!" Jess shouted. He grabbed my wrists. "You are going to have to make your way around to the side of the boat," he said. "I can't get you up over this rigging."

While Jess held my wrists, I inched my way around to the side. Sig managed to steady the boat. When he had tied up, he had pulled the boat so high onto the mud bank that it rocked instead of riding flat on the water.

"It's cold, Jess!" I cried. "It's so cold!"

I could not help to pull myself into the boat; I was all dead weight. The heavy knit sweater I was wearing had stretched below my knees and hobbled me so I could not lift my leg. My tall hiking boots, filled with water, threatened to pull me under.

Poor Margaret—I can see her now—standing in the boat, tears streaming down her face and wringing her hands. Jess tried to pull me into the boat, all 250 pounds of me, but he couldn't do it. "Give me a hand, Sig," Jess yelled. "We will have to roll her in." The men grabbed my clothes and rolled me into the boat like a log. I came out of that water sputtering and shivering. Never have I been so cold in my life. My teeth chattered so hard I couldn't talk. Jess and Sig took one look at me and ran ashore to start a fire.

As I stood over the blaze, I thought I would never be warm again. My hands were blue, and my feet felt as if they were imbedded in ice.

"You are going to have to get out of those wet clothes," Jess said.

While Sig and Margaret went off into the woods to pick berries, I pulled off my wet clothing. Fortunately Jess had an extra suit of long underwear in the boat. So many times I had complained about all the junk Jess packed with him. We never had a clean boat like other people because Jess insisted on carrying tools, extra gas, a first aid kit, pieces of wire, bolts and screws and such things. "If you ever need anything on the river, ask Jess Rust," people said.

Now I was grateful that Jess brought all his odds and ends with him. The long underwear felt warm and dry next to my skin. Then I put on Jess's long black slicker—which didn't take any fashion prizes—but at least I was covered up.

"If I had something to wear on my feet, I'd go pick berries," I told Jess. I was just dying to get my hands on all those luscious cranberries.

"I'll give you my socks, and you can wear them inside your shoes," Jess said.

Thus decked out I headed for the nearest patch while Jess stayed by the fire to turn my clothes as they dried. He never was very fond of picking berries, and this was a good way to get out of it.

In about an hour Jess joined me in the woods. "You better put your clothes on before Sig and Margaret get back," he said. "It will be dark pretty soon, and we should start home."

Jess took my bucket and said he would pick berries while I dressed. When I got back to the fire, I couldn't find my clothes. Another one of Jess's jokes, I thought.

"Jess, where are my clothes?" I hollered.

Jess came running from the woods, followed closely behind by Sig and Margaret.

"Where did you hide my clothes, Jess?" I demanded.

"I didn't hide them," he said. "They are right there by the fire."

But they weren't.

"Well, I'll be——" and he looked at the Magnussons.

"We haven't seen them," they said.

I was beginning to feel a little silly standing there in Jess's long underwear. "Well, someone has run off with my clothes," I said, starting to get mad. "Jess, are you sure . . ."

My husband started laughing. "Here they are," he said, holding up a smoldering piece of my gingham dress which had been burned by sparks from the campfire.

"Is that all?" I cried.

"Well, there is this," Jess said, pulling one of my corset stays from the coals. The only thing we salvaged was my heavy knit sweater which had been folded over a log.

There was nothing to do but to load up the boat and head for home. By then it was inky black on the river, and in those places where the sweepers hung over the water, it was like traveling through a tunnel. After going a short distance, wouldn't you know it, we hit a sand bar. When we heard that old familiar thud of the boat bottom hitting the mud, we all groaned.

Jess was used to such emergencies, though. He pulled on his hip boots and waded out into that cold water to push the boat off the bar. Just as he got the boat free, he stepped into a drop-off and plunged into water above his waist.

Sig jumped out and helped Jess anchor the boat to the sand bar, which stretched halfway across the river. Then the rest of us piled out and began gathering driftwood for a fire. Since I was wearing Jess's emergency set of underwear, we had to dry out his clothing before we could go on. While we waited we boiled up another big pot of coffee—thanks again to the supplies Jess carried in the boat.

By now we were all hungry again, since our supper had been interrupted by my dunking, so we finished the sandwiches and pie within the warm circle of firelight that jumped into the dark sky.

What a night! I had to go home in that union suit and old black slicker. We got a good laugh out of it though, and along with plenty of berries, that made the adventure worthwhile.

In those days berries and wild meat were an important part of our food supply. Whenever we went upriver I spent my time berrying while Jess fished. I knew where all the good patches were for currants, both red and black; the thimble-size strawberries, the sweet-flavored dewberries, the tangy blueberries and the glistening high- and lowbush cranberries.

Across from our house, along the banks of the old slough, the wild raspberries grew. In the afternoon, while my babies were asleep, I could slip out and pick berries. Sometimes I would take little Lila with me. As I stopped here and there to put a few berries in my bucket, Lila would pull my skirt and say, "Me want to pickle berries too, Mama." I would find her a nice low bush, set her beside it and let her eat to her heart's content. We would both go home scratched and berry-stained, and with sunburned noses, but my bucket was always brimming full.

For days I would stand over the wood range stirring the jams, jellies, sauces and syrups.

Next, the woods yielded up wild mushrooms—the shaggy manes, orange delicious, puffballs and meadow mushrooms. One year I had 50 cans of orange delicious. How we loved them with our moose steak.

Every fall Jess went hunting until he got a moose and a caribou. After he cut and wrapped the meat, we left it in the N.C. cold storage until the weather was cold enough so we could put it outdoors in our cache.

Nothing went to waste at the old house. The moose bones were boiled for bouillon, which I canned; and the scrap meat from the bones went through the grinder with onions and spices for headcheese. One treat my family loved was canned caribou heart with stuffing. If we got a young and tender piece of bear meat, I canned that too.

In late August or early September Jess and his friends took their boats down the Tanana River to Linder Lake. He returned home with a full load of mallards, teals, widgeons, and my favorite of all the birds, the butterballs.

Before canning, I stuffed the ducks and browned them in the oven. My canning outfit—a pressure cooker and a sealer for a #2½ tin—was one of my most valued possessions, and at that time of the year it was in use day and night.

Sometimes Jess brought home Canada geese. I boiled the legs and wings for soup, adding garden vegetables and rice before canning. The birds were then stuffed and frozen, a succulent meal for a Sunday dinner.

The girls unwillingly helped me pluck the down from the ducks and geese. From the down I made quilts for all the beds, first stitching the quilt squares on my old White treadle sewing machine, which Jess had bought for me at the Pirate Ship store on Second Avenue. I also made calico slipcovers for the quilts which could be removed for washing. Today, my daughters still have those quilts and the small goose-down-filled pillows of German ticking.

After harvesting the garden, there was more canning and preserving to be done. My kitchen and back porch overflowed with boxes of parsnips, peas, cabbages, carrots and potatoes. The long white parsnips (so good cooked in butter and sprinkled with sugar) as well as the shelled peas and the small potatoes, were canned in Mason jars, making a colorful display on my storage shelves.

In the cool basement we stored the carrots in a mound of sand and the potatoes in a large bin.

The cabbage was shredded into a 50-pound wooden butter barrel, which we used year after year, for sauerkraut. To the cabbage I added apple slices and salt, covered the barrel and let it ferment about a week before moving it to the basement. We ate that good kraut all winter.

Each year we stopped at Fish Mike's on the Tanana River and got salmon to can. To keep our larder full, we had to make all our trips pay by hunting, fishing or berrying. It was not unusual for me to have 500 cans of food on the shelves when winter began.

Our little family of three girls was growing, and when I became pregnant again we realized we needed more room. Jess and I gave up our bedroom so we could have bunks in there for the girls. Jess built large drawers under the bunks to store shoes and toys, and then he installed a much-needed closet in the bedroom. In those days storage space was always a problem; we had no basement or garage for a catchall, and the little house got mighty cluttered.

In the dining room Jess made us a wall-bed, which I covered with flowered curtains. He built shelves across the top where I displayed the fine china we had received as gifts—the golden Pickard, the cut-glass crystal, the hand-blown wine decanter. At the N.C. store, I put my name on the list for the banana crates when they were available. During those days when lumber was scarce and expensive, the sturdy wooden boxes were in demand as end tables and cupboards. My house was furnished with them for years.

When it came to house improvements, one thing always led to another. The bottom logs of the house, which rested on the ground, were rotting away. Jess set about to replace them, which meant new banking was needed. We replaced the dirt banking with sawdust and wood shavings, which was warm and dry and did not rot the logs.

Next we built a screened porch across the front of the house. In summer the oldest girls slept out there, taking their bedding and making a nest on the folding cots. On hot nights we had our meals on the porch, luxuriating in the cool breeze and safe from the marauding mosquitoes. Always we had a tin can lid burning with Buhach to ward off the insects that found their way into the house through the many cracks and crevices. I still associate summer with that pungent smell of Buhach burning.

In the meantime Jess had changed jobs. He had become tired of lifting the heavy cordwood to feed the boiler at the power plant. When the job of foreman of the Northern Commercial water and steam lines opened up, he took it. This meant more money, but as it turned out, the working conditions were worse. Jess thawed the frozen steam and water lines, which entailed crawling through the dirty underground tunnels to reach a trouble spot. Also, he had to

The old house during renovations. The front porch was removed and bottom logs replaced. Clara, Lila, and neighbor Mardy Thomas stand in the yard.

Neighborhood kids visit in 1915. From left, Cora Rust, 3, Louise Gillette, 4, Lila Rust, 4, and Louis Gillette, 3.

dig up the streets, thawing as he went, to get to other frozen pipes. Many times he was called out of bed in the middle of the night—at 40 and 50 below zero—for some emergency. Even with a crew working under him, it seemed to me that Jess was most often stuck with the worst jobs.

"How can you stand it, Jess?" I asked him when he came home after a long night of work, clothes caked with mud, hands chapped and red.

"It is part of my job."

That was my Jess, never afraid of work, and ready to do for his family, no matter what the cost. Although money was always short in our household, we never went hungry, nor did we want for the necessities of life. In those days, everyone was in the same boat.

When I think back to our neighbors on Eighth Avenue, I remember how our lives were intertwined with everyday living, and trying to get by. We shared the good times and the bad times. We helped each other through difficulties and rejoiced at another's good fortune.

Next door to us was the Louis R. Gillette family with their 12-year-old daughter, Mardy Thomas, and two younger children the same age as my Lila and Cora. I remember one afternoon Mrs. Gillette and I were sewing in her living room while the youngsters played on the front porch. I heard Cora say, "One for you and one for me. Here is a nice fat one for you."

I got up to see what they were doing and found them eating flies off the screen door!

Oh, our life was never dull. There was the day my kids pulled all the rhubarb out of our neighbor's yard, and followed that up by painting the woodpile green. And who could forget the day one of the girls, all dressed in white, fell in the outhouse on a hot summer's day?

When young Mardy was not babysitting for her mother, she would come to my house to help me with my three children. At first she didn't know how to take Jess's teasing, but when she caught on, we had good times together. Mardy, a slim, pretty girl with black hair and merry eyes, loved the outdoors and came with us on many trips upriver. We grew fond of Mardy and thought of her as one of the family.

There was another young girl, Cleora Casady, whom we thought of as one of our own. Her parents, John and Mrs. Neilson, were miners at Livengood, and when she came into town for school one winter, she lived with us. Cleora was a wonderful help with our small daughters. Even though our house was small, it didn't seem crowded with her in it. Cleora and Mardy became great friends and Jess was in his glory when he had both of them to tease.

After Cleora moved back to Livengood, she married George Bachner. When she became pregnant she made arrangements to have the baby in Fairbanks. Jess and I invited her to stay in our house until it was time to go to the hospital.

Once she was in the house Cleora said, "I am not going to the hospital. I want to have the baby at your house."

"Oh, no," I said. "I couldn't possibly deliver your baby."

Cleora was insistent. "I am having my baby here, and not only that, I am going to have a boy and break the jinx in this house."

When we realized we could not change her mind, I made arrangements for Doc McCollum to come, as well as our neighbor Lillian Shafer, who had been a midwife.

Then, wouldn't you know it, Cleora had a boy, just like she predicted, and she named him Jesse.

Later the Bachners had two more children, and when they moved into Fairbanks they bought a lot across the street from us and built a house. We spent many happy hours visiting back and forth, enjoying holiday parties and outings together, and Cleora was a great help to me many times. I missed her when they moved to Anchorage.

On the other side of our house lived the Godskis with their son Bill. Mr. Godski worked for the N.C. like so many Fairbanksans did at that 'time. Mrs. Godski loved flowers, and every year she planted red geraniums in her window boxes, which I enjoyed from my yard. When her husband died she had little money and found it necessary to take in laundry from the girls on the Line. Sometimes in the evening, when I wasn't too busy, I went over and helped her iron. I knew she was in poor health and suffered a great deal of pain. Within a year of her husband's death, she died of cancer.

Up the street, in the next block, lived a recluse, Kitty Hensley, with her daughter, Hazel. They had lived in a tarpaper shack almost camouflaged by a thick growth of alder and willow until a riverboat captain named Smythe (with whom Kitty was romantically linked) built her a snug, proper two-story house with painted window frames and a fireplace. After Hazel went Outside to school, Kitty became more and more withdrawn.

One morning a very distraught Captain Smythe came running to my house. "I can't wake Kitty. I can't wake Kitty," he said.

When I followed him back to the house I found Kitty wrapped in a bundle of rags, her small hands curled like claws, and the waxy pallor of death on her face. "She is dead, Captain," I said.

"Oh, no! She is just sleeping. She can't be dead."

After Kitty's body was removed, the captain ransacked Kitty's house for the money and jewelry she had hidden there. Years later when the house was sold, the new owners found a bag of gold poked behind the imitation fireplace.

Across the street from us in a low-slung log cabin bordering the thicket of the slough, lived a Mormon family, Roy and Lillian Shafer with their two daughters and one son. Roy built a barn, using culled lumber to keep the horses, pigs and chickens they raised. Their house had only the bare essentials, and Lillian waited in vain for her husband to finish the kitchen.

Every year the Shafers put in a huge garden, which was tended by the whole family. Whenever I went to their house Lillian and the kids were down on their knees weeding in the hot summer sun. Roy sold vegetables to the grocery stores and had a woodsawing business on the side. After a time Lillian became discouraged with her way of life and took jobs housecleaning.

In those days divorce was not common, but it did happen. When the Shafers split up, Roy and his son Frank went back to Salt Lake City. Lillian and the girls took a place next door to us after the Gillettes moved closer to town.

The old neighborhood was a wonderful place for children to grow up. Out back of our house was a large wooded area with a small pond where the children launched their rafts and sailed toy boats. One winter Lila and her friends hauled water through our house to make a skating rink in the front yard. There was a hill nearby where the kids went sliding, using a wooden mixing bowl for a sled.

Just beyond the Gillette house, in a sparse grove of willows, was Joe Brinkman's abandoned wellhouse. First thing in the morning the kids were over there. To them the old shack was a castle, or a haunted house, or a fort, or a store—whatever they wanted it to be. When I asked the kids where they had been all day, the reply was always, "Over at old Joe's."

One day Mr. Gillette walked over to Joe's to see what the kids were doing. It was the first time he had been in the wellhouse. When he saw the gaping waterhole, without any covering, he nearly had a fit.

"Jess, have you seen that wellhouse?" he asked.

"Not lately."

"It is a wonder no one had drowned over there."

The kids were aware of the well opening, but they considered it part of the fun the old shack offered. They could holler into its depths and their voices boomed back, and rocks thrown into the water made a wonderful splashing noise.

"We were always careful," the kids explained while Jess and Mr. Gillette boarded up the hole.

Not far from our house lived Ed Clausen and his wife, Myra. He started as a delivery boy for the N.C. and worked his way up until he became store manager. The Clausens had four children, which added to the ever-increasing number of kids in the neighborhood. One day Jess and I counted 20 kids within two blocks of our house.

Two bachelors, Andy and George, lived in a small cabin across the street from us. On occasion one of them babysat for us when Jess and I wanted to go to the Eagles Lodge or take in a movie.

Andy and George kept five sled dogs, which they would let me hitch up and take out on the trail. It was good exercise for the dogs—and me, still fighting the battle of the bulge.

Behind our house, and beyond the wooded lot, lived a German family by the name of Wehner. Their log cabin was built very close to the ground. In fact, it was so low that I had to duck my head when I walked in the back shed. The long, narrow house was typical of the times when people added on a room at the back as need dictated. This kind of telescoping construction—always a patchwork of odds and ends of lumber—was an economical way to add another room.

Walking through the Wehner house from the back, the first room was the bedroom, curtained off from the hallway. Next came the kitchen, and then the living room, all in a row like cars on a train. The house was "make-do" like ours, with painted wooden floors, banana crate shelves and second-hand furniture. In spite of our modest surroundings, we were never ashamed of our homes, nor did we apologize for the makeshift arrangements. Rather, we prided ourselves on every new invention to utilize the materials available.

Along the low eaves of the Wehner house were wooden troughs that hung down at the corners to direct the rainwater to the barrel below. This was used to water the garden, and the Wehners, like most of our neighbors, had a big one. They spent their summer talking of cutworms and aphids, too much rain or not enough, and how the celery was bitter and going to tops.

"Pop," as Adolph Wehner was known, played the trumpet in the Fairbanks City Band. He also drove the honey wagon, year after year, to pick up the slop buckets in the night hours. The rattle of the cans in the back of his old truck, was familiar music to us all. Later he was known as the Sanitary Engineer. Pop's wife, Barbara, was a tall, angular woman who always put the coffeepot on when she saw visitors coming down the path. The Wehners had four daughters and a son.

As a member of the band Pop took part in many community affairs. One year the band members decided it was time the city had a public park and campground. They selected a spot a mile below town, at Leah Bar (where I first landed in Fairbanks in a rowboat) on the banks of the Chena River. It was a lovely wooded spot with many tall birch and spruce trees left standing. With donations of lumber, equipment and labor, a bandstand and barbeque pit were built, as well as tables and benches.

On July Fourth the park was officially opened with a picnic. The long tables were spread with food, a tempting array of salads, desserts and homemade bread, while a side of moose cooked on the spit, sending out the most glorious smells on the air. At yet another firepit, coffee was bubbling in big pots.

Our good Mayor Tom Marquam gave a speech in recognition of the holiday and the people who had built the park. While the Fairbanks City Band played patriotic songs, many voices joined in.

For several years Leah Bar was a popular place for family picnics, but later it fell into disuse when people got cars and began building cabins at Harding and Birch lakes.

As our children grew older, we established a permanent camp upriver where we pitched our tents and left our gear all summer without worrying that anyone would steal or misuse our belongings. That is a part of Alaska that is gone forever. In those days we were all like neighbors, whether we lived next door to each other or not. Our way of life created a feeling of mutual respect and need—even among strangers—that is hard to find today.

About this time Mother Madole Meyers moved into town and took a small cabin on Second Avenue across from the house where Jess and I had been married. Mother and her husband, Fred, had not been happy together. He went Outside to find work, saying he would send for her, but I think Mother knew then that their marriage was over. She had been on her own before; she would be on her own again. That was all there was to it, no looking back and no regrets. I continued to be amazed at her strength and resilience.

Her fortunetelling sign appeared out in front of her cabin. Madame Renio was back in business. Since she was always in demand as a seamstress, she took in sewing again, and as always she got by on her own, never asking favors of anyone.

Those were days of change. I was busy with my family and lost touch with many of my old friends. It came as a surprise to me when Mary Anderson closed her shop, selling out to Gordon's across the street, and moved to Seattle. Mary had become ill, and her daughter Gudrun, whom she had not seen in years, came to Fairbanks to help her move.

Although work on the railroad continued, when the roadbed from Seward to Fairbanks was completed in 1923 there was no great upsurge of activity in Fairbanks. The railroad town of Nenana, 80 miles south of Fairbanks, had sprung up, but our population was reduced to about 1,200 people, with an additional 200 in the outlying gold camps. When I first came to Fairbanks the camps alone had maintained a population of 1,000 people.

The outlook was not totally bleak. Due to the foresight and persistence of the people of Fairbanks, the United States Congress and the Territorial legislature appropriated funds for the land-grant college, the Alaska Agricultural College and School of Mines, to be located 4 miles from town on a hill overlooking the Tanana Valley. Construction began in 1918, but it took 4 more years before the school opened. The college later became the University of Alaska.

There were other compensations, too. Fairbanks, as the seat of the Fourth Judicial District, supported the administrative offices of the U.S. district courts. In addition there were the activities of the Bureau of Land Management, the Alaska Road Commission, the U.S. Department of the Interior, the Division of Forestry, the Alaska Geology Branch and the Agriculture Experiment Station.

After the decline of gold mining, many men took up farming for an income. By 1920 there were 1,700 acres under cultivation. One year the Fairbanks farmers harvested 700 tons of potatoes. They experimented with different strains of barley, wheat and even corn. Each fall a large fair was held in Gordon's Roller Rink where the public came to view the agricultural prizes. Several dairy farms were started in the area to provide fresh milk.

Despite the hard times, there were some improvements to be seen in Fairbanks. The old wooden bridge over the Chena that was regularly swept out with each spring breakup was replaced by an overhead steel bridge, with the crossing at Cushman instead of Turner Street. There were no walkways provided for pedestrians, so a catwalk was built on both sides with ramps to the street. Over the bridge approach was a sign which read: "Please walk your horse." If a horse trotted, it caused the bridge to vibrate dangerously.

Improvements on existing roads were made by the Alaska Road Commission which also maintained the Fairbanks-Valdez Trail, now open to motor traffic. Mail reached Fairbanks via that route, as well as shipments of freight. The bulk of the town's supplies were still carried in by sternwheeler. Until the railroad came through we were dependent on that seasonal service.

As my baby's due date approached, Jess and I couldn't help but think about the boy we had always wanted. This time we did not pick out a name for either a boy or a girl. We had been disappointed too often to try that again. I made arrangements with Dr. McCollum to assist with a home delivery. Money was still a big consideration in our house.

August 3, 1920, dawned golden and warm, one of those rich days of early fall when the flowers outside my kitchen window were blooming luxuriously, and the vegetables were coming on ready for harvest. The minute I woke up that morning I knew that was the day the baby would be born. Jess made arrangements to be off work and notified the doctor and nurse. A neighbor took the three little girls—Lila, Cora and June—while our fourth child was born.

It was a boy! A boy! A boy! I couldn't help but think of Cleora. She said the jinx was broken, and it was.

Jess couldn't hide his pride. "I suppose you will think me foolish," he said grinning from ear to ear, "but I would like to name our son Jesse Worthington Rust Jr."

I held back a smile. "That's fine with me, Jess," I answered. For years Jess had made fun of people who carried on the family name to the third and fourth generation, but I did not remind him of that. "Jesse Worthington Rust Jr. it will be," I said.

"We have waited so long for a boy," Jess said, "and now I want him to have my name."

And so it was.

We made room for little Jess's basket in the bedroom with the girls. We had our boy and all was well.

chapter 18

Looking back puts things in a new perspective, and your evaluation of what is important changes. I can see now that it doesn't matter what problems you have, but how you react to them that makes the difference.

There were times when Jess upset me so. We had our share of quarrels, as most people do, and it was usually over the little things.

Take Jess's rabbit raising venture, for example. He got it in his head one day that he wanted to raise Belgian hares.

"I raised rabbits when I was a kid in Butte, Montana," he said. "It was a lot of fun and good eating."

Maybe they were good eating, but from the very first I doubted that raising rabbits was a lot of fun, knowing full well who was going to get to do all the work. Nevertheless, Jess set about building a shed in the corner of the yard with a fenced-in pen. Then he bought two rabbits, a male and a female, from Emil Van Raes, and we were in the rabbit raising business. Well, it wasn't so bad in the summer. I didn't mind cleaning the pen then, but in winter when the water pans froze solid, it was a lot of work to thaw out the mess and clean it. How I hated that job, and I had a few choice words for

Jess every time I had to do it. Whenever Jess had a few spare minutes, he helped me, but the responsibility was mine.

There was an old stove in the shed, but the fire went out every night. It was just one more stove to chop wood for, haul ashes and worry about whether it was still burning. With four young children to care for, a hutch of hatching rabbits was the last thing I needed. On top of it, we didn't make any money off the deal, but I had known from the start that we wouldn't.

One Easter when we had a large litter of bunnies, Frank Dunham asked to have a few in the window of the Red Cross Drug Store. They were a big attraction, and as a result we sold quite a few rabbits. After a while Jess lost interest in the whole thing and abandoned the scheme.

But that didn't stop him from thinking, a little while later, that it would be a good idea to convert the rabbit hutch into a chickenhouse.

"They will be real good eating, and think of all the fresh eggs we will have," he said.

Despite Jess's sales talk, I was not in favor of the idea, but Jess went right to work building nests and roosts. One day he came home with half a dozen Plymouth Rock hens and a Rhode Island rooster the kids named Sig because we got it from Sig Magnusson. This deal turned out as I knew it would: All the work of caring for the chickens fell to the kids and me.

Quite often when Cora and Lila were sent out to gather eggs, they came back empty-handed.

"There are no eggs," Cora would say.

"No eggs," Lila repeated.

When this went on two days in a row, Jess became suspicious and went to the chickenhouse to investigate for himself.

"All the nests had eggs in them," he ranted when he came in the door. "Cora! Lila! Get in here." They came shamefaced, holding their hands behind them, knowing full well that they were going to get paddled.

"Daddy, we just hate to put our hands in those messy nests," Cora tried to explain.

"Don't you lie to me when I ask if there are eggs," Jess said, and he gave both girls a spanking. He was a strict father, too strict I sometimes thought, but I never interfered when he was disciplining the children.

I could sympathize with the girls' feelings about the chicken pen; I hated to go in there, too. When I went to gather eggs or feed the chickens, Sig flew at my ankles and made loud noises. I knew he was going to attack me like that every time, but I never got used to it. I built up a great dislike for that rooster.

Chicken raising wasn't all bad, though. We did like the fresh eggs and fryers (Jess was right about that) and the children delighted in watching the fluffy little chicks emerge from their shells.

Even with these advantages, after a couple of years I told Jess I had too much work to do and I wasn't going to take care of the chickens any more. In the fall of the year we killed them all and put them in the cache to freeze. We tried to sell Sig, but with no luck and he went under the ax too.

One Sunday after we had eaten all the other chickens, I decided to cook Sig for dinner. The kids knew the minute I put the food on the table that it was Sig. They wouldn't touch one piece of that bird. I must admit I felt the same way. That night the dogs had a fine feed.

There were always cats and dogs around our house, but none could ever take the place of Diamond and Murphy. They had been special. It still hurt me to think of Diamond. After all we had been through with him, we finally had to sell him, too. There were other dogs, like Stubby, the lively black cocker spaniel Jack LaRough gave Jess when Lila was a baby. Stubby and Lila dug holes together in the backyard, and when Lila fell in them, Stubby grabbed hold of her dress with his teeth and pulled her out.

A few years later, we had one unusual pet: a wild raven that Jess brought home as a baby from its nest. The kids named him Jim and treated him like one of the family. Jess built a roost for Jim in the shed. He loved to sit on the kids' shoulders and walk around with them. We kept his wings clipped so he couldn't fly too far, but one day he got on a neighbor's roof and they shot him.

It was hard on us when something happened to our pets because we felt the loss so keenly. Then I would say, "This is the last time. No more pets." The kids would look at me with swollen eyes and tear-streaked cheeks and not really believe me. Somehow, no matter what I said, we always got another dog or more kittens, but Jim was the only pet raven we ever had.

When I look back it seems to me that Jess and I spent a lot of our time at the dining room table while the children were tucked away in their beds, talking for hours on how we could fix up the old house and make it better. We were either talking about the improvements or doing the work ourselves. I would look at the walls we had papered so often, the floors we had sanded and painted, the curtains I had made, the cupboards Jess had built, and I realized that our whole life together was wrapped up in those walls.

So much of our happiness and heartache, laughter and tears went into that house, trying to make it better, trying to make it bigger for our growing family to enjoy. Every improvement in the house was a special landmark, a sign of accomplishment, of getting ahead. When I looked at the washing machine, still sitting in the same spot against the wall in the kitchen, I couldn't help but smile. I had been old-fashioned enough to think it wouldn't wash the clothes clean enough, but it had served me well, and after four children it was still going strong.

There was the hand pump and the 50-gallon drum which we had painted inside and out with white enamel. And there was my prize possession, a new Lang stove, another one of Jess's surprises. It was a brand-new stove, mind you, not second-hand. It had lots of gleaming chrome and a warming oven on top. It was a big improvement over the old iron stove, which was parked in the back yard until Jess hauled it away.

I remember all those Saturday nights when Jess got out the old washtub and put it in the middle of the kitchen floor, and the girls took their baths within the warmth of the stove. How could I ever forget the time Lila got out of the tub and backed into the stove, leaving the "Lang" imprint on her wet bottom?

Sometimes my heart just overflowed with joy when I looked at this special place we called home. We had so little of the material things, but yet we had so much.

During the first 10 years we made many changes in the old house. Those changes were usually prompted by a new addition to the family, and 1921 was no exception. When Jess Jr. was just a few months old, I became pregnant again.

Once again Jess and I sat down with a pencil and paper at the dining room table to make a plan. Our fifth child would be born in November and we had to make room for him—we just knew it was going to be a boy now that we had broken the jinx.

After sizing up the old house, Jess and I decided to build an extra

Jim, the pet raven, with the children. This is 1928; by then George and Beth had arrived. From left—George, Jess Jr., Bobbie Ginther, June and Beth.

bedroom alongside the kitchen to fill in the ell where the living room wall jutted out. We bought two-by-fours of culled lumber and went to work on the foundation. It was early summer, giving us plenty of time to finish the room before the baby was born.

As soon as Jess got home from work at night, he started pounding nails. After dinner I helped him, working late into the evening, thanks to the long hours of sunlight. As the summer days flew by, the little room took shape. Soon we had the frame up and the walls in; the roof was slanted like the kitchen, making the room very low at one end. The kitchen window was cut larger for a doorway into the new room. Heat from the kitchen stove would provide enough warmth. The outside of the building was covered with tarpaper, which was not very attractive, but that was all we could afford.

While we were in the middle of this building project Jess came home one Saturday night saying, "I invited a young man for Sunday dinner. His name is Olaus Murie. He just came to town to study caribou migration around the country for the U.S. Biological Survey."

"That's fine, Jess," I said. Jess was famous for bringing home company, but I never minded. It gave me a chance to meet new people. We didn't have fancy meals, but we always had enough food and room for one more.

Olaus and Jess hit it off right away and became lifetime friends. They had many of the same interests and could talk for hours about their experiences with wild animals and their theories on animal habitats, mating, reproduction and migration. Since they were both hard-headed Norwegians, they didn't agree on everything, but they both learned from each other.

So many times while I was working in the kitchen I would look in on Jess and Olaus, seated at the dining room table, deep in conversation. Close at hand they always had a cup of Ghirardelli's chocolate mixed with canned milk and sugar. They liked to eat it that way, first by spoon, and then adding hot water to drink it down.

Olaus was tall and slender, like Jess, and walked in the same loose-jointed way, as if he were forever stalking animals in the woods. Olaus's blond hair was brushed back from his square face. He had deep-set blue eyes and a prominent Norwegian nose. I had never met anyone as shy and withdrawn as Olaus, but once he and Jess started talking, Olaus came alive; then he was a different person.

We both liked Olaus (and the children adored him) so we invited him to stay with us between his trips out of town. On those occasions he bunked on the couch in the living room. I think our noisy house was a shock to him at first. It wasn't long before he seemed to thrive on the bustle and activity, such a contrast to the quiet, scholarly life he had led.

Olaus came at just the right time for us. He pitched in and helped paper the new room, which became Jess's and my bedroom. At long last we did away with the wall-bed in the dining room.

In our room we covered the floor with methoid roofing paper and then we painted the floor maroon, mixing it with a little Fels Naptha soap at someone's suggestion. That paint job lasted longer than any we ever had.

When Olaus needed a team of dogs for his expeditions out of town, Jess helped him select the animals and train them. We kept those dogs, and many more to come, in our back yard, which sometimes took on the appearance of a zoo as well as a junkyard.

The Neilson family at the Rust house in 1921.

Jess continued to bring home old pieces of equipment which he intended to fix, but never did.

In the years that followed, Olaus became a world authority on elk, in addition to being a nationally recognized wildlife artist and writer. Before he passed away in 1963, Olaus was director of the Wilderness Society.

Jess was just itching to play the matchmaker between Olaus and our dear Mardy, who was attending her first year of college at Simmons, near Boston. "I have just the girl for you, Olaus. You just wait and see," Jess promised.

It took two years for them to meet.

When winter came in 1921 the new room was finished, covered with tarpaper and standing stark, like a sore thumb, in the white snow of the yard. I had harvested our garden and made winter clothes for the children. Mother Madole came to our rescue, as always, with knitted sweaters, wool slacks and skirts. Just before the baby was born, Mother left for a cooking job.

On November 10, our fifth child was born in the old house. A boy! Another boy! Jess and I could hardly believe our good fortune. Now Jess Jr. would have a brother. We named him George Franklin. Dr. McCollum had again made the delivery. My nurse, Mrs. John Burnette, stayed on several days to help take care of the children.

Lila, who was now 9 years old, was a big help to me. She was a serious child, though, as if all the troubles in the world rested on her little thin shoulders. Her sister Cora, a year younger, was just the opposite—a lively, happy-go-lucky child with her father's brand of humor—always up to some mischievous prank.

Our June, who was 4 years old when George was born, was my little daydreamer. She would wander around in circles until I told her what to do. The two older girls liked to pick on her until they made her cry. Thankfully, little Jess was a good baby, and I was grateful for that now that I had the fifth one to care for.

Before George was born, I took baby Jess off the bottle and started potty training him, only to find that he was as stubborn as his father. George was trained before Jess Jr. finally learned to obey. By today's methods I suppose we were wrong to paddle Jess to train him, but washing diapers for two babies in my household was not easy. Necessity is not always the mother of invention.

Fortunately Jess was good about helping with the children, even in those days before it was fashionable for a man to take on those responsibilities. It amazed me at how different each of our children were. They had their own unique and special personalities, as well as looks, but still there were those basic similarities that bound us together as a family.

Two new babies, almost within 15 months, put serious strains on our budget. We were no longer making ends meet; we were going into debt every month. One night Jess and I got into a loud argument about it.

"You are going to have to cut down," he said, as if that would solve our problem.

"Cut down," I said. "Where do you suggest I cut down?"

"I don't know what you do with the money, but it isn't going to last much longer the way you spend it."

I burst into tears; I couldn't help it. Jess could be so unreasonable sometimes. We had two more mouths to feed on the same salary we had before Jess Jr. and George were born. It was impossible. I was never extravagant or wasteful with Jess's money, and he knew that as well as I did.

The lack of money plagued us most of our life together. I was sick and tired of going without, too. How did he think I liked scrimping and cutting down all the time, buying furniture second-hand and going without new clothes?

I was the first to admit that Jess worked hard and that it must be discouraging to him that we never got ahead, but it wasn't easy on me either. I yelled those and other things at Jess until he walked out of the house. I spent an hour feeling sorry for myself and another one getting mad. Why I'd show that Jess Rust, just see if I wouldn't.

I went to the telephone and called Nina O'Gara at the American Hand Laundry. We were both members of the Eagles Ladies Club. One time she told me that if I ever needed a job to call her.

"Do you still want me to work for you?" I asked.

"Hell, yes," she said in that brusque, down-to-earth way she had of talking. "When can you start?"

I agreed to start the following week. She said, "Now, I don't want you coming to work for a month or so and then quitting. If I'm going to train you, I want you to stay a year."

At that point I would have signed away the rest of my life. I agreed to stay the year. Jess was as mad as a hornet when I told him what I'd done, but it was too late to turn back.

Going to work with five children at home to cook and clean for was not easy. In fact, during those first few weeks, I wasn't sure I was going to make it. I worked 5 days a week, 10 hours a day. I had to be at work at seven in the morning, which meant Jess had to get the older children ready for school before he went to work. Lila and Cora were to take the two babies to the sitter's house in the morning and pick them up on the way home from school.

I walked the 12 blocks to work every day, winter and summer, through the rain, through the mud, through the snowdrifts, wind and 50-below-zero temperatures. Often when Jess got off work at 5 o'clock he came to the laundry, on Third Avenue behind the Nordale Hotel, and we walked home together, two mighty tired people whose day wasn't yet over. By the time we got home everybody was hungry, just crying for dinner.

For a whole year I went to bed tired and got up tired, over and over again, as if I were on a big merry-go-round and I couldn't get off. When I first started, my job was to sort the laundry at the front counter, marking each garment and piece of linen with an identifying mark before taking it to the washer. Behind the counter was a wall of cubicles where we stacked the laundry after it was washed, pressed and folded. Then on Friday night I helped wrap the bundles of clean laundry in paper, pulling the lengths off a huge roll, fastening them with string from a large ball that hung from the high ceiling. Mr. O'Gara gathered the bundles into his Plymouth sedan and made deliveries on Saturdays.

The American Hand Laundry was housed in a two-story frame building owned by Bob Bloom, with storefront windows and an apartment upstairs where Jack and Nina lived, and where he made home-brew which he served to his friends when they came visiting in the afternoon. On Friday, when we worked late to get all the laundry out for the weekend, Nina cooked a big dinner for the employees and we ate upstairs at midday. I always looked forward to the day she served corned beef and cabbage. It was the best I ever tasted.

Nina, with her brownish-gray hair twisted back in a bun, was stout, with round, red cheeks and a temper that flared fast like a bonfire, and she swore like a trooper. We learned to stay on the good side of her, as did her lanky husband, Jack. Nina was a worker, and she expected the girls to keep up with her. They were a jolly bunch, those girls I worked with, and the spirit of camaraderie and cooperation made the long days pass easier. There was always work stacked up for us; we never seemed to get ahead of that mountain of laundry. When the bags full of napkins and tablecloths came in from the Model Cafe, and when the dozens of towels came in from the barbershops and hotels, we pitched in and got the job done.

The only thing in the laundry that really bothered me was the heat. In order to be somewhat comfortable while working, I wore sleeveless and collarless dresses, changing before I came home at night. There was a bath and shower room in the building, which I was free to use. That was a big help to me with our primitive, bath-by-the-stove arrangement at home.

Mrs. O'Gara let employees wash their own linens, along with the regular laundry loads. That saved me time and work at home. All the linens, including the towels, went through the mangle with one girl feeding the machine and another girl folding.

It was Jack O'Gara's job to keep the fires fed. There was a large furnace downstairs to heat the building and the water tanks. In the drying room, which was bigger than my entire house, was an airtight heater that operated at full capacity. Whenever I went in there, the damp heat nearly took my breath away.

Along one wall in the main room of the laundry were five square windows with an ironing board in front of each window where the girls stood, hour after hour, ironing the starched shirts. After I had worked a couple of months I was "promoted" to hand-washing the silk lingerie of the girls off the Line and the silk shirts and pajamas of the miners and gamblers. There I was, back on the scrubboard. For that I earned 75 cents an hour. It doesn't sound like much now, but I wondered how we ever managed without it.

Even though I was working and had very little spare time, I still tried to take part in the Eagles Club activities and amateur stage shows. In that respect I guess I was like my mother. The clubs needed volunteers, and it was always the busiest women who got the work done.

One Sunday in February 1922, I was rushing around trying to get the housework done and the dinner ready so I could get to the Eagles Hall to practice for a minstrel show. I put a dishpan of water on the stove to heat so I could scrub the kitchen floor before we ate. The three girls, Lila, Cora and June, came bursting in the front door, home from Sunday School and complaining of how hungry they were.

I was on my hands and knees scrubbing the floor and could not stop to fix them anything. Little George, tied in the small rocking chair, was in the kitchen with me so I could rock him while I cooked dinner.

"Well, go down in the basement and get an apple for yourself and your sisters," I told Lila. "That should tide you over until dinner."

I lifted the trap door that was cut in the floor between the kitchen and the dining room. While I stood guard, Lila went down the narrow wooden stairs to the root cellar; June and Cora were in the living room with little Jess and a neighbor boy. Just then the telephone rang.

"Jess, you'll have to get that," I hollered. "I can't leave the trap door."

The children in the living room were making so much noise that Jess couldn't hear on the phone. He motioned to the kids to be quiet, or to get out of the room. At that moment 5-year-old June came dancing from the living room into the dining room, and before I could grab her she fell through the trap door into the basement. I ran down the stairs to get her, and as I was carrying her limp body up the stairs, I saw Jess Jr. topple into the pan of hot water.

"Jess! Jess! Jess!" I screamed.

He came running and slammed the trap door shut. June was lying motionless on the floor. I rolled the baby's steaming shirt up his back, which was the wrong thing to do because it concentrated the heat in one area, making the burn worse than ever. But I was so distraught and afraid, I hardly knew what I was doing. All the kids howling around me, and I was blinded by my tears. In my hands was the scalded body of my 2-year-old boy.

Jess took one look at him and said, "Get those clothes off."

With shaking fingers I peeled off the wet clothes. While I put olive oil and baking soda on the baby's blisters, Jess called Lila Shafer for help. She came running and took June to her house. Thankfully, our little girl got through the mishap without any broken bones, although she was badly bruised.

In those years Fairbanks did not have a clinic. There were only two doctors to take care of all the people in town. At the time of Jess's accident, our doctor was out of town, so we had to call the one that was available. When I first contacted him, it was 1:30 in the afternoon.

"I will be there soon," the doctor said.

"Please hurry," I begged.

Two hours passed, and there was no sign of the doctor. Little Jess writhed in pain. We could hardly hold him down. It broke my heart to hear his pitiful cries and to see the suffering on his small face.

I called the doctor again. "You have to come right now," I said. "My baby is in great pain."

"Keep calm," he advised. "Now, what happened?"

After I told him for the second time, he promised he would come as soon as he could. Our vigilance continued. While I stood over the baby's bed, Jess paced the living room floor, watching the road for the first sign of the doctor. An hour passed. Then two. By this time the baby had become quieter, making only small whimpers as he twisted his head back and forth. I watched helplessly, afraid he was dying before my eyes.

"We can't go on like this much longer," I said to Jess.

"Call that doctor again," he said.

When I called for the third time I no doubt sounded hysterical, because by then I was. The doctor acted as if I was some mother getting excited about a little burn and interrupting his Sunday at home. He started telling me how I could treat the burn, naming medications we did not have in the house.

"Doctor, my baby needs help right now," I said, interrupting him. "I have four children, and I know what I am talking about. If there was another doctor in town, believe me, I would call him."

By the time the doctor finally arrived, it was nine o'clock at night. We had waited eight hours for him to respond to our call. Later we learned that the doctor and his wife had been entertaining guests, and they went to a movie after dinner. For that we waited all those agonizing hours while our baby suffered.

As soon as the doctor put his foot in the door, Jess burst out, "What in the hell took you so long?"

There was no time for arguments. The doctor took one look at little Jess and called the hospital. "Have a room ready right away. I am bringing in an emergency burn victim." He turned to me and said, "Why didn't you tell me how bad it was?"

"I tried, but you wouldn't listen."

Very quickly I wrapped our baby in a sheet and soft blanket. His little body was racked with spasms of pain. Jess carried him to the doctor's car and we rode, without speaking, along the slippery streets to St. Joseph's Hospital.

Many times within the next few hours it looked as if the end was near. The doctor prescribed a teaspoonful of whiskey every 15 minutes to keep the baby revived. I fed him the liquor, sitting by his bedside all night.

At one point the nurse said, "Doctor, there is no more whiskey."

It was Prohibition and Fairbanks was dry.

"I wish I knew where I could get some moonshine," the doctor said. "Some of that stuff is top quality."

Jess headed for the door. "I know where I can get some," he said. "I did a favor once for a bootlegger when the Feds were after him."

Jess made a telephone call, and within an hour, two bottles of moonshine were delivered to the hospital, free of charge.

For two days and two nights I never left the baby's side. Jess took time out to run home and take care of the girls and put in his shift at Northern Commercial Company. It was a week before the doctor pronounced Jess Jr. out of danger. I was off work during that time, but when I started back, Nina let me take an hour off in the afternoon to visit my baby.

From the first moment of the accident, I felt it was my fault. If I hadn't been in such a hurry, taking on too many things, it never would have happened. I should have been more careful. I went over every detail in my mind, again and again, thinking if only . . . if only I had done things differently. I almost made myself ill thinking about it.

During the six weeks Jess Jr. was in the hospital, he became the nurses' pet. They gave him so much attention that by the time he got home, I felt swamped by all his extra demands on my time.

For several months we had to take Jess Jr. to the hospital to have the bandages changed. At first the doctor drove us in his car, and then Lila and Cora took him over in the buggy, along the wooden sidewalks.

The doctor, regretting his neglect, did not charge us for his services. When our doctor returned to town he was upset that no skin grafts had been made on the baby's badly scarred legs and back. By then it was too late. Jess Jr. suffered much pain from those scars, which he carries to this day.

After the accident we decided that the trap door in the floor must go. We would build an entrance to the basement outside the house. Jess removed part of the banking and dug under the bottom log. There he installed a stairway and built a small room where we put a chemical toilet with a ventilator going out through the roof. How modern we were! No more going down the path to the little house with the half-moon cut in the door.

Now the only problem was that Jess had to carry the buckets up the stairs and out to the backyard. In winter he stashed them behind the fence and when spring came, he dug a hole and buried them.

Jess also bought a second-hand sink, which was hung on the kitchen wall, with a bucket under it. Then, tired of carrying out those slop buckets, Jess started digging a cesspool in the back yard. It was two years before it was finished, but at least the end was in sight.

 **chapter 19**

I remember well July 16, 1923. First, it was the hottest day in the history of Fairbanks. The temperature reached 105 degrees. The sun stung down out of a sheer blue sky that was totally cloudless. The heat shimmered off the muddy water of the Chena in blinding pinpoints of light. The few downtown concrete sidewalks (that were slowly replacing the wooden ones) were hot enough to fry eggs on, or so I thought as I stood on Cushman Street with George in the buggy waiting for the parade to begin. Cora and Lila, all dressed in white and carrying American flags, stood with the schoolchildren at the foot of the bridge.

There were hundreds of people lining the streets. For the first time in the history of Alaska, a president of the United States was visiting the Territory. The occasion was the completion of the Alaska Railroad from Seward to Fairbanks. President and Mrs. Warren Harding, Secretary of Commerce Herbert Hoover and other dignitaries were due to arrive on the train from Nenana where the Golden Spike ceremony had been held.

Fairbanks always loved a celebration, and the one marking the completion of the railroad was no exception. Months before the president was due to arrive, our mayor, Tom Marquam, initiated a tree-planting project to show our visitors that "Seward's Folly" was not an icebox. Everyone in town got busy planting birch trees along the parade route up to the Weeks Field ballpark, where a grandstand had been erected for speeches and ceremonies.

All the car owners were asked to meet the train and help transport the dignitaries to the ballpark. George Preston, manager of the N.C. store, had a new Dodge open touring car which he let

Jess drive to chauffeur Herbert Hoover and his assistants. After the ceremonies President Harding and his party were taken by car 70 miles out the Richardson Highway (named after Major W. P. Richardson, President of the Alaska Road Commission) to the Richardson Roadhouse for a dinner of roast moose, bear, caribou, Alaska king salmon and wild berries. The Richardson, which was originally the Valdez-Fairbanks Trail, was open to motor vehicles in the summer.

Once the Alaska Railroad was in operation, linking us with the port city of Seward, Fairbanks was never the same again. Our quiet town, which had been buried in winter isolation and cut off from the outside world, was entering a new era. There was talk that the Fairbanks Exploration Company (F.E.) would soon begin placer mining in Fairbanks, bringing money, engineers and gold dredges, with consequent work for our men. The railroad, with cheaper freight rates, would make it possible. The lean years were over.

About this time there was in Fairbanks a man named Carl Ben Eielson, an aviator and stunt pilot, who was teaching science at the Fairbanks High School. A group of Fairbanks men became interested in aviation and bought a Jenny airplane, which Ben used for exhibitions. These dazzling displays took place at Weeks Field ballpark, not far from our house.

In 1924 some businessmen in town bought a DeHavilland plane with a Liberty engine. This plane was not for entertainment only. Men with foresight, including Jimmy Rodebaugh, who was a conductor for the Alaska Railroad, realized that the plane would open up the vast regions of Alaska.

In the spring of that year, Ben Eielson made a trial run to McGrath, 280 miles from Fairbanks. The idea was to check out the possibility of providing mail service to that community which was then receiving mail by dog sled in the winter and sternwheeler in the summer. When Ben returned to Fairbanks after flying to McGrath, darkness had fallen. People waiting at the field were asked to turn on their headlights to light the field. That was a big mistake; the lights blinded Ben and he had a difficult time landing. Nevertheless, the flight was successful and the post office awarded the mail contract.

On the day of the first official mail flight to McGrath, there was a large crowd at the field to see Ben off, including a Pathe news crew who had come to Fairbanks to film the event.

Jess, who was grooming a team of Victorian Land Huskies for one of Olaus's expeditions, was asked to bring the team to the airfield so the Pathe men could get a picture of the old and new mail delivery methods. Jess was so proud to be in the picture that he didn't mind hitching up the team at 5 o'clock in the morning. I was so excited that I went out to the field with him. Later we saw the film at the movie house, and other pictures of Jess and the team in newspapers and magazines.

Not long after that a young man by the name of Noel Wien came to town to work for Jimmy Rodebaugh, who had formed the Alaska Aerial Transportation Company. During the summer of 1924 Noel flew a Hisso Standard from Fairbanks to Anchorage. He was the first pilot to make that trip. Since no maps existed at that time, he followed the railroad tracks.

Noel was soon joined in Fairbanks by his older brother, Ralph, who was a mechanic. Ralph was hired by the N.C. to help Jess deliver coal to the powerhouse, which was no longer burning wood. Noel taught Ralph to fly, and they were joined by their brothers Fritz and Sigurd. After the Wien brothers were flying commercially for several years, Noel went into business, forming Wien Airways of Alaska, which has developed into a multimillion-dollar business.

When I looked around, it seemed as if everything was changing, and yet many things stayed the same. I had put in my year at the laundry and I was happy to be home with my family again.

Now there was time to work in the yard and develop the beds of native flowers, shrubs and trees I loved so. From the Experiment Station I learned which wild plants could be transplanted and cultivated. When Jess went on fishing trips he dug up varieties like the baby orchid and wild crocus and brought them home.

In the front yard were beds of wild white and yellow daisies, and violets—both blue and white—that came up every year. The columbine in yellow, purple and cerise bloomed profusely. Then there was the lovely lupine and larkspur and lady slippers.

Along the fence grew the wild rose bushes whose small, saucer-shaped flowers attracted swarms of bees in June and July. The yellow Arctic poppy, which was prevalent along the roadways, was another perennial. Close to the house, under the shade of the roof, I planted the fiddleneck ferns we had tracked down in the swampy bogs. Wild spirea and cinquefoil provided flowering bushes against the house.

In the fall the leaves of the plants and berries (I also had dogwood and cranberry) turned rich tapestry colors, ruby red and deep wine. We had three kinds of spruce trees, tamarack (which lost its needles in the fall) and several kinds of willow. I remember one weeping willow which had fuzzy little "pussies" in the spring that turned into the prettiest yellow flowers.

On our hunting expeditions we not only brought home flowers, but rocks too. I was fascinated by the multitude of colors and surfaces. "Mother and her rocks" became a family joke. Sometimes our boat was loaded to the danger level with them. I used them to encircle the flower beds and to march along the boundary of the lawn where a constant battle raged between me and the crabgrass. When I ran out of places to put the rocks, I built a wall.

One week we took Mardy and Olaus on a boat trip upriver and that's where Jess's matchmaking began to pay off. In the fall Mardy went to Reed College in Oregon, and later she and Olaus were engaged. When Olaus's brother Adolph, who was also a biologist,

At a camp upriver, Olaus Murie teaches the children how to draw pictures of fungi. Seated from left: Olaus, Lila, Edson Moody, Cora and June. Standing: Clara (left) and Mabel Moore.

joined him, the two men rented Mother Madole's cabin on Second Avenue. Mother Madole, who was still working in Kodiak, had divorced Fred Meyers.

During the 1920's the Fairbanks Exploration Company (F.E.), a subsidiary of the U.S. Smelting, Refining and Mining Company, set up large-scale operations in Fairbanks, making Garden Island their headquarters. Gold dredges began operating at Fox and Cleary. Under construction was the Davison Ditch, one of the largest pipeline projects in the world, to bring water from the headwaters of the Chatanika River to the gold fields.

Due to the improved mining activity, a highway system was developed with the Steese linking Fairbanks with Circle City, 135 miles to the north, and the Elliott to Livengood, 80 miles to the east. More and more cars were seen on the streets of Fairbanks, replacing horse-drawn wagons and dog sleds.

With the influx of mining and railroad personnel, a new social strata was introduced. The F.E. Company built a two-story office building in Garden Island as well as a number of stately homes—some with verandas and gabled windows—for their executives. Many of the Fairbanks elite constructed new homes, frame structures of imported lumber, to replace the log dwellings. They installed furnaces in the basement, an electrical system and indoor plumbing, and decorated the houses with the finest of carpets and furniture. It cost as much to ship an expensive item as it did an inexpensive one, so "buy the best" was the prevailing philosophy.

After spring breakup in 1926, when the roads had dried, Jess decided it was time I learned to drive. We had use of Claude Denny's car while he was Outside. One evening after work Jess and I started out. What a disaster! I advise every woman not to let her husband teach her how to drive. Jess was so impatient with me that I was in tears all the time.

With just a few vague explanations about how the car worked, Jess thought I should be able to get right in and take off. He never bothered to tell me exactly how the gears worked or how I should shift.

"Push the handle down!" he would holler. "Now push the handle up! Step on the gas. No! Step on the brakes!"

"I give up," I yelled. "I am never going driving with you again." Every time we went out in the car it was like that. But I wanted to learn to drive so badly that I swallowed my pride and put up with Jess's swearing and sarcasm.

One day, nervous as a cat and not really knowing what I was doing, I ventured out alone in the car. I was going to lick this driving business if it was the last thing I did. I took a firm grip on the wheel and started off. Somehow I managed to guide that car down the street without running into anything. Of course I killed the motor more than once, but I kept trying, and finally I gained the confidence I needed.

About this time I knew I was pregnant. Jess was pleased and said, "We have three girls and two boys; now we can make it even." Here we were, hoping for a boy again. I wasn't as happy about the event as Jess; in fact I was mad at myself for being so careless. Fourteen-year-old Lila surprised me by her reaction. "Oh, Mother," she said accusingly, "why did you do it? Now Cora and I will be tied down to babysitting again. Oh, Mother!"

That year was an eventful one for the family, with good times and bad. We received news that our old friend Sam Jensen the boatbuilder had passed away at a hot spring near Fairbanks. He and Jess had spent many hours together building dog sleds and riverboats. Our two boys, Jess and George, used to visit Sam and go swimming in the slough near his house. Sam always invited the boys in for milk and sandwiches. Our friendship with Sam was a special one, but still we were surprised to learn that he had left all his cash to Jess and me. When the estate was settled, we received $550 each.

"Just imagine, Jess," I said, "we have never had $1,100 in all our lives."

"It seems like a million," he said. "Now we can get out from under some of these debts."

We were sitting at our favorite place, at the dining room table. The house was quiet with sleeping children. "Well, Jess," I said, chewing on my pencil. "I have an idea."

"What's that?" he said, leaning back in his chair.

"Let's buy a car."

"A car!" he exploded.

"Yes, a car. A brand-new car."

"You must have lost your senses," he said, thumping his chair on the floor. "Do you know how much it costs to run a car?"

"No."

"I didn't think so," he said. "It's like having a baby. The original investment isn't much; it's the upkeep that gets you."

"It seems everyone in town has a car but us," I said. "The Clausens and Hunters have a car, also the Petersons and the Kramers. This is probably the only time in our lives we will ever have enough money to buy a new car."

"A brand-new car!" Jess exploded again. "Did you say a brand-new car?"

I guess I looked a little downcast because Jess came around and gave me a hug. "You mean a car like this?" he said, whipping out a colored brochure of the Dodge cars that were sold at Northern Commercial Company.

"Oh, Jess, you were pulling my leg." That Jess, he knew me better than anybody, and I still fell for his tricks.

I guess we pored over that brochure for hours. We finally decided on a Dodge Star open touring car in a beautiful shade of blue. It cost $780.

After we put the order in at the N.C. there was that agonizing wait for it to be shipped up from Outside. I think we were more eager for the arrival of the car than we were for the new baby.

Right away Jess converted the old chicken house into a garage. The day he got word that our car was at the depot, ready for pickup, he did not tell me. That afternoon he came home, sober as a judge, and said, "The car is here."

I wiped my hands on a dishtowel and stared at him. "Well, what's wrong with it?"

"You won't like the color."

"What color is it?"

"It isn't the color we ordered."

I blew my top. "I might have known our first car wouldn't be what we wanted. Why couldn't they just send what we ordered? Well, I don't care if you do work for the N.C.; if I don't like the car, then you will have to send it back." After this ranting and raving, I saw the twinkle in Jess's eyes. I whipped off my apron and ran out the door.

Behold! A shiny new car was standing in the yard. It was a lovely shade of blue.

"Oh, Jess! It is beautiful," I cried.

Our kids—and half the neighborhood—came running to see this wonderful gift. We all piled in and Jess took us on a ride around the block. I gave a little prayer of thanks to Sam, and hoped he knew how much happiness he provided our family.

All the excitement about the car took place at the same time Mardy and Olaus returned to town. They had married after she graduated from the University of Alaska in 1924. While they were Outside Mardy gave birth to a fine boy, whom they named Martin.

For several months Olaus had been corresponding with Jess to enlist his help in preparing a 4-month expedition he and Mardy were going to take up the Yukon, Porcupine and Old Crow rivers into Canada to observe the mating habits of ducks and geese. They asked Jess to go with them as a guide and riverboat captain. After he got permission from his boss, Jess had reservations about leaving me alone to have the baby.

"Don't worry about me, Jess," I said. "I will be fine, and I think the trip will be good for you."

"I was with you when all the babies were born, and I hate to leave you alone this time."

"There is nothing to worry about," I said. "I am going to the hospital for this one."

With that Jess and Olaus threw themselves heart and soul into getting ready for the trip. They overhauled the riverboat and built a small barge to carry the equipment and supplies. The list of things to buy grew longer. Mardy and I were the errand girls running all over town in the new blue car.

Even though everyone tried to discourage Mardy from taking 9-month-old Martin with her, she would not give up the idea. Jess fixed a traveling pen for the baby and a harness so he could not crawl out of the boat.

It was a warm, sunny day in May 1926 when the boat and barge was launched in the Chena. Friends lined the riverbank to wish the travelers bon voyage. Their journey of several thousand miles was about to begin. As soon as the boat was out of sight around the bend, a terrible feeling of loneliness hit me, and I could hardly control my tears.

"What is wrong, Mama," Lila said, taking my hand.

"Oh, nothing. I will be all right," I said, brushing the tears away. When I saw the sad faces of my five children worried about their mother, I said, "I know. Let's go on a picnic."

"Oh, boy. Let's go to a gravel pit so we can swim," said Jess Jr.

It was a good way for all of us to spend the day. We would do fine while Jess was gone, I knew that, but it was the first time in 16 years of marriage that we would be separated for several months.

During that time I got ambitious and decided to fix up the old house to surprise Jess when he returned. Tom Pierson, a local carpenter, agreed to put a larger window in place of the small one in the living room. Then I had him cut a long, narrow window on the side wall, which gave the room more daylight, but then it showed up the faded wallpaper. How one thing does lead to another!

The paperhanger, Slim Heiges, came to hang the pretty, light-patterned paper in the living room and dining room. When he was finished, it looked so nice that I had him put fresh paper in both bedrooms. I knew I was spending too much money, but the results were so splendid, I could not help myself.

Once the walls were bright and clean, then the old flooring looked worse than ever. I ordered enough Congoleum to do the four rooms. After waiting in vain for Pete Deiser to lay it, I decided to do the floors myself. Time was getting short, and I wanted to have all the work done before I went to the hospital.

One afternoon I was down on my hands and knees measuring and cutting the floor covering when my two neighbors, Barbara Wehner and Sylvia Ringstad, stopped by.

"Clara, what in the world are you doing?" Barbara cried.

"Laying the floor."

"You can't do that in your condition," Sylvia said.

"Yes, I can," I said.

"But the baby is due any day," Barbara said.

"I know," I agreed. "That is why I have to do it now."

They both pitched in and helped me, and came back the next day to finish the job. After that Cora, Lila and I painted the woodwork and hung new curtains. How fresh and clean the house looked! We were so proud of our work. I splurged further and ordered a bed-style davenport for the living room so we would have an extra bed when the Muries came to visit.

August can be an extremely hot month, and so it was in 1926. The day was hot and humid when I went to the hospital to have my sixth child, and I was one uncomfortable gal. This was the first baby I had had away from home, and the first one without the help of Dr. McCollum. I was apprehensive, but Dr. Sutherland, an old family friend, gave me confidence. The delivery was not difficult, but after the birth an infection set in, and I had to stay in the hospital 9 days.

We did not get the boy we wanted to make the family "even." Since Jess and I had not picked out a name for the baby, I asked the children to name their new little sister.

Lila, who had been so opposed to the new baby, fell in love with the little one and said, "Let's name her after Aunt Beth."

"Oh, yes," Cora agreed. "Let's call her Elizabeth Frances."

My sister and her husband, John Francis, were living in California. After her marriage we began corresponding and became acquainted again through our letters. She had two boys, both older than mine, and she sent us their outgrown clothing. At Christmas Beth sent wonderful gifts. We looked forward to her packages that were exquisitely wrapped and held surprises of nuts and candies.

When Beth was born, Jess was hundreds of miles away in the village of Old Crow. He did not receive the doctor's telegram until he reached Fort Yukon on his return trip.

In early September I received a telephone call from Jess in Nenana. He and the Muries were planning to put their gear on the train for Fairbanks. The night they arrived, the kids and I met them at the depot. We stayed up past midnight talking about their trip. Jess told how the crankshaft broke on the motor and he and Olaus had to pole hundreds of miles upriver; how they were nearly eaten alive by the mosquitoes, and how the Native women loved blond-haired Martin. It took weeks before we were caught up on everything that happened.

After a week's rest the Muries left for Michigan, where Olaus did postgraduate work at the university. Then, wouldn't you know it, our davenport arrived. It was a beautiful thing in delft blue tapestry, our very first piece of new furniture.

It gave us additional sleeping capacity, which we needed with the new baby in the house. After a bit of musical beds we got everyone situated. Lila and Cora took our bedroom, and we put the baby in the room with the three bunk beds. That meant Jess and I were sleeping in the living room on the davenport, but at least it wasn't a wall bed.

Even though Jess agreed that the house looked much better with the new windows and fresh paint and wallpaper, he was mad at me for spending every penny of our savings on it.

"You shouldn't have done it, Clara," he said. "You know we have been planning to put a second story on the house, and we are going to have to tear up those walls and floors you just had fixed."

"I know, Jess, but I wanted to surprise you."

That was the first time I had undertaken such a major project without talking it over with Jess, and it turned out to be more of a shock than a surprise. In November when Ed Clausen asked me to work at the N.C. during the holidays, I jumped at the chance. That way I would be able to earn money for Christmas and make up for my spending spree. Mrs. McClosky, the marshal's wife, agreed to take care of Beth while I worked.

The N.C. had just put in a line of yard goods and a gift section (which the male employees refused to handle) that included things like English bone china, cut glass, bisque, Pickard and crystal. I couldn't help feeling like a queen bee since I was the first woman to work in Fairbanks's largest store.

For the holidays the N.C. stocked gift baskets that we packed with fresh fruits—oranges, apples, bananas and grapes—that came in by train, as well as packages of hard candy, dates and nuts. A few days before Christmas, Mark Sells, a local tailor and old family friend, came into the store and told me to pick out the biggest basket I had and to fill it with things a family would enjoy.

"Do it up right," he said. "Don't worry about the cost."

While I was working on the basket I thought, what a lucky family to get such a wonderful gift. When I arrived home, the basket was on our kitchen table! The children were so excited; we had never had such a lavish present before. We had that basket for years and years, always filled with fruit and candy at Christmas time. Although the giver of that gift is long gone, I shall never forget the night the basket arrived and the joy it brought our family.

Now that we had a new car we spent our weekends driving the roads rather than boating on the rivers. Our favorite place was Birch Lake, 60 miles from town on the Richardson Highway. I use the word "highway" in the broadest sense. It was a dirt and gravel trail, and in some places it was so narrow that two cars could not pass. The road wound around and over the hills clad in white birch and spruce, crossed rickety, one-way bridges that rattled and shook, and followed many a little slough and stream. In spring it was fender-deep in mud, and in the summer it was a billowing dust bowl. It took us five hours to travel the 60 miles.

The lake was small enough that the ice melted off in early June, yet it was big enough for boating and canoeing. Our favorite spot was on the west side of the lake on a promontory where the beach was soft sand and the water shallow for wading.

As soon as school was out in the spring Jess took us out to the lake, where we set up a summer camp. If the weather stayed reasonably dry, we lived there until fall. We had one tent for sleeping and another for cooking. I cooked on the Yukon stove and over the fireplace, where Jess put up stakes and a bar so we could hang pots. By the time summer was over I could bake beans, corn bread and even cakes in the coals. When Jess came out on weekends he brought food supplies and one or two of the neighbor kids, much to the delight of our brood.

One evening while the birds called from the trees and the ducks were quietly quacking on the mirrorlike lake, the kids and I started talking about how nice it would be to have a cabin on that very spot. It was no sooner said than Lila and I grabbed an ax and saw. We went into the woods where the tall birch and spruce grew, and in no time at all we had felled 12 trees.

All week we worked limbing those logs and hauling them out with a rope tied around our waists. What a tough job that was. We could only move two logs a day even with June and the boys helping us.

By the time Jess drove up the road Friday night we had cleared a wide area on the bluff and the logs were ready to go up. With Jess's help we had three rounds of logs up by Sunday night.

"Don't try and drag out any more logs," Jess said as he left. "You could hurt yourselves that way. I'll pull them out with the car when I come back."

All summer the girls and I spent our spare time cutting and limbing trees. By the time fall came, we had the walls up. The cabin wasn't much to look at, that was for sure. There were open spaces between those crooked logs big enough to throw a cat through, and we got plenty of razzing over that. Since we couldn't afford lumber for the floor and roof, the walls stood alone for a couple of years. We put the tent inside the enclosure for protection.

That was our country house, and like our town house, it had a lot of heart, soul and sweat in it.

chapter 20

In the spring of 1927 we received a telegram from Hilbert Anderson of Kodiak, Mother Madole's new husband. Cora was very ill, he said. They would arrive in Fairbanks by train that week. Hilbert instructed us to have a doctor and nurse meet them at the depot.

"It sounds serious, doesn't it?" I asked Jess.

He nodded solemnly.

Even at that, we were not prepared. Both Jess and I were shocked by Mother's condition. She was so ill she had traveled that long way on a stretcher.

"It is good to be home," she said, clutching my hand. "I had to come back." Her eyes, bright with fever, had dark circles under them. Her once vibrant olive complexion had turned sallow, and there was more gray in her hair than I wanted to see.

Jess and Hilbert helped transport mother across the street to St. Joseph's Hospital. "I want to see the children," she said to me as we left her room.

"Yes, Mother; I will bring them over."

We had never met Hilbert before, but Jess and I found him a pleasant man of simple ways. He was a stockily built fisherman who had lived in Kodiak many years. We invited him to stay with us while he was in town.

That night at dinner Jess asked Hilbert, "How long has Mother been ill?"

"Several months. At the first I had a nurse taking care of her, but one day I came home and found the nurse going out the back door with an armload of your mother's clothes and her fur coat. After that I stayed home and took care of her myself."

"Mother said you have been very good to her," Jess said.

"I hope you will not think badly of me if I leave tomorrow," Hilbert said. "I have been out of work a long time, and I must get back to my boat."

"We understand," I said. "We want to thank you for taking the time to bring her home."

After talking with the doctor, Jess and I knew there was little hope that mother would recover. That week she was in the hospital her condition deteriorated rapidly. It was as if she had used her last reservoir to come home to die. On Easter Sunday in 1927 Mother Madole Anderson passed away at the age of 69 years. She was buried in the small cemetery near the river where my brother Thayne was interred. Her grave is marked Cora Anderson.

Even though we had not been with Mother for several years, both Jess and I felt the loss, knowing she was no longer with us. My life had been greatly influenced by her, and she still lives in my memory. I shall always admire Mother Madole's strength and courage, and my gratitude to her goes on.

As soon as the children were out of school that year, we made plans to spend the summer at Birch Lake. The N.C. was rebuilding their boiler house, and we got permission to take the discarded lumber and windows. The boards, after many years of use, were as black as coal, but they were boards and we needed them for the cabin floor.

We bought enough two-by-fours for the rafters, and we cut three logs for ridgepoles and braces. The only door in the cabin was the one left over from the old house when we remodeled it. The door has this inscription: "Wipe your feet." That dated back to the years when Cora and Lila hung a sign on the door every time they scrubbed the floor. One day Cora took a knife and carved the message in the wood to make it permanent.

For several years we had saved wooden boxes of every size and description. These we split into slats to nail over the gaping cracks inside the cabin. Then we stretched cheesecloth over the logs, and after sizing it, we painted the cloth a light green.

Across the lake was a place where the moss grew luxuriously thick and deep in the woods. One day George and Jess Jr. rowed over to get a load. They were so long in returning that Jess and I began to get worried. Finally we could hear them singing and laughing across the water, but we could not see them until they were almost to shore. What a sight! They had filled the boat so full of moss that they were buried to their ears in the stuff and the boat sat so low in the water I thought they might go under.

"The boat could never sink with all that moss to hold it up," Jess said to quiet my fears.

We used the moss to insulate the cabin, stuffing it in between the logs on the outside and even layering it under the floor. It kept us warm and cozy and didn't cost a penny.

As always Jess's ingenuity was at work when it came to fixing up the cabin. All his life he was building something, making something over, or tearing something apart. He seemed to thrive on that kind of project. There wasn't anything Jess couldn't do. One weekend he installed a row of low cupboards, made out of old gasoline crates, under the side window. In no time at all, he built bunk beds so we had enough sleeping room for the whole family.

Our cabin at the lake was a bit of heaven for our family, and for our many friends who came visiting. Out back in the woods were plenty of cranberry and raspberry bushes where the fruit hung heavy in early fall. Sometimes we rowed across the lake to pick red and black currants, coming home with our precious cargo in time to fire up the old wood stove so I could make jams and jellies.

Jess put a swing between two tall spruce trees and cut the branches off for rungs so the kids could climb to their hearts' content. The girls and I built steps of birch logs down to the water's edge and cut the grass short to discourage the mosquitoes.

With the help of friends, Jess put a large porch across the front of the cabin, using logs from our property. One night when we arrived for the weekend, someone had left a roll of wire screening for our porch. Another time someone left a roll of canvas, which I made into curtains for the porch to protect us when the weather was rainy and cold.

We used the porch for our dining room and outfitted it with a lovely table with drop leaves that Jess made out of a large packing crate, which I painted red. He used gasoline crates to make benches and I painted them green with a red trim. Everyone who saw the benches said, "Oh, I want one." Jess was busy all summer supplying the demand.

When he wasn't working on our lake cabin, Jess was involved in repairing and remodeling our house. For several years we had talked of putting a second story on the house, but we didn't get serious about it until we knew my mother was coming for a visit.

"We must have more room," I told Jess. "I don't see how we can manage without it."

Jess scratched his head and began scribbling plans and figures on a piece of paper. "If I can get Cap Smythe to do the carpentry work, it shouldn't cost too much except for the materials."

"How long do you think it will take?" I asked. "Cap Smythe is pretty slow."

"Oh, it should be finished by the time your mother gets here this summer."

In January of 1928 I went back to work at O'Gara's American Hand Laundry so I could help pay for the remodeling of the house. Since I would be working while Mother was visiting, I wrote her that I would pay her a small wage and buy her clothes if she would take care of baby Beth. She liked the idea and we made plans accordingly.

For a number of years Mother had been living with my sister Beth and her husband and three sons and a daughter in California. Jess

Caribou hunting in the Star, 1929—Clara, Jess and Nina O'Gara.

and I invited her to stay with us as long as she wanted. From Beth's letters I gathered that Mother was an unhappy woman. I knew it would not be easy living with her. It had been almost 20 years since I had seen her, but I felt we were both mature enough to handle whatever might arise.

We didn't have enough money to pay for Mother's trip North, but Beth said she would drive Mother to Seattle to catch the boat bound for Valdez. We agreed to meet Mother with our car and drive her over the trail to Fairbanks. Jess would have his vacation at that time and he could hunt and fish along the way. Mother wrote back that she loved camping and was looking forward to the trip.

As soon as the weather was warm enough, we tore the front porch off the house and put down new logs for a better foundation. Just as I expected, the work went very slowly. Cap Smythe was an old country carpenter, extremely particular, and time meant nothing to him. When we got word that Mother was on her way, we were in a big mess. No matter how hard we tried we would never have the construction finished before she arrived. Nonetheless Jess, Cap and I worked long hours on the house until we had to leave. The children stayed home since there wasn't the room for all of us in the car. We planned to take our time coming back, camping along the way.

When I saw Mother coming down the gangplank, dressed like a doll with her snow-white hair curled so fancy, I wondered if she remembered what it was like to rough it in Alaska. Unfortunately, she didn't. Even though she knew we were going to camp out, she hadn't even brought a warm coat. Our first night on the trail we knew the camping idea had been a mistake. We should have waited until we had enough money for her to travel to Fairbanks by train instead of driving 350 miles over a rough trail.

The Richardson Highway was a narrow, gravel road with many shaky bridges to cross. To make matters worse, the weather was rainy, and the road was thick with mud and riddled with deep holes. Jess and I were in for trouble. Mother was cold and uncomfortable all night.

When Jess stopped to fish the next day, Mother complained about the wet ground, the mosquitoes and the threat of rain. Again that night it rained. Since it was too wet to put up the tent, Jess fixed a place for us in an abandoned roadhouse. Mother didn't like that either because it was dirty and had a bad odor.

As luck would have it, the rain started in again the third night. Jess tried to get Mother to stay at Paxson's Roadhouse, but she wouldn't stay there unless we did, and we didn't have enough money for the three of us, so we continued the long ride straight for home. I knew Jess was disappointed to have his vacation cut short, but he said, "It will give me a few extra days to work on the house."

Looking back I can see how difficult things were for Mother. She was used to modern conveniences, and we had few of them. We still had to pump water into the barrel and carry out the slop buckets. Bathing took place in a rubber tub in the kitchen, and we had to go down the basement stairs to use the chemical toilet. On top of that, the house was in a big mess with the front porch torn off, then the roof, and the constant banging and hammering that went on day after day, week after week.

In order to give Mother a room of her own, Lila and Cora moved out of their bedroom and slept in the dining room, with a screen for privacy. Mother clashed often with the children. One time she refused to come to the dinner table until Lila apologized for something she had said. It was one temper tantrum after another.

By the time we tore the roof off and began building the three bedrooms upstairs, it was late summer. When the weather turned cool Jess hired Tom Pierson to help with the work so we could finish by freezeup.

In order to construct the stairway, we had to tear the bunks out of the children's bedroom. Since Lila and Cora were the oldest, they had to move outdoors and sleep in a tent while the boys slept in the dining room. It became quite cold, with snow on the ground, before the new addition was ready. The girls were so anxious to have a new bedroom that they never complained. Later they told me that there were many nights they were too cold to sleep.

As the days went along Cap Smythe and Tom did not get along too well. Cap had drawn up the plans with Jess so he thought he was the boss. When Jess told Tom to follow Cap's orders, Tom quit. Of course that happened before they got the new roof on. That meant Jess had to take time off from work to help before it got any colder and snowed again.

Both Jess and I knew that Cap had some funny and old-fashioned ideas about house building, but there wasn't much we could do about it. After he tore out the bedroom wall to make the dining room larger, Cap built an elaborate archway of inlaid wood between the dining room and front room. It looked lovely when it was finished, but we were nearly going out of our minds with the construction dragging on and on.

"Jess, how much longer is this going to take?" I asked him one night when we were alone.

"I don't know, Clara. Cap can't be hurried."

"I'm getting tired of this big mess and everything taking so long."

"You'll just have to put up with it," Jess said shortly. "I'm doing all I can. I don't know what more you expect."

I felt myself coming close to tears. I hadn't meant to criticize Jess. We were all on edge, along with being tired, and Jess and I rarely had any time together. Maybe that was what was bothering me.

As the weeks passed, Cap took time out to build a platform landing with rounded stairs and a balustrade so we could go up the stairs from either the dining room or front room. Later the children used the platform for a stage when they put on plays. Under the stairway Cap built a closet and installed a fancy-shaped door, European style, with wide hinges and ornate design.

After the roof was finally on, the upstairs bedrooms began to take shape. There were three rooms up there, each with a clothes closet and an additional cubbyhole for storage space under the eaves.

We gave Mother the large front bedroom that looked out over the street. Cora, June and the two boys shared the long room with a screen to divide them. Cora wanted the room painted green with black trim, of all things. It was a French style, she said.

"Maybe she doesn't like to wash woodwork," was Jess's explanation. "Let the girls have what they want. They have waited long enough."

We all have, I wanted to add, but I held my tongue. With his job at the N.C. and building at home, Jess had been working day and night for several months.

Sixteen-year-old Lila, at long last, had a room of her own, which she promptly painted blue. After I helped the girls paint their rooms and get them in order, Jess and I and baby Beth moved into the bedroom off the kitchen. It was wonderful to have all that extra space. We hardly knew how to act. We had come a long way from the log and lean-to cabin of 1908.

Now that we were settled I thought things might go more smoothly for Mother, but there was no pleasing her. She became very unhappy and stayed in bed all day. Many times Jess had to leave his job, go home, and stoke up the fires before Mother would get up and take care of Beth. She complained often when the girls practiced their piano and violin. Also, having two active boys, Jess Jr., 9 years old, and George, who was a year younger, plus a very vocal baby underfoot, did not add to her well-being. It bothered me when she criticized Lila and Cora because they were good girls, and they were always a big help to me around the house.

During the time Mother lived with us, I served as president of the Pioneer Women of Alaska, a group of women who had lived in Alaska, or the watershed of the Yukon, on or before 1908. Our organization bought an old grocery store near the library on First Avenue, and with the help of the pioneer men, we remodeled it for use as a meeting hall. There we entertained with teas and card parties, and once a year we gave an open house reception for the townspeople.

When the president went out of office she was given a choice of a gift or a $50 check. When my time came, I wanted one of the new Hoosier kitchen cabinets that had just come into the stores. They were gray enamel with cupboards and shelves above and below, as well as a white enamel work board that could be extended. There was a flour bin—with a sifter—a sugar bin, drawers for cutlery, and a tin-lined breadbox with a sliding cover.

The night the cabinet arrived, Mother and I were on our way to a neighbor's house for supper and a card party, so we left the cabinet sitting in the middle of the kitchen floor. I hadn't quite figured out where I wanted to put it.

During the evening Lila called me at the neighbor's. "What time will you and Grandma be coming home?" she asked. "I wondered if I could go out a little while."

"No," I answered sharply. "You stay home. We are going to be quite late." I was a little provoked with her for calling me.

When Mother and I got home that night the lights in the garage and in the kitchen were blazing bright.

"What in the world is going on in here?" I asked as I opened the back door.

"Surprise!" said Lila and Cora.

All on their own they had transformed the kitchen into a different room. They had sawed off the top of the old cupboard, covered it with new oilcloth and placed it under the window. The shining new

Clara's mother, Mrs. Hickman, with George, Cora and June during a visit to Fairbanks in 1928. The Godski house is in the background.

cabinet sat against the wall where the old one had been. The bins were filled with flour and sugar and the pots and pans were all in place. To top it off, they had scrubbed and waxed the floor. The girls loved doing things like that and were always happy when they could pull a fast one on me.

I remember one night, it was my birthday, and Jess came to pick me up at the laundry. He was always in such a hurry to get home, but for some reason he stood talking longer than usual. When we pulled into the garage he diverted my attention for a few minutes before we went into the house.

In the kitchen I found the girls rushing around as busy as bees. They had the dining room table out to its full length with my best linen tablecloth on it. At each place setting was new green crystal glasswear, long-stemmed goblets, sherbet glasses and fine china. A lovely dinner warmed in the oven and the affair was complete with a large birthday cake with candles on it.

Just as I was wondering who was going to share this feast with us, in walked the folks we had just left at the laundry. The girls had used their own money for this special birthday and talked their dad into helping.

"What a lucky mother I am to have such thoughtful daughters," I said, hugging my girls.

During the time Cap worked on the house he had his dinner with us in exchange for his services. We also bought his tobacco and other personal items, as well as hay for his goats. He was a great believer in the nutritional value of goat milk, and our June thrived on it.

Cap was a handy man, but careless in his appearance. His baths came few and far between, and he was strongly flavored with the smell of goats. The clothes he wore, week after week, were soiled and frayed. His head of black hair was bushy and wild, as was his long beard. When he ate soup or drank coffee he made loud slurping noises that annoyed my fastidious daughters. There was always a big argument about who would have to sit next to Cap at mealtime.

All the while the improvements on the house continued. Cap built a large front porch using tongue-and-groove planks he had saved from the decking of the *Florence S.* That wood was four inches thick and never did wear out. The porch, stretching the width of the house, had a pitched roof and an open veranda where we sat on hot summer evenings.

There were times when I wondered how long all of us could go on living with Mother's unhappiness and constant complaints. Somehow we managed to get through the holidays, but as the cold, gray days of late winter settled upon us, I felt as if something was going to erupt. Jess borrowed $175 for her fare home. When he offered it to Mother, she said she didn't want to be sent away like an unwelcome guest.

"We want you to do whatever will make you happy, Mother," I said.

Not long after that I came home from work, and Mother met me at the door with the news that she was leaving.

"I have a chance to get my way paid Outside, plus $5 a day for expenses," she said.

"That is wonderful, Mother," I said, unable to hide my pleasure and relief. "How did that come about?"

"I am going to be a matron in the marshal's party taking a woman in custody to a mental institution in Oregon."

We insisted that Mother take the money Jess had borrowed, and we all parted on pleasant terms. When she returned to California, she settled in an apartment near Beth. It was 11 years before I saw her again.

That summer after Mother left, Cap Smythe became very ill and was unable to continue working. He still had his dinner meal with us, but we had to hire Tom Pierson to complete the remodeling of the house. By this time the old kitchen and back bedroom, part of the original structure, had become quite dilapidated. Since the new addition was larger, Tom built the foundation, walls and roof around the old structure. The roof was built with a gable to match the one in front.

When the new kitchen was finished, Jess and Tom tore out the old part and literally carried it out the window and the door. Tongue-and-groove flooring went down with a bright new linoleum in a black and white checked pattern. Now we had a lovely large kitchen, as well as a new bedroom, and a small room which would become our bathroom when we could afford the plumbing.

In the kitchen, Jess and Tom built new cupboards and a cooler—which I needed badly. There were no refrigerators in those days. For people who could afford it—and we weren't among them—there were iceboxes that were kept filled with blocks of ice. Our cooler was a narrow cupboard from floor to ceiling with holes cut through to the outside wall at the top and at the bottom. Those holes were covered with screening. The air circulated in and out and kept the food cold. The shelves were made of slats for better air circulation. In cold weather we could not put anything in the bottom section that we did not want to freeze.

For the time being, the future bathroom was the laundry room. The old wood washing machine was gone, and in its place was a gleaming Thor, which we bought on the installment plan at the N.C.

The new downstairs bedroom was for the boys so Cora and June could have the narrow upstairs bedroom to themselves. At last Jess and I were situated in a nice bedroom, the big one upstairs.

Our next project was a large back porch with two windows and a glass door that could be exchanged for a screen insert in the summer. The old chicken house, that served as the garage, was rebuilt and attached to the side of the house. Then, wonder of wonders, Jess and Tom began recovering the house with shiplap to match the new addition. Every trace of logs was gone. Then the house was painted yellow with a brown trim.

Coming home from work one night, Jess and I sat in the car to admire our house that had been more than 20 years in the making. The long rays of the summer sun shone on the front windows until they gleamed like burnished gold. The pitched roof was outlined against the pale blue of the summer sky.

My flower beds, the yellow of the daisies, the ruffled pink of the petunias, the green foliage of the crocus, made a colorful border around the house and along the white graveled sidewalk. The grass, freshly cut, lent an expansive air to our little corner of the world. The spruce and birch we had planted earlier fanned tall and vibrantly green.

"It was worth it, wasn't it?" I said, taking Jess's hand. "All our hard work was worth it?"

He nodded his agreement. Through the years his thin frame had become thinner, the lines creasing his face had deepened, and his hands were thick-jointed and rough. We had been through a lot, my Jess and I. Now we had the home we had always dreamed of as children. It hadn't come easy. Our sweat, blood and tears had gone into the house, but that only made it more precious to us.

"There is only one problem now that we have the second story on," Jess said.

"What's that?" I asked.

"We need a new heating system," he replied.

Sitting in the car with the warmth of the fine June evening pouring in the window, that didn't seem like much of a problem, but I knew Jess was right.

"What are we going to do?" I asked. All the years we were married Jess and I talked over our plans. We shared everything, not only the decision making, but the labor too, as well as earning the money to finance the projects.

"I'll have to dig out the basement to make room for the furnace and the coal bin," Jess said.

Once the plan was made, Jess had to order the materials so they would be there when we were ready for them. Just before winter in 1930, Jess installed a Sunbeam circulating furnace in the basement. What a luxury that was. When we came in from the cold, the first place we headed for was the register in the living room, where we would stand and let the warm air blow around our ankles.

The long stovepipe for the furnace went up through the main floor, the living room ceiling, through the bedroom upstairs and the attic. Sometimes when the temperature was 40 and 50 degrees below zero, that stovepipe turned red-hot. There were many nights I worried about fires, but Jess was careful; he never took any chances. Every winter the stovepipe was replaced. If it wasn't, the creosote would gather on the inside and eat away the pipe. Before retiring at night, Jess knocked on the pipe to loosen the creosote that had formed during the day so that it would not start a fire.

Now that we were burning coal it was less expensive and less work, even though we still had to carry out ashes and the clinkers. At least there was no more wood to chop.

As always, one thing led to another when we remodeled the house. Now that the living room and dining room were larger, we needed more furniture. It just so happened that Mrs. Ralph Kuban, of McIntosh and Kuban Drug Store, had for sale a large oak table that extended to seat 15. She also had an oak buffet with a large mirror that fit above it. I bought all that furniture for $50.

By that time we had bought an apartment-size piano. That helped fill the living room, along with our davenport, which Pete Deiser recovered with gray mohair. At one end of the dining room there was a corner reserved for Jess. There he had his large leather chair and magazine shelf. The second-hand bookcase was remodeled by Jess so he could use one side as a gun case. The floor, varnished hardwood, was kept polished with O'Cedar and covered with scatter rugs.

Even though there were many days I did not feel like getting up at 6 o'clock in the morning and going to work for 10 hours on my feet, it was the only way we could afford the house improvements and take care of our six children. It was just as well that I didn't know when I started work that it would be 24 years before I was a lady of leisure again.

chapter 21

One minute my children were babies, and then, before I knew it, Cora and Lila were almost ready to graduate from high school. Looking back can be deceiving: A year seems like a minute in my memory, and 10 years like a day.

While my children were young it seemed as if the same duties of washing diapers, wiping runny noses, bandaging cuts, hemming dresses, knitting scarves and packing lunches would go on forever. But they didn't. All things come to an end. In such a short time the children became self-sufficient, then independent, and then gone.

Jess and I enjoyed our children at all stages, but more so as they got older. Like all small towns, our boys and girls went through grade school and high school with the same kids they had grown up with. At that time the population was stable and families lived in town, even in the same house, for 10 or 15 years.

Somehow our house was the place where all the kids gathered. Everyone seemed at home there. It had that "lived-in" feeling. There was no fancy furniture to worry about, and best of all, we had a big living room with hardwood floors that were perfect for dancing.

It wasn't unusual for Jess to come home from work on a Saturday night and find 30 kids dancing the Lindy Hop, the schottische or the polka in the living room. He would take one look at that gang and hurry to the basement, where he put several braces to hold up the floor.

At first the girls furnished a lunch of sandwiches and cake, but as the parties became more frequent and the numbers grew, I told Lila and Cora that we just could not afford to provide all the food. Then the girls took turns bringing the snacks and the boys made sure there was plenty of Coke and phonograph records.

Since our record player wasn't too reliable and the girls wanted a new one, Jess made a proposition to them.

"If you save your babysitting money and pay half the cost of a new record player, I will pay the other half," he said.

Lila and Cora were jubilant and worked hard to get extra jobs. They had their share saved long before Jess and I did. Since they were so eager to have the new machine, Jess took them to the N.C. to pick out a new cabinet Victrola, and we paid the balance by installments.

Guy Rivers, an attorney, bought his daughters, Muriel and Virginia, an old Ford car to drive. Our girls were a bit jealous, but that didn't stop them from going out riding whenever they had the chance.

There was just one thing about the Rivers girls and their driving. They didn't know how to shift properly. Sometimes they couldn't stop, so when they came to our house they would toot the horn and circle the block. Lila and Cora would run out and jump into the car.

Jess watched that performance until he'd had enough. "I don't like the girls getting in the car like that," he said. "One of these days someone is going to get hurt."

When the girls returned home that night Jess was waiting for them. He stood in the street and hollered directions to Virginia on how to stop the car. Somehow she got the lever in reverse and the car backed up and began going around in circles and got dangerously close to our two boys, who were playing across the street in a vacant lot. I got scared and ran to warn the boys.

"Watch out!" Jess yelled.

"What's wrong?" I called.

"Look behind you!"

"Yipes!" I screamed.

The darn car, still out of control, was coming after me, and I had a hard time getting out of its path.

Finally Jess jumped on the running board, reached inside and turned off the motor. He had tried to tell Virginia how to stop the car, but in her panic, her foot froze on the accelerator. All she could do was grip the steering wheel while the car continued its dizzy course.

Those were three mighty scared girls when they piled out of the car but Jess made Virginia get back in and he gave her lessons on how to shift gears. He wouldn't let our girls ride with the Rivers girls until they could properly start and stop the car. This caused our girls to put up a fuss, and pretty soon Cora and Lila wanted a car of their own.

Jess scouted around until he found one for $100. It was a Ford sedan with a high fabric top that looked like a hearse. In fact, it was owned by our local undertaker, Hosea Ross, who had just purchased a new car. When Jess showed the girls the old sedan they were so excited.

"Can we buy it, Dad, please, can we buy it?" Lila pleaded.

"It costs $100," Jess reminded them. He didn't tell them that he had already put $50 down to bind the sale.

"We will work for it," Cora said. "We'll pay it off."

In no time at all they paid Jess the full cost of the car. He would not let them take it out until they knew everything about driving, including how to patch and change a tire. After the girls started driving it seemed that at least once a week Jess was running to their rescue when the car broke down or they were out of gas.

Our girls called the car Nellie, and since they didn't like the black color, they got busy and painted it blue. Then someone painted "Seeing Nellie Home" across the back. That was so appropriate because many people had to do just that when the car broke down. The girls never gave any thought to maintenance or repairs; as long as the car got them out of the driveway, that was good enough for them.

One Sunday, Cora and a boy from college and Charlotte Wehner drove to Birch Lake to visit us for the day. On the way home the boy was driving too fast. When he started to pass a car he went off the road, throwing Charlotte out through the fabric top and Cora out the door. Fortunately, the bank was grassy and no one was hurt, except for a few scratches.

With the help of a passer-by, the kids got old Nellie out of the ditch, parked it alongside the road and caught a ride back to the lake.

It just so happened that the kids had a fresh watermelon and a bag of peaches in the car that day. After the accident, that smashed fruit looked amazingly like flesh and blood. When some of our friends drove by and saw the Ford, they thought someone had surely been killed. They wondered how they were going to tell Jess and me about the accident. How surprised they were to learn that no one had been hurt.

Jess managed to drive the car to town, but it was beyond repair. If the truth were known, I think Jess was glad. He was getting tired of going out on emergency calls at all hours of the night.

With our teenage daughters, little Beth and our two rambunctious boys, there was never a dull moment around our house. Sometimes when the kids started fighting, I thought I would go out of my mind. The boys were the worst by far. Out of desperation Jess went downtown one day and bought them both a pair of boxing gloves and told them to go out in the yard and get the fighting out of their system.

There were times when I seriously wondered what little boys were made of. Just what made them tick, anyway? One day at the laundry I got a frantic call from Lila.

"Oh, Mother," she said. "You'll never believe what Jess and George have done."

"What is it, Lila? Tell me," I said.

"They broke all the windows in Gus Conradt's garage."

"Oh, no. I'll be right home."

It seemed that our boys and their friend Jim had a disagreement. Jim threw a rock at George, but missed, and the rock went through Gus's garage window instead. The sound of that tinkling glass incited the three boys. Their disagreement forgotten, venturesome George picked up a rock and threw it through another window. There was that tinkle, tinkle of falling glass again. The boys were intrigued by the sound. Before they realized what they were doing, all three of them were throwing rocks as fast as they could. There were two windows, and each window had eight panes. That glass kept falling until the ground was covered with it.

As it turned out, Gus was very nice about the incident, but he did insist that the glass be replaced. There were at least twelve broken panes. Jess cut the glass to size, bought a can of putty and instructed the boys how to put glass in the frames.

It was a tedious job, and it took the boys two days. How they sweated that one out, being careful not to complain when their dad was within earshot. After that Jess made them clean up all the broken glass that had fallen in the garage and on the ground. We thought they had learned their lesson, and that would be the end of the broken windows. But it wasn't.

Carrying out the garbage is a loathsome job in most families, and our boys disliked it more than most kids. They dumped the garbage in the barrels which sat beside the garage door so Jess could haul it away in the old N.C. truck. One day when there was lots of debris on the ground, 10-year-old George was sent to pick it up. To say that he approached the job reluctantly is a mild description indeed. Noting his attitude, Jess and I watched from the dining room window just in time to see George pick up an old tin pie plate.

He puzzled over it for a minute, then lifting his arm, he sent it sailing away from him. That pie plate acted like a boomerang and came circling right back over his head and through the dining room window. Jess and I ducked just in time.

It was worth the price of the windowpane to see the expression on George's face. He was flabbergasted. Finally he managed to say, "I didn't mean to throw it through the window, honest, Dad."

"I know you didn't, George," he said, "but after this when you are sent to do a job, you do it, and no fooling around."

There was an old German fellow in town in the early days who taught our girls to play the piano and violin. His name was Otto Hoppe. He had music students all over town, for that was how he made his living. I can see him to this day, a small, slightly bent man with smooth cheeks and thinning gray hair. As soon as Cora and Lila came home from school, Mr. Hoppe soon followed, moving briskly up the path and knocking sharply on the door.

"Hello, Mr. Hoppe," I always greeted him.

"Ya, ya. Are they ready, those girls?"

Mr. Hoppe was a good teacher, but he became very impatient if the girls had not practiced their lesson. Sometimes he knocked their knuckles with a short ruler. I put a stop to that when Cora's hands became red and swollen.

"It is a teacher's privilege to hit his students when they do not play well," he said in his broken English.

"Not in this house," I said.

It wasn't long before Cora and Lila were playing duets on the piano and performing at programs for the Pioneers and Eagles lodge. Later Cora took violin lessons from Gladys Bell and joined the school orchestra. June started lessons, but soon lost interest and quit. I never forced the children into music, but once they started, I insisted they practice every day. How they grumbled and complained over that. Later—much later—they were glad for it.

Beth wasn't interested in piano, but she did want to play the drums. (All I needed in the house was a little more noise.) Mr. Hoppe brought a sanded block of wood and two drumsticks to practice with until she got the rhythm. When she joined the school band, she used a real drum and later became a drummer in the Elks Girls Drill Team.

On lesson night I always asked Mr. Hoppe to stay for dinner, and I gave him a loaf of bread to take home. Before leaving, he would go into the kitchen and get the used coffee grounds, putting them in a can he brought for that purpose.

"You Americans waste too much food," he said. "I can make good coffee on what you throw away."

Mr. Hoppe was a collector of junk. His small cabin on the edge of town, where he lived alone, was surrounded with boxes stacked as high as a fence. The open end of the boxes faced his house and there he stored all those things he collected and thought would be of use someday—rusted pots and pans, old newspapers, tin cans, used clothing, broken furniture and more boxes, boxes inside boxes.

One day when Mr. Hoppe came to our house he was very upset. A neighbor had complained to the authorities about his junk, saying it was a fire hazard and a rattrap. Then the city moved Mr. Hoppe into another cabin and burned down the old one, even before he had a chance to save his precious music he had brought from Germany.

While in high school, both Cora and Lila went in for basketball and played in many competitive games. Jess Jr. liked basketball and boxing, while our tough George took on things like tumbling and ice hockey. All six of the children liked to ski, although George went at it more seriously than the others. When he went with the school team to Anchorage for competitions, George came home with first prize in downhill skiing.

With her brothers and sisters to teach her, Beth started skiing when she was in the first grade, and went on to win many prizes. She was also an excellent figure skater. I shall never forget the day

Jess and I stopped by the school skating rink to admire, from a distance, a young girl doing figure eights and pirouettes.

"That kid is darn good," Jess said. "I wonder who she is."

"That's your daughter Beth," I said, unable to hold back a smile and gloat at the same time. Just a few weeks earlier Jess had raised the roof because I bought a pair of $12 figure skates for Beth. Since she was the baby in the family she had been the recipient of hand-me-downs all her life. When it came to figure skates, I thought it was about time she had a new pair. After Jess saw her skate, he could not help but agree.

It seemed that June always had problems when she was growing up; she was never very strong. When she was a freshman in high school, she went to visit a classmate who hadn't been to school for a few days. The girl was in bed with a high fever. Then a few days later June became very ill and soon she was delirious with fever. Dr. Sutherland said it was infantile paralysis. He advised us to isolate her from the rest of the family, and said every cup, dish and piece of silverware she used should be sterilized. Her fever ran high for many days. We were all so scared. I barely slept at night, listening for June's call.

At last the fever abated, but June was left with paralysis on her right side. After working with her, giving her exercises and treatments with the vibrator, June regained full use of her arm and leg. All in all, my children enjoyed good health and for that I am grateful. Maybe the diet of beans, moose and rabbit had something to do with it. We sure had plenty of that.

One Easter morning the fire siren sounded. Jess immediately dropped what he was doing and ran to the N.C. powerhouse with young Jess close at his heels.

The Alaska Hotel, on the corner of First and Wickersham, was blazing out of control. The yellow flames shot hundreds of feet into the air while the black smoke rolled over the town like a shroud. Residents of the hotel were leaping out of the windows. People in the streets were screaming. Jess and Jess Jr. arrived on the scene just in time to see our friend Bob Taylor jump out of the third-floor window and fall to his death.

When the fire broke out, Bob ran from room to room, banging on doors and yelling, "Fire! Fire!" After saving the lives of many people, Bob became trapped on the third floor. He ran to his room and grabbed the end of the rope that was coiled under the window for a fire escape. In his confusion, instead of sliding down the rope, Bob jumped, holding the wrong end.

The hotel was a total loss. It was one of those frame buildings that was covered with corrugated tin, and burned like a matchbox. There was no chance that it could be rebuilt. When I first came to Fairbanks in 1908, that hotel, then named the Shaw House, stood at the corner of Second and Wickersham until it was moved to First Avenue. I remember on my first Sunday in town, Dad took Mother, Beth and me to the Shaw House for dinner. It had a lovely dining room and plush lobby with high-backed leather banquettes, black and white tiled floor and potted palms. Mom and Dad Shaw ran the hotel then, and many lonely people were invited to share a meal with them. I know because I was one of them after my folks went Outside.

After the fire, the hotel owners, Tom and Leona Foster, sold some of the fixtures they had salvaged. Jess came home with the blackest looking bathtub I had ever had the misfortune to see. He was so proud of his new possession and that he got it for $10. "Just wait until I clean it up," he said. "It will be as good as new."

I had my doubts about that, but he spent hours scraping until the tub was clean enough to paint—a pretty orchid color, inside and out. It was a magnificent tub, standing on clawed feet, filling one end of our bathroom. We put down linoleum in shades of lavender, orange and green, and painted the walls and woodwork a pale green. With a washbasin and toilet we had, for the first time in our lives, an honest-to-goodness bathroom. Jess had also been working on the cesspool, so it was ready when the bathroom was finished.

There was one more problem to overcome—getting water to our bathroom. Jess, always the resourceful one, located a second-hand pump. Admittedly it was in pretty bad shape, but fortunately Jess could fix anything, and after nights of tinkering, the pump was in working order and installed in the basement near the well. If Jess hadn't been able to do all the plumbing, we never would have had those modern conveniences.

When the plumbing system was ready to go, complete with a hot water tank, we were in for a big disappointment. With all the iron in our water, we had to have a water softener. More expense, but we were lucky because we got it at the N.C. on credit. No more lugging buckets outdoors or having the hand pump and the water barrel sitting in the kitchen. How modern can a person get?

chapter 22

In September of 1931 when I had a 2-week vacation from the laundry, I felt as if I needed to get away for a while. Earlier that year I had received word from my sister, Beth, that Dad had passed away in Inglewood, California. Zacharius Fremont Hickman's running was over. Strangely enough, the same day I received a letter telling me of my father's death, Jess received a letter from his stepmother, saying that his father had died in Portland, Oregon.

I decided to take a trip and visit our friends Joe and Eileen Bowman, who had a mink ranch near Curry. Beth was not in school yet so I took her with me. Since the train stopped overnight at Curry (it was the halfway point between Fairbanks and Anchorage) we stayed in the modern, two-story hotel. Everything was a delight to 4-year-old Beth, especially feeding the mink. Every day I went hiking and fishing and enjoyed myself without a single thought about work or home duties.

When it was time to go back, Beth and I had to stay overnight at Curry to wait for the train. It was then I learned that heavy rains had caused the Tanana and Chena rivers to overflow and that both Fairbanks and Nenana had been flooded.

"The railroad tracks are washed out along the Healy River Canyon," one man told me. "The train will be delayed 3 days."

"Are you sure it is that bad?" I asked.

"It sure is, lady," he answered.

There were many conflicting reports about conditions in Fairbanks, but I was not too concerned. Our house was eight blocks from the river and stood on high ground. When we finally reached Nenana, my optimism was dashed. There the railroad tracks were underwater, and a boat was tied to the platform to transport people to town.

My next surprise was waiting for me in Fairbanks. Jess met Beth and me at the depot with a pair of tall rubber boots.

"What are these for?" I asked.

"To wade to the car," Jess said as he picked up Beth. "Haven't you heard there was a flood?"

"Yes, but I didn't think it was this bad."

"It is," Jess said.

But I still didn't believe him.

When we reached home the girls were paddling around in our front yard in the King canvas canoe, and the boys were sailing on a raft they had made out of pieces of wooden sidewalks that had floated by the house. Our garage, Jess informed me, had four feet of water in it.

"Oh, what a mess," was all I could say.

"It isn't all that bad," Jess said, trying to console me. "We just have water up to the top step in the basement."

"The top step!" I cried. "That means the furnace, the pump, the water softener and everything else is underwater.

"I know," Jess said, "but some people have four feet of water on the main floor."

Since it was late in September and cold at night, Jess set up the Yukon stove in the living room. When the floodwater receded, four days later, we were faced with the real mess. Not only was everything sopping wet, and no way to dry it, but the basement was thick with river silt and mud. Water was a problem. The pump Jess had worked so hard to repair apparently was ruined, and we had to go back to hand pumping as well as boiling all the water for drinking and cooking.

The floodwaters had come so fast that Jess had not been able to save anything in the basement. My winter supply of jams, jellies and canned vegetables was spoiled. Gone too was our old trunk full of mementoes—my gray taffeta wedding dress, old pictures Jess had taken in Dawson, and letters from my family.

So often during those days of cleanup I was close to tears. We were not the only ones with problems; other families suffered losses too, but it was so discouraging after all the work we had put in the house. Fortunately Jess could do the repair work necessary, so before it got too cold that winter, the furnace was fixed and the water pump working again. For months afterwards, however, our house was permeated with a damp, musky smell coming up from the basement.

By this time the kids had started back to school, and I was working five days a week at the laundry with Saturday and Sunday off. On the weekends the girls pitched in and we all cleaned and cooked and did the laundry. Each week I baked eight loaves of bread as well as a large pan of sweet rolls.˙ After school the girls baked cakes or cookies, and sometimes a pan of corn bread for dinner. We really did manage quite well, but it took organization and teamwork. Everyone said that the man who married one of the Rust girls would get a good cook, and that was true.

The first bride in our family was Lila. After she graduated from high school in 1932 she went to work at the American Hand Laundry for a few months. After Christmas of that year she married Nels Jorgensen, whom she had been dating for some time. Theirs was a Christmas wedding at the First Presbyterian Church with a beaming Jess escorting his daughter down the aisle.

Not long after Lila was married, I got a call from Cora Weir, who was superintendent of the telephone operators. The office was located at Second and Turner behind the N.C. store. This municipal service, along with lights, water and steam heat, was owned by the N.C. Cora asked me to stop by on my way home from work to see her. Since I was quite curious about her request, I agreed.

"How would you like a job as a telephone operator?" she asked. "We are going to need someone pretty soon to take over the night shift."

"Oh, I don't think I could handle it," I said, noting the complicated equipment.

"Sure you could, Clara," she said encouragingly, "and it would be much easier than the work you do at the laundry."

I could not help but agree with her there. After 9 years at the laundry, I was beginning to feel worn out from the heavy lifting, and from the long hours on my feet.

"I hadn't thought of changing jobs," I said hesitantly.

"Why don't you at least try it," Cora insisted. "Come back tonight after dinner and watch me work the switchboard."

I did watch her for several hours that night, and the work was interesting. But how in the world would I ever know what to do with all those flashing lights on the board? What would I ever do with all those cords that plugged into the holes? And would I be able to remember the telephone numbers the way Cora did?

"I just don't think I can do it," I said sadly.

"Yes, you can," she said. "I will make you up two cross-reference

Top—*Waechter's meat market on Second Avenue was among Fairbanks's businesses.* Bottom—*Pete Menzel, in the white coat, worked there a number of years.*

telephone directories, one by name, and the other by number, and you can study it."

After talking it over with Jess, I decided it was time for a change, and with a little help maybe I could master the switchboard. I told Nina O'Gara at the laundry that I might be leaving soon.

Within a few days Cora Weir called, "You will have to come to work tonight."

"But I haven't memorized any of the numbers yet," I said.

"That's all right. Bring your books with you. We need you now."

At that time there were two small PBX switchboards with approximately a hundred holes to plug in. Most of them were party lines with two or four different numbers for each line. When a call came in, little disks dropped with a buzz and a light came on. My earphone fastened to a spring band around my head, and the mouthpiece hung from a cord attached to the top of the switchboard.

When I first started, the operators worked a 10-hour shift alone. At times we were extremely busy handling all the calls. Since there weren't many printed directories in town, most people called in and said, "Give me the Tom Jones residence." Then I would ring the number. We not only had to learn the name and number of each subscriber, but we had to know the number of rings required for the party line.

On my first night at work, I was one mighty nervous person knowing the full responsibility was on my shoulders from 10 o'clock at night until 8 o'clock the next morning.

"The main thing for you to remember is how to handle a fire call," Cora said as she left me that night.

Knowing the importance of that, I had memorized the procedure and felt confident that I could handle it. As soon as a fire call came in, I was supposed to get the location of the fire and call it to the fire station. They in turn would push a button that was connected to the powerhouse to indicate which siren to blow to alert the area where the fire was occurring.

Then I would call the powerhouse so the engineer could start the water pumps. If it was a large fire in a critical area, I was to call the managers of the telephone and utilities company. The minute the siren sounded, the switchboard lit up like a Christmas tree with people inquiring about the fire. I was instructed to open as many lines as I could and repeat over and over where the fire was located.

On my very first night on the job, a fire call came in at 2 o'clock in the morning from St. Joseph's Hospital. My hands were prickly with sweat as I tried to remember all the things I was supposed to do and the people I was supposed to call.

After calling the engineer at the powerhouse I waited for things to happen, but nothing did. No siren, no noise of the fire engines coming down Cushman Street. Then I got a call from Bill Hunter, the engineer at the powerhouse.

"Why didn't I get a signal from the fire hall?" he asked.

"Ye gods!" I screamed. "I forgot to call them!"

Fortunately it was not a serious fire, just a furnace smoking, but I never pulled that stunt again, and Bill Hunter never let me forget my first fire and how I forgot to call the fire department.

In those days before dialing systems, everyone in town knew the operator by name. Many of the operators did special favors for people, making morning wake-up calls and delivering messages. In an emergency the operator was one of the most important people in town, and we "Hello Girls," as we were called, were treated with a great deal of respect.

At Christmas time we were showered with gifts. I never saw so many boxes of candy—most of them came from our local candy man, "Sticky Griffin," and were his chocolates ever good. We received stockings, handkerchiefs and perfume and hand soap. The banks sent each of us a check for $5. Almost every store in town remembered us with a gift. All Christmas week it was so exciting with everyone calling to wish us a Merry Christmas.

For 9 years, 5 days a week and 10 hours a day, I was at my appointed place at the telephone office. We worked straight through the shift, without a break for lunch. Sometimes the Model Cafe would send over a hot lunch by the night patrolman, and I would eat it between calls.

My daughter Cora graduated from high school in 1934, went to college for a while and then got a job in the messhall at the Cleary Hall Quartz Mine.

It was there she met Pete Snet, a young man of Russian birth. He was a quiet person who spent most of his time working his mining property on Happy Creek and building a cabin.

It didn't take Jess and me long to figure out that Cora and Pete were serious about each other. When Cora had any extra time she would spend it helping Pete work on the cabin, riding one of the boys' bicycles 15 miles on gravel roads. When Cora came home she chattered gaily about "Pete this" and "Pete that," and what a wonderful place Happy Creek was, and what a beautiful cabin they were building.

In October of that year, they were married in the old house. Lila and Nels drove the newlyweds out to their cabin while Jess, Charlotte and I followed with the wedding gifts in our car. When I saw that "beautiful little cabin" Cora had talked about, I was shocked, and couldn't help feeling resentful toward Pete for bringing my daughter to such a place.

The cabin was only 12 feet by 14 feet, with one door of rough lumber and two small windows. The floor was hard-packed dirt, and the bed was made of poles without a mattress. I had had my share of pioneering, but never like this.

"Calm yourself down," Jess kept saying. "Everybody has to start someplace."

"But not like this," I said, looking around at the crude dwelling.

Beauty as well as ugliness is in the eye of the beholder. Cora was as happy as if she were living in a mansion. This was a home of their own and they didn't owe anybody anything. Later in the summer they built another small room and put down flooring.

When they weren't building on their house, they were working the mining claim. Cora helped Pete sink the shaft, and when that was done, she turned the windlass to bring up the buckets of dirt. Cora had to pack water from Happy Creek for every need. When the creek froze over she had to shovel snow and melt it. There were times when I worried and fretted about her out there in that cabin, but I knew she had to lead her own life. Later when Cora had her first baby, Noel Michael, on Christmas Day in 1936, she took the little one out to the cabin on Happy Creek, and I couldn't help but think it was like my life happening all over again, struggling without modern conveniences while raising a family.

After Cora married, June moved into the blue room and Beth had the long bedroom to herself. Then Jess and I decided that the yard was too big so we sold 50 feet of property to Bill Hunter, who built a fine, modern house there.

Now that our family was smaller we didn't need such a large garden so I planted some lettuce, onions, carrots and two hills of potatoes, that's all. I also kept my strawberry bed; we had to have that. We put the rest of the yard in lawn with shrubs and flowers.

At last I had my rock garden in one corner, just the way I always wanted it, with a rock wall the width of the yard which bordered Seventh Avenue.

Not only was our family changing, but Fairbanks was changing too. This once-upon-a-time gold rush town was losing its frontier appearance. The new three-story concrete Federal Building, located on Cushman between Second and Third (where it stands today), housed the post office and court office. Fairbanks's only tycoon, Austin E. (Cap) Lathrop, built the first concrete commercial building on Second Avenue. Cap also built the first movie house. The talkies had come to town and could be seen at the Empress Theater where Don Adler played the pipe organ at intermission. Many of the downtown buildings were taking on a more sophisticated appearance. Gone were many of the false storefronts and the saloons with sawdust on the floor. Wooden sidewalks downtown were rare.

The revival of the Fairbanks economy that had started with the coming of the railroad and the F.E. Company operations continued for a decade. The population nearly doubled, with approximately 2,500 residents in Fairbanks in the mid-thirties. With a new gold strike in the Cripple Creek area, 10 miles from town, the F.E. dredging flourished during the depression years. Healthy economic conditions prevailed in Fairbanks, with only two unemployed people in the Fourth Judicial District. Gold production was the highest it had been since 1913, and gold was selling for the top price of $35 an ounce.

In 1937, June graduated from high school and went to work at the Curry Hotel, where she renewed her acquaintance with Bruce Savage, who was working for the Alaska Railroad. Bruce had been a guest in our house during his high school days when he was on the Anchorage basketball team. When summer was over, June and Bruce told us of their plans to be married.

They made arrangements to have the wedding in the Presbyterian Church and the reception at the house. June and I got busy right away cleaning, painting and fixing up the place. We painted the living room and dining room and varnished the floors. Next we made drapes, and much to my surprise, June bought a new wing-back chair with cushions to match the drapes.

"It is for you, Mother," she said. "Dad has his leather rocking chair, and now you have a chair of your own."

Not only that, but June got together with the buyer from the N.C. store and ordered a beautiful black lace dress for me to wear to the wedding. It was hard for me to find clothes in my large size and I was grateful to have such a thoughtful daughter.

After the wedding, June and Bruce moved to Palmer, and Beth fell heir to the blue room. About this time, Jerry Whelan, a young school friend of Jess Jr., came to live with us. We thought of him as our son. It seemed the old house was meant to have young people in it, and as soon as one moved out another came to fill the empty place.

Once again Jess and I had become grandparents. Lila and Nels had their first baby, a girl, whom they named Karen. She was born in December of 1937. Earlier that year Cora's second child was stillborn. It seemed our family always had its ups and downs, and we all helped each other through the difficult times.

Then tragedy struck again. In March of 1938 Cora's 2-year-old son, Noel, was scalded by hot water in an accident similar to the one we suffered when Jess Jr. was a baby. Little Noel did not survive. At that time Cora was pregnant with Peter Jr., who was born in the fall of that same year.

Jess and I had both known for a long time that we were in need of a new car. In the spring of 1938 I made arrangements at the N.C. to buy the Plymouth sedan they had on display. This was going to be my personal project. I paid $75 down and agreed to pay that much per month. Some months I even managed to pay $100, and by carefully budgeting my money, I paid off the car. Our new sedan was much more comfortable than the open Star—which had seen us through many a rough and rugged mile.

As soon as we got the Plymouth, Jess Jr. and George began clamoring for a car, so Jess fixed up the Star for them. With reasonable use it could have lasted them a year or more, but they drove it across the countryside, over the hilltops and through streams. Within a few months they had burned out the bearings. Jess helped them repair it, but they still hadn't learned their lesson and soon the car was broken down for good.

Never content to let anything go unused, Jess took the chassis out of the Star and made a trailer with it to haul our boat back and forth to the river. So the old Star—what was left of it—still had a few more miles in her.

In the fall one year when Jess and I both had some vacation time, he said, "It's about time we went off on a camping trip, just the two of us. We will take a leisurely jaunt out the highway and stop whenever you wish."

"I'm ready to get away for a while," I agreed. "Let's go."

"It will be a good time for us to get our moose for the season, too," Jess said.

Early one morning with the car packed full of food and camping equipment, we started off. It was one of those exquisite fall days with the Alaska Range etched indelibly against the blue sky with the foreground flaming vibrantly with the colors of scarlet and bronze, gold and copper. The air was crystal clear; it almost crackled, and I felt as if I could reach out and touch the snow-covered top of Mount Hayes. There is a certain place along the highway, after you pass Harding Lake, where you come face to face with that flamboyant spread of mountains. I always looked forward to that sight on a clear day, and I was never disappointed.

We took our time, stopping at friends' cabins and visiting with highway travelers to see if anyone got a moose or caribou. At Richardson we stopped to see Galen Frye, the postmaster, who invited us to have lunch with him.

"It's getting pretty late," I said. "I think we should move on so we can get to Summit Lake before it gets dark."

Jess said, "Oh, don't worry. We will get to our campsite and we will get our moose. There is one waiting down the road for us."

We finally got on the road again, and as we came down Richardson Hill and hit the straight stretch, there was a huge moose with a beautiful rack standing in the middle of the road.

"What did I tell you?" Jess said, grabbing his gun and easing out of the car. "There's our moose."

I sat right where I was. As Jess began creeping toward the moose, that brute turned nonchalantly and ambled off into the brush.

Jess raised his gun. I heard two shots. Then he motioned for me to come. "Bring the ax, rope and my camera," he yelled.

That moose had fallen about 50 yards off the road behind some logs. He looked as big as a sternwheeler spread out there on the forest floor. He weighed more than 1,000 pounds. Jess and I sure had our work cut out for us. This "vacation" turned out to be the hardest work I had done in years.

By the time we had that animal cleaned, quartered and pulled out on the road, it was after midnight. I pulled the car closer so we could load the meat. About this time a car came along and we recognized our neighbor, Ed Clausen, and a couple of fellows on their way home from an unsuccessful hunt.

"Lucky Jess," they said. "He always gets his moose."

"Why don't you take a quarter and divide it among you," Jess offered. The men pitched in and loaded the meat into their car. It was a job even for them and I wondered how Jess and I had managed to drag it as far as we did. When there is a job to be done, you do it without thinking how hard it is.

After the men left Jess and I sat down and looked at each other.

"Are you thinking what I'm thinking?" Jess asked.

"I sure am. We let those guys drive away without helping us load the meat into our car."

"We sure did," Jess said. "Wait until I see them."

It was nearly 2 o'clock in the morning by the time we got the car loaded and headed back to Galen Frye's cabin. Galen was waiting for us with a hot dinner on the stove. Ed had told him of our luck and how badly they felt when they realized Jess and I had to load our meat alone. Galen helped carry the meat and hang it in an old barn where there was plenty of cold air circulating to keep it fresh until we picked it up on our way home. After a most welcome hot meal, Jess and I fell into bed, totally exhausted.

The next morning we started out for Summit Lake, some 60 miles beyond.

"I don't care if we do see another moose," I told Jess as we got under way. "Don't shoot it, because I won't help carry it out."

"Don't worry," Jess said with that big grin that still made my heart happy. "I wouldn't go through that again either."

Summit Lake was as gorgeous as I remembered it, nestled between the wooded hills that were meticulously reflected in the clear, still water. At moments like that my heart just sang with happiness. How I loved Alaska!

There was nothing I liked better than to watch the leaping fish, the twirling colored leaves and the puffs of white clouds move across the sky. When we got a taste of the pure outdoors like that, it made living in Alaska all the more worthwhile.

Dressed as I was in faded overalls, scuffed shoepacs and a heavy plaid shirt, it was hard to believe that I had once been a city girl. I guess Jess was right, oh, so many years ago when he said I had the makings of a sourdough.

After Jess pitched our tent on the edge of Summit Lake, he built up the campfire that was most welcome in that high elevation. While I settled close to the fire's warmth, Jess took his fishing pole to "get some big ones." We were going to have fresh trout fried over an open fire or his name wasn't Jesse Worthington Rust Sr.

It wasn't long before Jess came back to camp.

"You just have to watch me pull out these big fish," he said.

A snooze by the fire was more what I had in mind, but I went with him instead. When we reached the banks of the fast-running Fish Creek, which we had to cross, I said, "Jess, I don't have any boots. Maybe I better go back to camp."

Jess was not that easily discouraged.

"Get on my back, and I will carry you across."

"You can't do that," I protested. "I am too darn heavy."

"I can do it," Jess insisted. He stooped over and said, "Come on. Get on my back."

I thought it would make it easier for him if I gave a little jump. Well, that was the wrong thing to do. Jess went head-first into the creek with me on top of him. Boy, was he mad! He came up spluttering and cussing, and then he saw how funny it was, and we both started laughing as we climbed out of that cold water.

"O.K. for you," he said. "Let's try it again."

"Oh, no, Jess."

"Yup, come on, get up here," he said, stooping over for the second time. "And no running jumps, dammit."

I got on his back, real easy-like, and we started across the creek. The water was deep and quite swift, but we made it to the other side without a tumble.

Needless to say, we were both soaked to the skin, with teeth chattering; we were cold in those clammy clothes. Even at that, I had to wait until he landed his prize trout. It was a beauty, too, and what a feast we had that night.

It was moments like those—and the many trips that Jess and I took together—that provide some of my most treasured memories. We were good companions, Jess and I, enjoying the same things out of life. How fortunate I was. When I think back to my early married years, remembering how naive I was about things, I wonder how I had managed to come so far.

chapter 23

As the years passed, I felt a longing to see my sister, Beth. It had been more than 30 years since she had left Fairbanks on the sternwheeler and said to Jess, "I bet this boat will just get around the bend, and you two will be married."

By 1940, she had four children and lived with her husband in Los Angeles. Mother lived near them, and a trip Outside would give me a chance to see my family.

There was just one problem: money. Even with both Jess and me working, it was hard to save enough for a trip like that.

One night when Jess and I were at the movies, the manager, Don Adler, stopped by our seats at intermission time with a box of tickets.

"Draw one, Clara," Don said. "Tonight the winning ticket is worth $200."

I pulled out a ticket, and gasped.

"What is it?" Jess asked.

"I can't believe it!"

"Whose name is it?" Jess wanted to know.

"It's mine! I've never won anything before in my life."

"There is your start for your trip Outside," Jess said.

After cashing a savings bond—and with a paycheck in hand and my movie money—I took a three months' leave from the telephone office. While I was gone, Beth would stay with Lila and Nels, and Jess and boys would "bach" at home. I couldn't help but feel guilty about running off and leaving them for such a long time.

"Don't worry about us," Jess said. "We can take care of ourselves. You know I wouldn't want to go Outside, even if we could afford it."

That much was true. Jess hadn't left Alaska for 35 years, and from the way he talked, he didn't care if he ever did.

After traveling by train to Seward, I boarded the boat for Seattle. Nothing was the same since I had left there in 1908, a lonely girl of 18. Gone was the clacking of the streetcars; gone was the candy store where I had worked; gone was the little cottage on Yesler Way.

In Los Angeles I was reunited with Beth. She was still my slim and attractive young sister, now with children of her own. Mother, as well-groomed as ever, was at the bus depot too. Those weeks at Beth's house were happy ones.

The Rust family, in front of the old house, just before Clara left for Outside. From left, Jess Jr., George, Cora, Lila, Beth, June, Clara and Jess.

When I returned North, Beth's son, Dick Francis, accompanied me on board the steamer *Denali* up the Inside Passage. It wasn't long before he got a job as a printer at the Fairbanks *Daily News-Miner,* my dad's old newspaper.

At this time the war in Europe seemed remote to us. However, Congress had appropriated money for military installations in Alaska, including Fairbanks. In 1940 surveyors located property for an air force base. Several homesteads along the Richardson Highway, including the Buzby Dairy, were purchased.

Soon the land was cleared and a runway built along with hangars, barracks and a powerhouse. The installation was named Ladd Air Force Base. Soldiers and flyboys poured in by the hundreds. With the construction work on the base and the influx of military personnel, the Fairbanks economy got a good shot in the arm. Our town would never be the same again.

About this time Cora and Pete moved to Mountain View, a small community near Anchorage. With the construction of Richardson Air Force base in that area, there was plenty of employment. It wasn't long before Lila and Nels joined them, soon followed by George. They had it pretty rough down there for a while, with the girls and their families living in a tent until they got established.

With all the military construction going on, my sister Beth decided she wanted to see Fairbanks before it changed too much. Since I wanted the house looking its best when she arrived, we launched into some construction of our own. We put oak flooring into the living room and dining room, and while the house was torn up, Jess put in a hot water heating system with a coal stoker. Now it was time to get rid of that tin stack. We hired a professional bricklayer to put in a block chimney. No more worries about the hot stovepipe going through the floors and ceiling, and there was no more knocking down of the creosote at night.

"Oh, Jess, why don't we really splurge while we are at it, and buy an electric stove and refrigerator?" I said.

"All right," he agreed. "We might as well. You have waited long enough for them."

That was in 1941. What a marvelous change in our kitchen. We did miss the old Lang range for warming up on a cold night, but we put it into service at the Birch Lake cabin, where it was badly needed.

All these changes around the house called for a new paint job.

The old house in 1940, with the Bill Hunter house at right.

Whenever I had a paintbrush in hand, I was in my glory. Every room, including the lavender bath, got a fresh coat. My redecorating did not stop until I had new drapes and rugs in the living room. When Beth arrived, she could hardly believe it was the same house she had lived in so many years ago.

When sister Beth was ready to return to California, my daughter Beth went with her for a visit. They stopped in Anchorage, where my George and Beth's Dick decided to go with them to California. That left just Jess Jr. at home with us.

On Sunday, December 7, 1941, Fairbanksans heard over KFAR radio that the Japanese had bombed Pearl Harbor. Immediately the town went on alert. Many people thought the Japanese would attack Alaska next. Guards were stationed at vital points—the powerhouse, telephone office, and radio station. Both Jess and I had to have passes to get into our jobs.

After the United States entered World War II, Jess Jr. joined the Air Corps at Ladd Field, and George joined the Navy in California. Jess Jr., who hoped to be sent Outside, spent his 4-year tour of duty in Alaska.

By this time Beth had returned from California and began dating Jim Aggi, who had been sent to Alaska to assemble airplanes. Jim and his buddies called themselves "Feather Merchants." During the war Fairbanks was the exchange point for the lend-lease of military planes destined for Russia. After the planes were

247

assembled, Russian pilots flew them over the pole to their homeland.

To accommodate this increased air activity, another airbase was built at Mile 26 on the Richardson Highway. This installation was named Ben Eielson, in memory of the early Fairbanks aviator.

For a number of years Alaskans had urged the U.S. government to build a highway linking the United States, Canada and Alaska. It wasn't until the war years that Congress realized the absolute necessity of such a highway in order to ship materials to the North.

In the spring of 1942, the government started the monumental task of pushing a road through more than 1,500 miles of rocky terrain and mountain ranges, through the muskeg and across rivers from Dawson Creek, Yukon Territory, to Fairbanks. By the summer of the following year, the highway was opened to military traffic only. Transportation has always been the key to the development of the Interior, and this was another turning point in Fairbanks's growth.

In 1942 I was offered the job as head operator on the day shift at the Ladd Air Force Base telephone office. After nine years on the night shift at the Fairbanks telephone office, I was ready for a change. About this time a telephone line was being installed along the Alaska Highway. When that was completed, the captain in charge asked me to take the job as head operator for the Alaska Communications System (ACS), which was housed in the federal building downtown.

"I don't think you should change jobs again," Jess said when we were talking it over. "I don't think you can trust the captain's promises. He has made promises to other people that he has never kept."

"It would be easier to work in town," I argued. "I wouldn't have to ride the bus every morning."

Jess could see that I had my mind made up, but he did say, "I think you are making a big mistake."

As it turned out, Jess was right, and I should have listened to him. I made a mistake that I regretted for a long time.

The captain's promises were empty. I was not made head operator, nor did I get the day shift. After a series of difficulties, I turned in my resignation. The captain and I had a heated conversation, during which he threatened to have me court-martialed. Since he had no grounds for that, he sent an ACS messenger to my house with a letter saying I was fired for insubordination.

Much to my disappointment, my days as a telephone operator were over. I could not get my job back at the Ladd Field office because I had quit during wartime. After 11 years of sit-down work, I went back to the laundry.

Then it was time for another wedding. This one was for Beth, our last daughter at home. Beth and Jim Aggi were married in July of 1944 in the First Presbyterian Church with a reception in the old house. Beth carried the Battenburg handkerchief Jess's mother had made for my wedding 35 years earlier.

Two months later—another wedding. Jess Jr. announced that he and Barbara Matson, whom he had known in Palmer, were going to be married. The ceremony took place in the old house with Barbara coming down the stairs while Charlotte Wehner Ames played the "Wedding March" on the piano.

During their first year of marriage Jess Jr. and Barbara lived with us. It was like having another daughter. Not long after that her brother, who was living in a children's home in Valdez, came to live with us. The old house was filling up again.

chapter 24

After the war was over, Jess and I received some very sad news. In the spring of 1946, Pete and Cora's 6-year-old son, Peter Jr., drowned in Bryte, California, a small Russian community where they had been living for several years. We were heartbroken, and I felt helpless being so far away. This was the third boy Pete and Cora had lost. Their little family now included two small daughters: Marta, who was born in 1943, and Sandy, who was born in 1946. It was a cruel blow to our Cora, who always said she wanted to raise six boys.

"I would give anything if I could be with Cora now," I told Jess. "If only there was some way I could get out there."

By this time airplane travel had been established between Fairbanks and Seattle, but I could not afford to fly both ways. Then one day an ad appeared in the newspaper.

"Wanted. Riders to Spokane, Washington, in privately owned bus, $100 per person."

That was my chance. When I signed up for the trip, I was told I would have to pay my own expenses en route. The bus would stop for picture-taking and picnics, which sounded like a fine idea.

It was a sunny morning in July when we started. In addition to the five men on the bus, there was my friend Kathy Wehner and her young son. The man who organized the trip, Fred, led the way in a station wagon with his wife.

At that time the Alcan Highway (later called the Alaska Highway) had only been open to public traffic three months. The road conditions were extremely crude, and the overnight accommodations were not much better. Not only that, but the bus was in poor shape and our driver, Ed, did not know very much about handling such a vehicle. Several times each day the engine overheated and we had to stop until it cooled down. There were many such delays. Some days we only made 250 miles.

One day when we were traveling in hilly country the brakes gave out and Ed had to pull on the emergency brake while we careened around the hairpin turns. As we came around a sharp curve we were suddenly face to face with a large truck parked in the middle of the road. When Ed finally got the bus to a safe stop, the brakes were on fire. We all piled out and Ed extinguished the fire.

At night when it was time to stop, we had to take whatever accommodations were available, and in most cases, that wasn't much. The food was terrible, too. I remember one night we were housed in a metal army hut without water or lights. There wasn't even a candle. We slept on army cots with thin mattresses and smelly blankets. There were no sheets or pillowcases.

We still had trouble with the brakes. Fred was afraid we might have an accident in the bus, so all the passengers had to ride in the overcrowded station wagon while he drove the bus. After several hundred miles of that, there were some mighty disgruntled passengers.

Once the brakes were fixed, we boarded the bus again, but engine problems plagued us all the way. We had to stop every 20 miles to pour water in the radiator. Fred got way ahead of us, and when we caught up with him at night, he was mad as a hornet because we had taken so long. He kept saying. "This trip is costing me $50 a day. We have to go faster."

By the time we reached Edmonton, Fred threw up his hands in disgust. "I will give you your money back," he told us, "and all of you can go the rest of the way on your own."

"I don't want all my money back," I said. "That wouldn't be fair. Give me enough to cover my bus fare to Spokane and I will be satisfied."

Ten days after I left Fairbanks, I was with Lila, Nels and their two children in Pasco, Washington. After resting there, I traveled by bus to California to be with Cora. My stay there was shortened when I received word that George was being married in Cathlamet, Washington. He wanted me there for the wedding.

The nuptials took place in the rose-decked Lutheran Church on Puget Island. My new daughter-in-law, Helene Danielson, was a blond girl who made a lovely bride. After the wedding I planned to visit friends in Seattle and then fly home.

Just before I left Cathlamet, George said, "Mother, I really want to drive back to Alaska, but we don't have enough money to make it on our own. I was wondering if you would ride back with us and share expenses?"

The thought of bumping over that miserable, rough highway the second time made me ill.

After talking with Helene, though, I decided they were both serious about the trip. Reluctantly, I gave in. It wasn't that I didn't want them to come to Fairbanks, but I had looked forward to my first airplane ride and not to another 2,400-mile highway trip.

"Just be sure your car is in good condition when you pick me up in Seattle," I told George. "That is a long, rough road, and the gas stations are few and far between. You should have two spare tires and carry your own tools so you can do your own work."

"Sure, Mom, sure," George said.

Despite my warnings, George was not too well prepared for the trip. When he pulled up in front of the Shannons' house where I was staying, the car was enveloped in a cloud of steam.

"It is nothing to worry about, Mom," George said.

"You are crazy to start out in that wreck," my friends in Seattle said. "You will never make it."

It was early September and I feared we would run into snow before we got home. Since the car was overloaded, we had to box up a lot of wedding presents and some of my clothes to be shipped ahead.

If the first day on the road was any indication of things to come (and it was), we were in for trouble. We had traveled only a few hundred miles when we had our first flat tire. George had to patch the patches. The next day we had two more flats, an overheated engine and dirt in the gas line.

By the time we had one problem solved, another one loomed up. After repairing the distributor, the brakes gave out, followed by more flat tires. The rough road rattled the car from stem to stern. With all the breakdowns, the trip was taking longer and costing more than we expected. To save on expenses, we slept in the car and bought food at grocery stores so we could make sandwiches along the road. I had had $200 when we started, but at the rate we were going, the money wouldn't last much longer.

"We will have to wire Dad to send money to us at Dawson Creek," I said.

The road became more desolate and rough the farther north we went. The nights were cold, and sleeping in the car was becoming more uncomfortable every night. This trip made my first one seem like a picnic. We seemed to spend as much time broken down alongside the road as we did driving. Despite the difficulties, Helene remained cheerful and I admired her attitude. It certainly couldn't have been the kind of honeymoon she had hoped to take.

By the time we reached Dawson Creek, I had enough money to pay the hotel bill and $6 to spare. There were 1,500 miles of bumpy road still ahead of us. We surely needed that money from Jess. We checked at the banks. Nothing. We checked at the telephone and government express office. Nothing. No money. No word. Nothing. I couldn't call Jess because civilians could not use the government lines for private use.

I could not understand why Jess would let us down. There must be something wrong at home, I thought, and that added to my worries.

"George, I've done all I can," I said. "It's up to you to get us out of this one."

I left George and Helene standing on the street corner and went back to the hotel. It wasn't long before they came bursting in the door.

"We found a man at one of the banks who will loan us enough money to get home," George said. "How much do you think we will need?"

We decided to borrow $80 from the bank clerk who had trusted us enough to give us a personal loan. I figured that would get us to Whitehorse, where our money from home would surely be waiting. After one good night's rest and a bath at the Regina Hotel, we slept under the stars again.

Five days later we reached Whitehorse. We went straight to the N.C. store, where the manager said he had been on the lookout for us for a week. He had the money. Jess had been unable to send it to Dawson Creek because the Fairbanks banks had no listing of any bank in that city. We got back in the car and drove straight through to Fairbanks, a long and exhausting 600 miles. It was 5 o'clock in the morning when we reached home.

There we found Jess and Beth busy packing the Plymouth. Since they hadn't heard from us (I thought the N.C. manager in Whitehorse would call Jess) they thought we were broken down somewhere, and they were going to rescue us. Jess was happy we were safe, but I think he felt a little cheated out of a trip. He had enough gas, oil and food in the car to last several days. Beth, who was pregnant with her first child, had come from Bethel, where she and Jim lived, to meet her new sister-in-law, Helene.

"It seems a shame to unpack the car now," Jess said. "I think we should go someplace."

"But Dad, we have been traveling two weeks," George said.

"I know, but why don't we just drive down to Birch Lake and stay in the cabin overnight," Jess said.

George looked at me. Helene looked at George. I looked at Jess.

"Sure, if that's what you want to do," I heard myself say.

"Good! Let's go," Jess said.

So we got out of the Packard, piled into the Plymouth and started down the gravel road we had just come.

There wasn't anyone in the world I would have done that for except Jess.

 **chapter 25**

Christmas of 1946, while George and Helene were living with us, we wanted to make a special occasion because it was Helene's first holiday away from home. We had a fine big tree, beautifully trimmed and placed in the living room with packages piled beneath the boughs.

Since Jess had to go to work early Christmas morning at the N.C. power house, we decided to open our gifts Christmas Eve night, Jess Jr., Barb, their daughter Donna, and 3-month-old Jesse Worthington Rust III, joined us for a family celebration. We missed Beth and Jim, who were spending the holiday in California with his family. Earlier that winter Beth had slipped on the ice in Bethel and lost her first child in a miscarriage.

To start the evening off, my Jess fixed a silver fizz—a concoction of whipped egg whites, gin and soda water. He made the best. While we sat around the tree I looked with anticipation on an especially large package for me from Jess.

"Go ahead," Jess said. "Open mine first."

Everyone watched while I opened the box, only to find another wrapped box inside the box. Inside that box was another wrapped box, and then another. The family was getting a good laugh out of this, especially Jess. It was his kind of joke. I wouldn't have been surprised to find a used light bulb inside. Just as I started opening the fifth box, the siren downtown and our phone sounded off at the same time.

Fire! The N.C. garage was burning. The three men—Jess, Jess Jr. and George—grabbed their coats, caps and mittens and away they went. By that time the sky was ablaze. It seemed to me as if the whole downtown was on fire. The sirens sounded again and again. It was an all-out alert. To make matters worse, it was 35 degrees below zero that night.

As the hours dragged on and the men still did not return, I became more and more curious about Jess's gift. I couldn't help it; I just had to open the next box. Inside was a small velvet jeweler's box. I lifted the lid and there was a beautiful diamond solitaire ring.

Then I was so sorry that I had opened the gift without Jess that I almost cried. I should have waited. Jess had taken his diamond tie screw and had it made into a ring for me. He had always said, "I want to dress you in diamonds." That was my Jess, always thoughtful and generous beneath a sometimes gruff exterior.

When the men finally got home, faces blackened by the smoke, they were wet and cold to the bone. We got busy and fixed a hot lunch for them. They said the garage was almost a total loss. In addition to the display room of cars and stockroom of parts, the building had housed the telephone exchange and several apartments on the second floor.

"Some residents barely got out alive, and most of them lost all their possessions," Jess said. "Gus Stewart lost his Sydney Laurence and Ted Lambert paintings."

When we began opening our gifts again, there wasn't the same enthusiasm with which we had started. The fire had saddened our holiday. By then it was almost time for Jess to go to work. With the telephone office burned, the town was without communications except for the ACS lines. In a short time, however, a new switchboard was set up in a temporary location.

When spring came, Helene wanted to go back to Washington. She could not get used to the cold, nor our way of life in Alaska. Not long after that George went Outside to be with Helene and their new son, Ronald. That left Jess and me all alone in that big house. Jess Jr. and family, who were living over in the Derby Tract, visited often, and we had dinner parties together, but it was not the same as having the family at home.

From time to time Jess had talked about building a "cabin in the woods" after the kids were gone. As the quiet weeks passed, he talked of it more and more often. I thought it was just talk. He couldn't be serious about leaving our house and all the comforts we had worked 40 years to get.

"You can build your cabin in the woods," I said to Jess, "but I am staying here."

There wasn't a single room or wall or floor or piece of furniture in that house that did not hold a special memory for me. In my kitchen I would look with pride on the electric stove and remember the old Lang range that had stood in its place. How many times had I polished the top with a piece of bacon rind to give it a lustrous shine? How many times had I made new curtains for the windows and papered the walls and painted the woodwork? I had been down on my hands and knees over every inch of the floors, tearing out old boards and putting down new ones. The water in the well, the basement the house stood on, the lumber that framed it, the paint that colored it—it was all a part of me. I could never leave that old house.

In the yard—the plants, the bushes, the trees, they were all put there by our hands. We had taken a crude cabin on the edge of the wilderness and turned it into a modern, comfortable house that anyone would have been proud of, and it hadn't been easy. Couldn't Jess see that it was the home we had both been denied as children? Surely he couldn't turn his back on it now.

Still, Jess's talk of a "cabin in the woods" persisted, much to my dismay. Then one day in March of 1948, Jess Jr. told his dad about a valuable piece of property—153 acres—that he should look over. The homesteader, Joe Konkle, could not prove up on his property in time to get his patent, so he was going to give up his rights to it the next day.

Jess was all excited. "Let's go look at the property right now," he said.

"Right now?" I repeated. There were little tremors of doom in my stomach. "In all this snow?"

"We have to look at it right now," Jess said. "If Konkle gives up the property tomorrow, we wouldn't have a chance to get it."

Already the events were going too fast to suit me. "All right. Let's go," I agreed reluctantly.

We piled into the car, Jess, Jess Jr. and I, while the March sun was blazing a spun golden glow over the glazed surface of the molded snowbanks. We traveled the two lane Richardson Highway until we reached the Badger Road turnoff. Here the road was narrower, bordered by tall, snow-laden spruce. There were a few scattered dwellings, small cabins, mostly, on partially cleared land. In a particularly lonely part of the road, Jess Jr. stopped the car.

"What is the matter?" I asked.

"This is where we get out," Jess said.

"But there isn't anything here," I said, glancing out at the quiet, empty spaces of snow dotted with trees.

"We have to snowshoe in. There isn't a road to the property," Jess Jr. explained.

What kind of a godforsaken place is this, I wondered. "I will wait in the car. I don't think I can get through the snow," I said.

After awhile—long enough for the yellow light to fade from the snow and blue shadows to deepen—Jess and his dad came trudging back to the car. One look at Jess and I knew: He liked what he had seen, and his mind was already made up.

"It is beautiful back there," Jess said, his face beaming. "There are lots of tall trees. It is a perfect place for a house right by the river. We are going over to Konkle's right now to talk about the property."

After talking to Konkle, Jess was in seventh heaven. Mr. Konkle told Jess to meet him at the land office the next morning, and he would sign the property over to him. In exchange, Jess would pay Konkle $1,000 for the improvements, a farm tractor and some building materials.

"Things seem to be moving pretty fast," I said. "Do I have any say in this matter?"

"Of course," Jess said. "I guess I got carried away by my own enthusiasm. How do you feel about it?"

"Where are you going to get a thousand dollars to pay Mr. Konkle?" I wanted to know.

"I will have to borrow it from the banks."

"How will you pay it back?"

"I will pay it back after we sell the house."

There it was. Sell the house. My head was spinning. "Oh, Jess, how could you, after all we have put in it?" By then I was crying.

"We can't have both," Jess said. "We can't afford the house and the homestead too."

"I just can't see it," I said, wiping my eyes and trying to control myself. "Just when we can relax and enjoy our home, you want to start all over again."

"Now, Clara. You know I have been talking for years about a cabin in the woods. It is so peaceful out there. I know you will love it."

"But, Jess, think of all the work," I argued. "It would be years before we got the house the way we wanted it. There is no water, no lights, no cesspool, no telephone—there isn't even a place to live. It's more primitive than when we moved in the old house, and we aren't as young as we used to be either."

Jess continued talking like a Dutch Uncle, praising the property to the skies, and bubbling over with more enthusiasm than I had seen him display in years. The homestead was what Jess wanted; it would make him happy. It was as simple as that.

"Can't we think about it?" I said finally, rubbing my head where it ached. "I am not ready to make a decision like that now."

"But we can't wait," Jess said. "If I am not at the land office tomorrow morning, we will lose our chance."

"Oh, Jess, I hate to do something like this in a hurry." It was late, and I was tired of arguing. "Why should we give up the house after all the hard years of work we put into it?"

"I will build you a better house. It will be just the way you want it, with a fireplace and everything," Jess promised.

I was weakening; Jess knew me well enough to see that.

"After we sell the house, I promise we will take a trip Outside," he said.

That did it. Jess hadn't been Outside since 1905. If he would go, that would make it worth selling the house. Besides, I knew Jess had his heart set on his cabin in the woods and he wouldn't be happy without it. And I wouldn't be happy if he weren't happy.

"All right," I gave in. "If you want the homestead, we will put the house up for sale."

First thing next morning Jess was at the land office, and before I had a chance to change my mind, the homestead was ours—all 153 acres. Even at that, I didn't really believe we would give up the old house. We belonged there. I couldn't imagine living in any other place.

When our friends heard about the homestead they said, "Why do you want to move so far out of town?"

I wondered the same thing, but it was too late to back out of it then.

While we waited for the snow to melt, Jess was busy with plans for the equipment and tools he would need for building. It had been a long time since he had been so eager to tackle a new project. As soon as the ice was off the river we took the *Clara III* out to the Chena Slough and headed upriver to our property. It was wet and swampy that spring, and the only way we could get to the homestead was by river.

The minute I saw that beautiful land, untouched in its natural state, I fell in love with it.

"Just think, all this belongs to us," Jess said.

I could picture the log house Jess would build there among the dark pointed spruce with the river flowing by. It would be a lot of work, there was no doubt about that, but it could be done. Jess was 63 years old, and I was 9 years his junior. Not the ideal age for homesteading, but we had experience, and that counted for something. Jess had plans for farming the homestead, raising potatoes for a retirement income.

The first thing Jess did was hire a dozer and cut a road into our place from the bridge. The road followed the river's edge, and was bogged down in mud, barely passable. Jess could hardly wait to set up his umbrella tent, his cot and Yukon stove. He took a two-weeks' vacation from the N.C. so he could start clearing the land. Even though the work was hard, he was in his glory. I hadn't seen him look so good in years—tanned by the sun, and those brown eyes flashing with good humor and excitement.

While Jess worked on the homestead, I stayed in town to sell the house.

"What should I do with all our belongings?" I asked Jess. "Where will we put them?"

"Sell everything," Jess said. "It will be cheaper than storing it, and we can get new for the house."

My heart gave a sudden lurch when he said "sell everything." It was as if he asked me to cut off my right arm. I thought of all the years I had worked to get the vacuum cleaner, my toaster, mixer and the furniture. Now to turn everything over to strangers was almost more than I could bear.

With a lump in my throat, I put the ad in the paper. My heart wasn't in it, and I was pleased when the first prospective buyer turned it down. I wasn't that fortunate the second time. A man who had just come to town to work for the Road Commission wanted it. He paid a good sum down and sent for his wife, who was living Outside, to look at the house before sealing the deal.

Just my luck; she fell in love with the place. The couple had three children—and one on the way. The house would be perfect for their family. She said it would be August before they would move in, which would give me time to get my things packed.

When Jess's vacation was over, he worked evenings at the homestead, usually staying overnight on the weekends. Thanks to the long summer nights, there was enough sunlight to work until 11 or 12 o'clock. He was hurrying to build us a rough cabin to live in while he worked on the big house.

My time was spent at the old house sorting through an accumulation of more than 40 years. Where, oh, where would we put everything—the old photo albums, the girls' wedding dresses, old Easter baskets, Christmas decorations, books, letters, schoolwork and report cards—those things that would not be of interest to anyone else but were too precious for me to throw away. It was hard.

I packed my linens and blankets, a few dishes and cooking utensils, just the necessities I knew I would need at the homestead right away. Beth stored some things for us, my sewing machine and silverware; I was not going to part with that.

Some evenings I rode out to the homestead with Jess Jr. and Barb, taking a picnic lunch to share with Jess. It was a time of upheaval and adjustment for me, and it was hard to match Jess's enthusiasm for the building that was going on.

Then, much to my bewilderment, the buyer's wife, her mother, father-in-law and three children arrived a month early on the Fourth of July and wanted to move in right away.

I rushed out to the homestead.

"Jess, what should I do? I haven't finished sorting things. I'm not packed, and I am not ready to leave yet."

"Oh, let them move in," he said. "You can move out here. We need someone to watch the tools and materials while I am at work."

"But where will I stay?"

"In the tent. We can buy two good box springs and mattresses and put them up on boxes so we will have a good place to sleep."

And haul water from the river, and cut wood for the stove, and wash clothes on a scrubboard, I thought.

My packing was finished in a hurry, and I left behind more personal things than I had intended. To this day there are many things I regret leaving behind. I was paying dearly for a trip Outside and a new cabin I did not especially want.

The day Jess and I handed the keys over to the new owners and drove off, I dared not look back at the old house. I doubt that I could have seen it anyway, I was so blinded by my tears.

We drove in silence out the rutted road that led to our homestead. The summer sun left a golden glow on the dusty green leaves and the thick underbrush. On the air was the sweet scent of wild flowers, and the gentle music the slough makes inside its muddy banks.

Up ahead in the rude clearing, circled by trees shoulder to shoulder, was our summer home—the brown umbrella tent with the dirt floor and the Yukon stove.

When Jess stopped the car, I thought: Here we are, right where we started from, 40 years ago. Is this what it was all leading to?

Only this time we didn't even have a little house with a half-moon cut in the door. All we had was a canvas wrapped around three birch trees and a hole in the ground, and I had to dig the hole myself.